# UNCONDITIONAL

# PIVOTAL MOMENTS IN AMERICAN HISTORY

*Series Editors*
David Hackett Fischer
James M. McPherson
David Greenberg

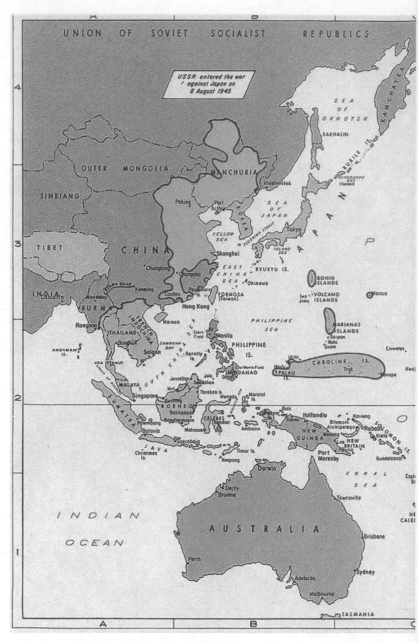

The Far East and the Pacific. Areas Under Allied and Japanese Control, 15 August 1945. Courtesy of Department of History, U.S. Military Academy.

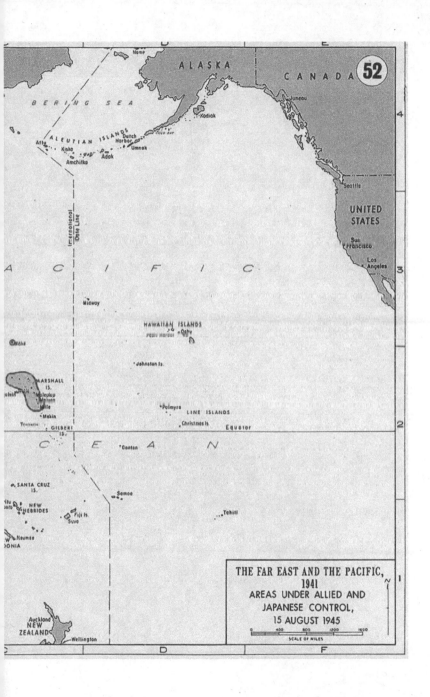

THE FAR EAST AND THE PACIFIC,
1941
AREAS UNDER ALLIED AND
JAPANESE CONTROL,
15 AUGUST 1945

# UNCONDITIONAL

## THE JAPANESE SURRENDER IN
## WORLD WAR II

### MARC GALLICCHIO

OXFORD
UNIVERSITY PRESS

# OXFORD
## UNIVERSITY PRESS

Oxford University Press is a department of the University of Oxford. It furthers
the University's objective of excellence in research, scholarship, and education
by publishing worldwide. Oxford is a registered trade mark of Oxford University
Press in the UK and certain other countries.

Published in the United States of America by Oxford University Press
198 Madison Avenue, New York, NY 10016, United States of America.

© Marc Gallicchio 2020

First issued as an Oxford University Press paperback, 2023

CIP data is on file at the Library of Congress
ISBN 978-0-19-009110-1 (Hardback)
ISBN 978-0-19-762184-4 (Paperback)


Paperback printed by Marquis, Canada

For Sam and Isabelle, unconditionally

# Contents

# Acknowledgments

I have worked on this project on and off for many years. I was able to present a very early version of it at Tohoku and Doshisha Universities in Japan as Fulbright Lecturer in 1998–1999. Other projects intervened, and in 2014, when I had started up again in earnest, I was called away by the opportunity of a lifetime: the chance to work with my mentor, Waldo Heinrichs. Waldo was also my friend and my first reader for nearly forty years. He passed away while I was working on this book. My enjoyment in finishing this project has been greatly diminished by not being able to seek his advice and share my findings with him.

I am very grateful for the funding I received to conduct the research for this project. I wish to thank the Provost's Office at Villanova University for two faculty research grants, the Department of History for use of the Albert Lepage faculty research fund, and the Harry S. Truman Library.

Two of my graduate assistants at Villanova, Thomas Foley and Christopher Mengel, were a great help in locating materials for this book. I am thankful for the support of my colleagues in the Department of History at Villanova who have made working there such an enjoyable experience. In particular, I want to thank Lynne Hartnett and Paul Rosier for their advice and wise counsel at the very last stages of this project, Vicki Sharpless for help with computer-related questions, and Frances Murphy for her invaluable assistance with the photographs that appear in this book.

I also want to thank my editor at Oxford University Press, Tim Bent, for being willing to take me on for a second book. I appreciate his toleration of my delays, his editorial judgment, and his careful attention to every line of the manuscript.

Finally, I am eternally grateful to my wife, Lisa Ross, for her support, encouragement, and sound advice. Lisa is the intelligent reader we all write for, but with a better sense of humor. Thank you, dear, for helping me through another of these books.

# Editor's Note

Visitors to Pearl Harbor today often begin their tour with the USS *Missouri*, the last battleship commissioned by the United States in World War II and now a popular museum. They learn about the elaborate ceremony staged in Tokyo Bay in September 1945, when Japanese officials capitulated to the United States and its allies on the hulking vessel's deck. On this historic spot, visitors can take in the full course of the war—or at least the American experience of the war—from start to finish.

Most Americans generally know that Japan's surrender was "unconditional." Yet few give much thought to what that freighted word means, beyond its connoting the decisive victory of liberal democracy over fascism and imperialism. But why was the completeness of the Allied victory and the abjectness of the Japanese defeat so necessary? And why is it so important?

Marc Gallicchio's book recounts the full story behind the Japanese surrender. From Harry S. Truman's ascension to office in April 1945, through the Potsdam Conference of July, and on into Japan's August decision to surrender just days after the second atomic bomb was dropped on Nagasaki, the narrative involves the concurrent military, diplomatic, and political developments with which the new American president had to contend. Braiding together these multiple threads, Gallichio allows us to understand the controversy that perpetually surrounds Truman's choices, and in turn to see why the question of unconditionality has remained central to our thinking about war and how to end it.

The original call for unconditional surrender came from Franklin D. Roosevelt. In Casablanca in January 1943, the thick of the war, FDR held a press conference after meeting with Winston Churchill at which he foresaw "absolute victory" for the Allies, explaining that the Axis Powers—Germany, Italy, Japan—would ultimately need to accept without reservation the terms the Allies would set down for concluding hostilities. Americans readily accepted this policy. Given the stakes, why should the Allies settle for less?

But when Roosevelt died in April 1945, passing the presidency to the untested Truman—who had been vice president for just 82 days—the picture had come to look very different. Few doubted now that the Allies would prevail in the conflict. It was only a matter of when, and at what cost. And on that subject consensus—among the American public, in the military leadership, and in the government—proved maddeningly elusive.

Within the Truman administration, rival factions vied against one another. Old hands believed Truman's inexperience would allow them to steer war policy in their preferred direction. Resolute anti-communists argued that a more lenient stance toward Japan would convert it into a postwar bulwark against the Soviet Union's geopolitical ambitions. And the ferocity of the fighting on Iwo Jima and Okinawa buttressed arguments that a policy of victory at all costs would sacrifice American lives needlessly.

Truman stood firm, and *Unconditional* is in large part the story of a statesman in the making. He turned out to be especially clear-eyed on the all-important question of the fate of the Japanese emperor. Despite pressure to allow Hirohito to stay on as emperor, he concluded that compromise would only encourage the Japanese to seek additional concessions. The dropping of the atom bombs brought about Truman's desired goal. Though the emperor remained nominally on the throne, he was so denuded of power that his survival in no way compromised American war aims.

Truman's decision proved to be pivotal in several ways. Uprooting Japan's militaristic ideology and replacing the imperial monarchy with a pro-Western democratic system led swiftly to a policy of thoroughly reconstructing Japan, down to imposing a new constitution. By putting its former adversary on this path, Truman not only served the interests of the United States but advanced peace and prosperity. Not least, he also enabled Japan itself to flourish in the postwar era.

Debate over ending the war did not end with the war. In the 1950s, anti-communists on the right argued that the policy of unconditional surrender had been a mistake, even tying it to the outbreak of the Korean War. In the 1960s, neo-isolationists on the left became the policy's chief critics, seeing it as a marker of America's own incorrigible belligerence. Today, as the peaceful liberal world order that the United States superintended for three quarters of a century is coming to an end, understanding its origins has become vital.

—David Greenberg

# UNCONDITIONAL

# Introduction

## "A Reasonable Assurance of Future World Peace"

On January 24, 1943, President Franklin D. Roosevelt and Prime Minister Winston Churchill wrapped up their ten-day conference at Casablanca by meeting with about forty reporters under the bright Moroccan sun. Security was tight. The Allies had landed in North Africa in early November and were fighting German forces to the east in Tunisia. This was the first time since the Civil War that an American president had been in a war zone. American and British planes circled overhead, and guards were stationed every twenty yards around a fenced perimeter. As Churchill and Roosevelt sat in chairs before the standing reporters, the president declared, "The elimination of German, Japanese and Italian war power means the unconditional surrender by Germany, Italy, and Japan."[1]

With that brief announcement, Franklin Roosevelt committed the United States to the unconditional surrender of the Axis powers. Almost immediately, that succinct statement of objectives became the most readily recognized policy of the war. Like most of Roosevelt's policies, unconditional surrender served multiple purposes, some diplomatic and others political. After FDR's death, however, the rallying cry of unconditional surrender became a lightning rod for Republicans and the growing number of Americans who were wearying of the war against Japan.

In the final months of the war, a vigorous public debate erupted over the policy of unconditional surrender and by extension, the very definition of victory. There was more at stake than a disagreement over the best and quickest way to end the war. The debate over unconditional surrender extended the ideological battleground of the New Deal into the international realm. The Japanese

understood this, as did most Americans at the time. To fully explain Japan's decision to surrender, we will need to understand what the participants knew then.

This story begins in the spring of 1945 as the debate over unconditional
surrender burst into public view on the American home front. When Harry
S. Truman became president upon Roosevelt's death on April 12, 1945, he
was beset with competing recommendations for achieving victory. Military
strategy, diplomacy, and domestic politics were closely intertwined in the
final months of the war. Binding them was the policy of unconditional surrender. By the summer of 1945, the policy that was supposed to unify the
American people in wartime had become the source of intense political
debate.

To the surprise of many, not least President Truman, the explosion of
atomic bombs over Hiroshima and Nagasaki, and the entry of the Soviet
Union into the war, did not end the debate over unconditional surrender.
The Japanese government refused to give up and continued to seek a
negotiated surrender. The final drama of the war crystallized the debate over
unconditional surrender in the U.S. and set the stage for future recrimina-
tion that would contaminate domestic politics.

The victory of the Chinese Communists in 1949 and the outbreak of
the Korean War in June 1950 provided the impetus for a renewed attack on
the policy of unconditional surrender. As a sequence of calamities unfolded
in Asia, one prominent journalist went so far as to call it the greatest political mistake of the war. Others alleged that it was part of a deliberate plot
by communist sympathizers to aid the spread of communism in Asia. The
strange afterlife of unconditional surrender took an even more surprising
turn in the 1960s when the policy came under fire from historians on the
political left. In response, conservatives, who had once been among the
leading critics of the policy, now defended it. It was as if two opposing
armies had moved silently at night, or in this case over several decades,
to occupy the other's terrain, only to continue the battle from their new
positions.

One need not choose sides in the rancorous partisan debates over the
merits of the policy or accept the conspiratorial interpretations of unconditional surrender to realize that something has been lost in our understanding
of the events that resulted in Japan's surrender seventy-five years ago. This
anniversary seems a propitious moment to explore the strange history of
unconditional surrender and illuminate a past that has been obscured by the
passage of time.

# I

# "Our Demand Has Been and It Remains—Unconditional Surrender!"

Beginning at dawn on April 1, 1945, the silhouettes of the enemy's ships could be seen stretching for miles along the Okinawa coastline. Standing on Mount Shuri, the highest point on the island, Colonel Yahara Hiromichi watched as more than a thousand landing craft plowed toward the Hagashi beaches. Though dazzled by the sight, he was hardly taken by surprise. For three hours the Americans had pounded the landing zone with nearly forty-five thousand shells 5 inches or bigger, twenty-two thousand mortar shells, and thirty-three thousand rockets. It was the largest concentrated naval bombardment ever to cover a landing. By 0830 the soldiers and Marines were reaching their designated beaches and the defenders were offering only occasional opposing fire. The Japanese had no intention of contesting the beach landings. Instead, following plans Colonel Yahara had drawn up, the Japanese Thirty-Second Army was dug in on the southern third of Okinawa, where it prepared to use the craggy terrain and tight maneuver area to wage a campaign of attrition against the invaders.

Yahara was pleased that he had deceived the enemy into expending so much ordinance on the undefended beaches. That moment of satisfaction vanished, however, when he realized that the landing craft were going to reach the beaches without any opposition from the Japanese Air Force. Where were the planes that had been promised? They had attacked the invasion fleet for several days before the landing. Why did they fail to strike the vulnerable landing craft as they lumbered toward the shore? The Japanese soldiers who had emerged from their fortifications to watch the landing asked each other the same question. Once ashore, the Americans moved inland toward Yomitan and Kadena Airfields, located on the western side of Okinawa. For the first time during the war, the enemy was on Japanese territory.[1]

Although the Air Force was absent at the crucial moment, the Navy was determined to do its part in the defense of Okinawa. While Yahara observed the uncontested landings, the battleship *Yamato* was preparing to leave the relative safety of Japan's inland sea and steam south. The pride of the Imperial Japanese Navy when it was completed in 1941, this marvel of naval architecture bore a name that proclaimed its special place. By the late nineteenth century, the Japanese referred to themselves as the "Yamato people," a name derived from an ethnic group in central Japan. The Yamato people were assumed to be racially pure Japanese, separate from and superior to the lesser groups that inhabited the fringes of the empire, including Okinawans, Koreans, and the Ainu of the northern islands. It would be difficult to imagine a more symbolically potent name for a ship. Almost as soon as it was ready for action, however, the *Yamato* was surpassed in usefulness by the new queen of sea warfare, the aircraft carrier. Despite its sophisticated armament and damage-control systems, without air cover the *Yamato* was as vulnerable as the Royal Navy's *Prince of Wales* and *Repulse*—also vessels of great national pride—had been when they were sunk by Japanese aircraft at the start of the war.

*Yamato*'s captain knew that he was taking his crew on a mission with virtually no chance of success. In fact, the ship left port with only enough fuel for a one-way run to Okinawa. This suicide run was the result of a brief exchange between Admiral Oikawa Koshiro and Emperor Hirohito. During this encounter, Oikawa, the chief of staff of the Imperial Japanese Navy and the emperor's advisor, explained the plans for using suicide boats and planes to attack the invasion force assembled off Okinawa. Puzzled, the emperor had asked, "But where is the navy? Are there no more ships? No surface forces?" It was a question and a command. With no more than the verbal equivalent of a raised eyebrow, *Yamato* was doomed. Stung by the emperor's rebuke and unwilling to subject the Navy to ridicule for protecting its most famous warship, Oikawa ordered *Yamato* to sea.[2]

On April 5, as the *Yamato* and its nine escort ships readied for their journey, Prime Minister Koiso Kuniaki formally announced his resignation. Koiso's term had been marked by one failure after another. In late 1944, he declared that the battle for Leyte in the southern Philippines would be the decisive engagement of the war, comparing it to the legendary battle

Imperial Japanese Navy's battle ship *Yamato* running full-power trials in Sukumo Bay, 1941.

of Tennozan (1582) in which the great lord Hideyoshi Toyotomi overcame heavy odds to emerge victorious and eventually unify the country. The Japanese Army poured irreplaceable resources into the campaign but had failed to turn back the Americans. In late December, the Army, without informing Koiso, stopped reinforcing Leyte and accepted its loss. That embarrassment was followed by the loss of Iwo Jima in February 1945 and the failure of Koiso's diplomatic effort to end the war in China on favorable terms. Now the Americans had successfully landed on Japanese territory. That was the last straw.

On April 6, a day after Koiso's resignation, the *jushin*, the six former prime ministers, met to select a suitable replacement. They settled on retired Admiral Suzuki Kantaro, a seventy-eight-year-old hero of Japan's first war with China and the Russo-Japanese War. Suzuki had other qualities that made him seem ideally matched to this perilous moment in Japanese history. He had remained above the ideological struggles that had riven military politics in the 1930s. In fact, he had seemed so dangerously apolitical that he was targeted for assassination by Army zealots; he still had shrapnel lodged in his body from the botched attempt on his life. Suzuki had also served as grand chamberlain to the emperor, and the two men remained on good terms.

The change in leadership in Tokyo convinced some diplomats in the United States that Japan was signaling its intent to end the war. They were mistaken. The *jushin* had not chosen Suzuki to redirect Japanese policy or seek an immediate exit from the war. Like the military, and Hirohito, Suzuki believed that Japan would need to achieve a major victory on the battlefield before negotiating an end to the war. The main figures in Suzuki's new cabinet shared his view, with the exception of Foreign Minister Togo Shigenori. Togo believed that Japan needed to end the war promptly. He agreed to serve in the cabinet on the provision that Suzuki would commission a thorough assessment of Japan's capacity to wage war. Suzuki agreed, but more time would be lost before the report was ready for the prime minister's review.

With the Americans ashore on Okinawa and a new prime minister at the helm, Japan had reached a turning point and refused to turn. Instead, the country continued its path toward disaster, with the military urging the nation to endure further sacrifice until they were rescued by the hoped-for victory.[3] On April 5, the day Koiso submitted his resignation, the Soviet foreign minister informed the Japanese ambassador that the Soviet Union would not renew its Neutrality Pact with Japan when the agreement came up for reconsideration in April 1946. The treaty would remain in force for another year, but the announcement sounded an ominous note for the Japanese. Two days later, on April 7, the same day Suzuki took up his new duties, the *Yamato* met its end in the East China Sea south of Kyushu, Japan's southernmost main island. American torpedo planes swarmed over the *Yamato* and slammed ten torpedoes and five bombs into the disabled ship. Only 23 officers and 233 sailors out of a crew of 3,332 survived. Many of those on board defied orders to abandon ship. Those who obeyed had to throw themselves to the mercy of the sea; *Yamato* carried no lifeboats or rafts.

On April 8, the day after *Yamato* went under, the Imperial General Headquarters issued orders for its revised plan for the defense of the homeland. Code-named *Ketsu-Go*, meaning "decisive operation," the plan divided the home islands into seven operational districts in which the decisive battles might be fought. For example, *Ketsu-Go No. 1* covered the defense of Hokkaido, the northernmost home island. *Ketsu-Go No. 3* was for the Kanto Plain, the area that included Tokyo. The *Ketsu-Go* operations integrated efforts by the Army, Navy, and Air Force, and were entirely defensive. They required the complete mobilization of the Japanese population and relied on the deployment of suicide weapons. The commander of the First General Army explained that "this was not just a simple defense, but the final, glorious struggle to preserve the nation, one in which the lives of men were of no consideration—men and officers would attack relentlessly over the bodies of their fallen comrades until the invaders were destroyed."[4]

One week after Koiso announced his resignation, Japan's main adversary also changed leaders. On the afternoon of April 12, Vice President Harry S. Truman was settling down for a bourbon and casual conversation in the chambers of House Speaker Sam Rayburn when he was abruptly summoned to the White House. As he entered the residence on the second floor, Eleanor Roosevelt met him and, placing an arm on Truman's shoulder, said, "Harry, the president is dead." The First Lady's calm pronouncement did not come as a complete surprise to Truman. In late February, Truman had been shocked by Roosevelt's gaunt appearance after the president returned from the Yalta summit conference. Like others who were concerned by the

Suzuki Kantaro. *Rekidai Shusho tou Shashin* (Courtesy National Diet Library).

clear signs of FDR's declining health, he allowed himself to hope that a few weeks at the spa in Warm Springs, Georgia, would restore the president's vitality. From that point on, however, the possibility that he might suddenly be called to the presidency was never far from Truman's mind.[5]

During the next several days, Truman was sworn in, attended the Washington memorial service for the fallen president and his burial in Hyde Park, met with his predecessor's cabinet, had several briefings on the global military situation with the Joint Chiefs of Staff, and moved his family into Blair House, which would be their temporary residence until Eleanor Roosevelt moved out of the White House. In private, Truman admitted to being overwhelmed by the immensity of the responsibilities he had assumed. Publicly, however, the new president conducted himself with a calm dignity that reassured an anxious citizenry. On April 16, he went to Capitol Hill to address a joint session of Congress. Truman's main purpose was to confirm that he intended to continue Roosevelt's policies on the home front and on the global stage. Specifically, the United States would go forward in hosting the charter meeting of the United Nations, which was scheduled for April 25 in San Francisco. Truman also pledged to bring the wars against Germany and Japan to successful conclusions, rejecting any thought of compromise or, as he put it, a "partial victory." He declared, "Our demand has been, and it remains—Unconditional Surrender! We will not traffic with the breakers of the peace on the terms of the peace."[6]

Press reports of Truman's brief speech noted that the congressional audience responded with enthusiastic applause. In pledging to seek the unconditional surrender of Germany and Japan, Truman had committed himself to the policy that FDR had announced two years earlier. Truman now not only endorsed the policy, he concisely defined it. The Allies would not negotiate surrender terms. The Germans and Japanese would have to lay down their arms and entrust their fates to the mercy of the Allies.

The policy seemed simple enough to explain; its implications, however, were not. FDR had first announced the policy of unconditional surrender when he and Prime Minister Winston Churchill gave a joint press conference on January 24, 1943, the last day of their meeting at Casablanca. At that stage of the war, the Americans had established themselves in North Africa and, in conjunction with British forces, were well on their way to eliminating the German presence on the southern shore of the Mediterranean. Partway into the press conference Roosevelt introduced the idea of unconditional surrender with remarks that seemed almost off the cuff. Noting that he and

Churchill had determined that peace would never return without the "total elimination of German and Japanese war power," he added that some of the "Britishers" among those gathered at a press conference might not be familiar with the story behind a famous American general:

> His name was Ulysses Simpson Grant, but in my, and the Prime Minister's, early days he was called "Unconditional Surrender" Grant. The elimination of German, Japanese, and Italian war power means the unconditional surrender by Germany, Italy, and Japan. That means a reasonable assurance of future world peace. It does not mean the destruction of the population of Germany, Italy, or Japan, but it does mean the destruction of the philosophies in those countries which are based on conquest and the subjugation of other people.[7]

In subsequent press conferences and reminiscences, both leaders did much to obscure the origins of the policy. At various times, including his original announcement at Casablanca, FDR breezily claimed that the phrase had just popped into his head before his press conference with Churchill. On another occasion, he recounted a dialogue between Grant and Confederate General Robert E. Lee about surrender.

None of it was true. Roosevelt had given the matter considerable thought before the Casablanca Conference. In May 1942, FDR informally approved the recommendation made by the postwar advisory committee he had established. FDR, like the members of the committee, believed that one cause of World War II was that World War I had ended in circumstances that allowed the Germans to think that they had not actually been defeated on the battlefield. Unconditional surrender, which would lay the country open to military occupation, would eliminate any chance that Germans would misinterpret the results of the war this time. The policy also meshed with Roosevelt's oft-repeated belief that the only way to ensure that the Axis powers would not disrupt the peace again would be to root out the sources of fascist ideologies; that meant going beyond punishing individual leaders and transforming societies.

Not surprisingly, domestic politics also figured in Roosevelt's approval of the policy. Roosevelt, who had been President Woodrow Wilson's assistant secretary of the Navy, remembered that Republicans had pilloried Wilson for rejecting their demands for Germany's unconditional surrender in favor of an armistice based on the Fourteen Points. Pursuit of unconditional surrender would, he hoped, inoculate FDR against charges that he was repeating his predecessor's mistakes.[8]

Roosevelt did not publicly announce his commitment to the policy until Casablanca, almost eight months later. By that time, military-diplomatic circumstances and political considerations turned the president's impulse to punish the aggressors into a concrete policy. On January 7, 1943, before leaving for Casablanca, FDR informed the Joint Chiefs of Staff that he was going to speak to Churchill about the advisability of informing Joseph Stalin that the Allies would not stop until they reached Berlin and "that their only terms would be unconditional surrender."[9] Roosevelt saw it as way of shoring up the alliance with the Soviet Union. In early 1942, the president had carelessly promised the Russians that the U.S. would open a second front in Europe by the end of the year. When that proved impossible, Roosevelt pushed hard for an invasion of North Africa so that Americans would be fighting Germans somewhere before the year was out. That offensive did little to satisfy Stalin. Therefore, FDR sought to assure the Soviet leader that the Western allies would see the war through to the end and not make a separate peace with Germany.

Unconditional surrender would also ease concerns on the home front about Roosevelt's willingness to negotiate with the dictators who had started the war. Those concerns were aroused when the Americans negotiated with the collaborationist Vichy French government in North Africa in order to minimize the French military's opposition to the U.S. invasion. The compromise, which was agreed to after brief but sharp fighting, left Admiral Jean Darlan, the commander-in-chief of Vichy French forces, in control of French North Africa. Many of FDR's backers saw this arrangement as a betrayal of the basic goals of the war. What was next, some in Congress asked, a deal with German *Reichsmarschall* Herman Goering or Japanese Foreign Minister Matsuoka Yosuke?[10] Roosevelt had been stung by these criticisms. His announcement of unconditional surrender was meant to assure voters that the Darlan deal was a one-off arrangement. There would be no compromises with the leaders of the Axis powers.

Like FDR, the Joint Chiefs of Staff had more than one reason for embracing the policy. They worried, with good reason, about the American public's willingness to endure the sacrifices demanded by a war fought on multiple fronts. Unconditional surrender, they hoped, would serve as a rallying cry, a statement of objectives that the public could understand and support. Moreover, the Joint Chiefs, like FDR, also believed that a lasting peace required the complete destruction of German and Japanese military power.[11]

FDR discussed the subject with Churchill on the second day of the summit at Casablanca on January 18. When he sent the proposal on to the cabinet, Churchill explained that the policy was being applied only to Germany and Japan because there was some hope that by omitting Italy, the Allies would encourage the downfall of the government in Rome and its replacement with one eager to surrender. Churchill's cabinet approved the announcement of unconditional surrender but rejected the argument about Italy. Churchill subsequently added Italy to the press communiqué that he and FDR drafted but, for reasons that remain unclear, never released. Instead, Roosevelt announced the policy in the press conference quoted earlier. Toward the end of the conference, Churchill asked the press to convey to the world the unity that characterized Allied policymaking and to assure their audiences that the United Nations would prosecute the war "until we have procured the unconditional surrender of the criminal forces who plunged the world into storm and ruin."[12]

Churchill later claimed that he had not discussed the policy of unconditional surrender with Roosevelt and that he had been surprised when the president announced it at the press conference. That clearly was not the case. Churchill also subsequently explained, more plausibly, that once Italy was included in the statement, he lost enthusiasm for it. There is, however, no record of his having objected to the policy at the time. For his part, Roosevelt muddied the waters by his references to Grant and Lee. Roosevelt's adoption of the term and the policy had nothing to do with "Unconditional Surrender" Grant. His subsequent references were fabrications but nevertheless succeeded in their main purpose—clearly communicating to the American people that, like Grant, the Allies were resolutely determined to compel the enemy's total defeat, without compromise, and despite the costs.[13]

Influential columnist Walter Lippmann agreed that Roosevelt's statement committed the Allies to pursue total victory. Lippmann also recognized the significance of the doctrine for relations with the Soviet Union. He viewed Roosevelt's statement as a renunciation of the "super-duper realists" who wanted to make the Darlan deal a model for diplomacy with Germany and its satellites because they feared the growing power of the Soviet Union in Europe. Lippmann said jeeringly that the "amateur Machiavellis in their sheltered bureaus who fondly imagine they are both military strategists and guardians against Communism have had their little fling at statesmanship."

Roosevelt's pronouncement had made it abundantly clear that there would be no "tricky deals" with the Germans or the Japanese.[14]

Roosevelt held to that approach publicly and privately over the next two years. In November 1943, the president, Churchill, and Generalissimo Chiang Kai-shek affirmed their support for the unconditional surrender of Japan after their meeting in Cairo. The Cairo Declaration, as the statement was called, promised to strip Japan of the territories it had gained through imperialist expansion, specifically Formosa (Taiwan), Korea, the Pacific islands acquired during World War I, and Manchuria, as well as "all other territories taken by violence and greed." Toward those ends, the three leaders pledged themselves to "persevere in the serious and prolonged operations necessary to procure the unconditional surrender of Japan."[15]

At various times, Churchill and some presidential advisors urged FDR to consider softening the demand. During one meeting with Roosevelt at the Yalta summit conference in February 1945, Churchill raised the possibility of shortening the war with Japan by delivering a four-power ultimatum demanding Japan's surrender coupled with an offer to mitigate the severity of unconditional surrender should the Japanese accept. Churchill left it to the Americans to decide what such mitigation might entail, but it appears that he had in mind some reassurance on the status of the emperor.[16] The prime minister emphasized the thousands of lives that would be saved if Japan capitulated, but he had additional reasons for seeking an early end to the war. Chief among these was his concern that Britain would be left alone facing Russia in Europe were the United Sates to redirect its resources to the Pacific following Germany's defeat. Roosevelt responded to Churchill's suggestion by saying that it might be worthwhile to broach the subject with Stalin, but he doubted the ultimatum would have much effect on the Japanese until they began to feel the full weight of American air power in their country.

The president was determined to make Germany and Japan suffer the consequences of their aggression. He made his last public statement on the subject in his March 1, 1945, report to Congress following Yalta. After repeating his assurance that unconditional surrender did not mean the enslavement of the German people, Roosevelt explained what it did mean. Germany would be occupied by the Allies, Nazi laws repealed, and Nazis put on trial and punished severely. The occupation would also eliminate militaristic influences in German society, dismantle the German military, and abolish the General Staff. Germany would pay reparations in kind to the countries it invaded, but, he added, "We don't want the German people to starve or to become a burden on the rest of the world." Later in the speech, Roosevelt spoke about plans for Japan. "The defeat of Germany will not mean the end of the war against Japan. On the contrary, we must be prepared for a long and costly struggle in the Pacific." Nevertheless, he added, "the unconditional surrender of Japan is as essential as the defeat of Germany. I say that advisedly, with the thought in mind that that is especially true if our plans for world peace are to succeed. For Japanese militarism must be wiped out as thoroughly as German militarism."[17] That was the last presidential statement on the topic until April 16, when Truman spoke to Congress.

Truman soon realized that Roosevelt had not indulged in hyperbole when he spoke of the need to remind himself, and the American people, that there were two wars being fought. FDR and the Joint Chiefs had long worried that the American public would balk at the sacrifices required to defeat both Germany and Japan. They were also concerned that the end of war in Europe would create a massive letdown in public support for the war against Japan. Those worries intensified as the defeat of Germany seemed only a matter of weeks away. After more than three years of war, many on the home front were growing more vocal in resisting government controls and questioning the fairness of the sacrifices they were being asked to make in support of the war effort. Labor unions broke their fragile truce with business more frequently; Congress vehemently rejected the administration's efforts to regiment the workforce through a national service law, known as the work-or-fight bill; and business leaders and consumer organizations called more insistently for the lifting of restraints on domestic production.

A number of developments fed the growing expectation of a dramatic shift toward production for the home front, referred to as "economic reconversion." On April 2, James Byrnes, the director of the Office of War Mobilization and Reconversion (OWMR), announced that he was stepping down from the post he had held since May 1943. The resignation of Roosevelt's "assistant president for the home front"—as he was called—came shortly after his office issued a quarterly report that contained an obligatory warning that after Germany's surrender, the stepped-up campaign against Japan would continue to place great demands on the economy. Nevertheless, most observers, including Byrnes's former colleagues in the Senate, saw the report as signaling greater emphasis on reconversion. Byrnes's resignation, which they viewed as indicating a new direction for OWMR, with greater emphasis on the "R," reinforced those perceptions.[18]

The civilian and uniformed inhabitants of the recently completed Pentagon resisted these calls and defended military prerogatives against encroachment from Congress, business, and labor. Undersecretary of War Robert Patterson epitomized the view shared by most military officials that there could be no let-up in military production until both wars were over. A corporate lawyer in civilian life, Patterson—dubbed "Washington's Number One Warlord" by *Time* magazine—proved more than a match for the advocates of reconversion. Disciplined and austere, he followed in the tradition of government service established by his patron, Secretary of War Henry Stimson, and proved to be an even more dogged bureaucratic warrior. "Bob Patterson has a one-track mind," complained Solid Fuels Director Harold Ickes, "and that one track is just a short spur."[19]

When Truman moved into the Oval Office, he found himself squarely in the middle of the battle between the Pentagon and the civilian advocates of reconversion. That conflict intensified on May 8 when the shooting war in Europe ended abruptly and Hitler's successors surrendered unconditionally to Allied forces in a schoolhouse in Reims, France. As the Allies maneuvered their forces into the occupation zones agreed upon at Yalta, the American commander General Dwight D. Eisenhower simultaneously initiated the first stages of a massive redeployment that, according to plans, would move three million GIs from Europe to the Pacific in time to finish the war against Japan. The redeployment—described by General George C. Marshall, Chief of Staff of the Army, as the "biggest administrative task in history"—began with a shuffling of troops into different categories based on their Adjusted Rating Scores, a number determined by several variables, including length of service, combat experience, and military valor. Men with scores over 85 points would move into divisions designated for shipment home and discharge from the service. Those with scores near 85 would move into divisions assigned to occupation duty in Europe. The remainder, excluding engineers and construction troops, would be assigned to divisions designated for service against Japan, following a thirty-day furlough in the United States. Engineers and construction units would head straight for the Pacific with no furlough.

Redeployment was necessary to carry out the planned invasion of Japan, which Marshall, for one, believed was the only way to compel Japan's unconditional surrender. Demobilization, the discharge of high-point men, was enacted to reward those GIs whose prior service exempted them from the final campaign against Japan. The program was also conceived of as a dividend payable to the home front once Germany was defeated. Marshall hoped that the orderly release of GIs would demonstrate that the Army was not insensitive to the public's desire to bring the boys home. To devise a system deemed fair by those involved, the Army took the unusual step of using modern survey techniques, polling GIs for their views on the subject. In effect, as one historian has noted, the Army took the extraordinary step of treating its soldiers like a political constituency.[20]

GIs overwhelmingly gave their approval to the process when it was unveiled. They continued to support the criteria used for awarding the Adjusted Rating Score when it was announced in May. They were less pleased, however, with what they perceived as the sluggish pace of discharges and seemingly haphazard availability of ships to carry them home. These complaints were nothing compared with the uproar at home. To Marshall's dismay, and the surprise of the officers administering demobilization and re-deployment, the announcement of the critical score for discharge touched off a public clamor to bring the boys home as speedily as possible. Feeling the heat from constituents, congressmen turned to the Army for answers. The Army urged patience and, at the risk of reversing its priorities, put more resources into demobilization than it originally planned. That, in turn, created a backlog in redeployment, which was already snarled by shipping shortages, miscommunication between transportation officers in Europe and the U.S., and the extraordinarily complicated process of sorting troops into their new units.[21]

Following Germany's surrender, the seemingly distinct programs of re-conversion, redeployment, and demobilization all became intertwined in the public debate. In many economic sectors, reconversion depended on the release of skilled workers from military service. That led to calls for modifications in the discharge system that the Army had painstak-ingly devised. Advocates of reconversion also questioned the large number of troops envisioned for the one-front war against Japan, as well as the enormous quantities of supplies they needed to carry out their mission. Legislators, business leaders, organized labor, and public commentators all complained that the military, the Army in particular, was devouring the materials and manpower needed to begin the process of reconversion to a peacetime economy. Lingering resentment toward the military over the "work-or-fight" bill and the Army's use of inexperienced eighteen-year-olds in battle, among other issues, gave the debates over manpower and materials a sharper edge than they might otherwise have had. When the national service bill went down to defeat, Alan Drury, the Senate correspondent for United Press, gleefully wrote in his journal, "The handwriting is on the wall for the roll-top regulars of the Pentagon and Navy Building and as much as they hate it, their little fling at ruling America is entering its final stages with the war."[22]

Despite the torrent of criticism, Undersecretary Patterson held firm in his commitment to the existing discharge system and the Army's manpower and materials requirements for the final campaign against Japan. General Marshall tried to defend the Army's position in closed sessions with legislators, but the Chief of Staff was finding the experience increasingly disagreeable, especially when he was able to read about his supposedly classified deliberations in the next day's papers. For the time being, the armed services could count on Truman's support in the debate over reconversion. In his role as chair of the Senate Special Committee to Investigate the National Defense Program, Truman had acted as a vigilant custodian of the taxpayer's money. As president, he was willing to defer to the military while he attended to other pressing business.

As senator and during his brief tenure as vice president, Truman acquired valuable experience dealing with the domestic side of national politics. He had little experience in foreign affairs, however, and virtually no insight into Roosevelt's policies beyond what he could glean from FDR's public statements. When he became president, Truman pledged himself to carrying out Roosevelt's policies. During his first weeks in office, he struggled to learn what exactly those policies were. As his first speech to Congress showed, Truman believed that unconditional surrender and leadership in the United Nations Organization headed the list. Beyond that, things got murky. Roosevelt's reliance on special representatives operating outside of the State Department bureaucracy and his penchant for acting as his own secretary of state left Truman with little institutional support. He would have to rely on Roosevelt's emissaries for assistance. There was no guarantee, however, that they would agree with each other. Nor was it clear that even they had more than a fragmentary understanding of their former boss's policies.

From the moment he took office, relations with the Soviet Union topped Truman's list of concerns. The Soviet-American alliance began in 1941 as a marriage of convenience, and three years of being allies had done little to change the contractual nature of the relationship. As early as summer 1941, Roosevelt had recognized that the United States would have to rely on Soviet assistance to defeat Germany in a reasonable amount of time. War plans drafted in the U.S. estimated that the Americans would need to mobilize more than two hundred divisions of approximately fifteen thousand men if Germany defeated Russia. The Soviets held and the Americans eventually mobilized only ninety-one divisions. Before the Western allies landed in France on June 6, 1944, the Red Army was responsible for 90 percent of German casualties. After June 6, German casualties on the eastern front exceeded by two hundred thousand the total number of German troops deployed against General Eisenhower's forces.[23] The political settlement in the areas occupied by the Soviets would reflect the harsh reality contained in those stark numbers.

Roosevelt had understood that Stalin would not leave Soviet security to the untried methods of the new United Nations. He appears, however, to have hoped that Stalin would refrain from imposing on Eastern Europe a Soviet-styled police state. Rather than rely on Stalin's nonexistent generosity, Roosevelt employed a carrot-and-stick approach, dangling the prospect of postwar reconstruction aid with one hand and withholding information on the Anglo-American atomic bomb project with the other, to make Stalin more cooperative. Finally, FDR had hoped that if the Americans and British made it plain that they would not challenge Soviet suzerainty in Eastern Europe, Stalin would oblige them by providing a fig leaf of democratic respectability on the governments in that area. Beyond that, there was not much that could be done. Confrontation was out of the question, especially while Germany and Japan remained unbeaten.

Unfortunately, Roosevelt's public depiction of American relations with the Soviet Union differed significantly from his private management of those relations. Fearing a return of isolationism after the war, FDR resorted to idealistic rhetoric to hide the spheres of influence agreements concluded at Yalta. For example, at Yalta the Allies agreed to an ambiguously worded Declaration on Liberated Europe that committed them to fostering democratic governments in the areas freed from Nazi tyranny. The declaration contained no enforcement mechanism, however, and its use of terms like "democracy," which meant different things to the Americans and Soviets, made it unenforceable in any case. The Yalta agreement on Poland in which Stalin pledged to create a representative provisional government was not much better.[24]

The Yalta arrangements presented Truman with the difficult task of reconciling Roosevelt's lofty depiction of them with their realpolitik underpinnings. The Big Three's agreements on Asia posed even more of a challenge because they remained secret to preserve the fiction of Soviet neutrality in the Pacific War. In the Agreement Regarding Japan, Roosevelt welcomed Stalin's pledge to enter the Pacific War within three months of Germany's surrender and his pledge to recognize only the Chinese Nationalist (Guomindang) government of Chiang Kai-shek. As compensation, Roosevelt and Churchill agreed that the Soviets would acquire a share in the Chinese Eastern and South Manchurian Railways, the southern half of Sakhalin island, the Kurile Islands, and leases to the port of Dairen and naval base at Port Arthur on the Liaotung Peninsula. By conceding to Stalin what he could take by force, Roosevelt hoped to avoid a scramble for influence in Asia after the war. The Soviet leader might try to seize more territory in northeast Asia after Japan's defeat, but in doing so he would lose international approval for the substantial gains he had made at Yalta. Roosevelt gambled that Stalin would not take that risk; with American forces scattered throughout the Pacific and with the first stage of the invasion of Japan half a year off, he saw few alternatives.

Roosevelt lived long enough after Yalta to see that as the Red Army moved into Eastern and Central Europe, Stalin cared little about pleasing the Allies. The Soviets did not impose their will uniformly in the areas they liberated from the Germans, but in crucial areas, notably Poland, they displayed a disregard for the letter of the Yalta agreements that proved difficult to ignore. Shortly before his death, FDR cabled Churchill with the assurance that military circumstances would soon permit the Americans and British to be tougher on the Soviet Union than "has heretofore appeared advantageous to the war effort."[25]

It was now up to Truman to decide how to turn an impulse to be tough with the Russians into a workable policy. He quickly learned that there was no shortage of advisors willing to encourage him to be firmer with Stalin. There were fewer, however, who could say how that firmness would yield positive results. Among those advocating a tougher approach to the Russians was the American ambassador to Moscow, Averell Harriman. Immediately after FDR's death, Harriman had rushed to Washington to warn Truman that he faced a "barbarian invasion of Europe" unless the United States forcefully opposed Stalin's flouting of the Yalta agreements in Eastern Europe. Secretary of the Navy James Forrestal welcomed Harriman's summons to action. Forrestal, an amateur boxer in his youth, sported a twice-broken nose that was emblematic of the combative demeanor he had carried into adulthood. Agreeing with Harriman, Forrestal advised Truman that if the Russians remained unyielding on Eastern Europe, "we had better have a showdown with them now, rather than later." Also pushing for stiffening of American policy were Admiral William D. Leahy, Roosevelt's and now Truman's representative on the Joint Chiefs of Staff, and Major General John Deane, the head of the American military mission to Moscow.[26]

The new president took his first step in that direction during the second of two White House meetings with Soviet Foreign Minister Vyacheslav Molotov on April 22–23. The Soviet official stopped in Washington on his way to San Francisco for the United Nations conference to pay his respects and take the measure of the new president. During their second meeting, Truman lambasted Soviet conduct in Eastern Europe and in undiplomatic language told Molotov that he would not tolerate what he viewed as blatant disregard for the agreements made at Yalta. That sharp exchange gave advocates of a firmer policy toward the Soviet Union a momentary thrill, but Truman quickly realized that the United States could not risk a break with the Soviets. Truman needed Russian cooperation to launch the United Nations and, as Secretary of War Stimson and Chief of Staff Marshall reminded him, they were counting on the Red Army to defeat the Japanese Army in Manchuria. Truman, like FDR before him, found himself in the uncomfortable position of needing Stalin to provide the appearance of cooperation in Eastern Europe.

Truman began to recognize that the Yalta agreements were susceptible to varying interpretations. In one instance, he referred to them as "purported to have been made at Yalta."[27] Later he complained that every time he read the agreements, he "found new meanings in them."[28] In mid-May, Truman dispatched Roosevelt's confidant and personal envoy Harry Hopkins to Moscow to meet directly with Stalin. Truman wanted to show Stalin that American policy had not changed after Roosevelt's death. For his part, Stalin was willing to give Truman the meager concessions he desired. Hopkins returned with the Soviet leader's promise to reorganize the Polish government and a compromise on voting rights in the United Nations that allowed the stalemated conference in San Francisco to move forward. Having papered over his differences with Stalin, Truman agreed to meet the Soviet leader and Churchill in July in the Berlin suburb of Potsdam.

While Truman was preparing to dispatch Hopkins to Moscow, others in his administration sought to determine what, if anything, could be done to prevent Soviet domination in northeast Asia once the Red Army rolled into Manchuria. Early in April, the head of the Navy's Strategic Plans Division, Vice Admiral Charles Cooke, recommended that the United States reconsider how its strategy for the defeat of Japan would affect the postwar balance of power in East Asia. "Savvy," as Cooke was called, worried about the vacuum that would be created by the wholesale destruction of Japanese power. He advised Chief of Naval Operations Admiral Ernest King that the best way to end the war would be with a "strengthened CHINA and a JAPAN thrown back to her homeland, incapable of aggression, on the one hand, but, at the same time not completely eliminated as a party to the stabilization in EASTERN ASIA and the WESTERN PACIFIC."[29] Navy Secretary Forrestal took a similar view during a meeting of the Committee of Three (the secretaries of state, the Navy, and war) on May 1. "What is our policy on Russian influence in the Far East?" he asked. "Do we desire a counterweight to that influence? And should it be China, or should it be Japan?"[30] Ten days later, Cooke and Deputy Chief of Staff Vice Admiral Richard Edwards met with Ambassador Harriman and Forrestal to discuss the potential problems of Russia's entry into the war against Japan.

Forrestal feared that Soviet behavior in Eastern Europe offered a preview of what the Americans could expect in Asia. Harriman suggested that the situation might even be worse than Forrestal imagined, warning that "there could be no illusion as to a 'free China' once the Russians got in, that the two or three hundred millions in that country would march when the Kremlin ordered." Admirals Cooke and Richards thought that China could be spared that fate if the United States reevaluated the assumptions on which its strategy was based. According to Cooke, the U.S. no longer depended on the Soviet Union's early entry into the war against Japan. It followed that ending the war before the Russians came in would facilitate the achievement of Cooke's previously stated objective of creating a strong China while leaving Japan reduced in power but still able to contribute to the "stabilization" of the region. The challenge, of course, was finding a way to end the war before the Russians came in. "The best thing for us," Richards added, "would be if the Japanese would agree to a basis of unconditional surrender which still left them in their own minds some face and honor."[31] Richards did not explain how a surrender that preserved the Japanese military's sense of honor could still be an "unconditional" surrender. It is telling that no one at the meeting pushed him to do so.

Others in the administration were thinking along similar lines. In fact, the prospect of Soviet entry into the war so troubled Undersecretary of State Joseph Grew that he was losing sleep over it. One morning in mid-May he rose early and jotted down his concerns in a memorandum on Soviet expansionism. Regarding East Asia, he wrote, "Once Russia is in the war against Japan, then Mongolia, and Korea will gradually slip into Russia's orbit, to be followed in due course by China and eventually Japan." A career diplomat, Grew had spent most of his professional life implementing policy and transmitting information to policymakers. With the secretary of state away at the UN conference in San Francisco, he suddenly found himself in the position of being able to initiate policy. On May 12, four days after Germany's unconditional surrender, Grew sent the secretaries of war and the Navy a memo asking their views on the political consequences of the Soviet Union's entry into the war against Japan. Grew worried that the Yalta Far Eastern agreements practically invited Soviet mischief in the region. Was there something the Americans could do about that? Did they still require Russian assistance against the Japanese? If so, were they in a better position now than they had been in February to modify the Far Eastern agreements and bring them more into line with American postwar objectives?

The son of a wealthy Boston manufacturer, Grew had entered the foreign service in 1904 and risen steadily up the career ladder to hold several ambassadorial posts including ambassador to Japan in 1932. When FDR became president in 1933, he kept his Groton and Harvard classmate in Tokyo. Grew served there until the war broke out and returned to the United States in an exchange of diplomats in 1942. Despite their shared experiences as products of two of America's most elite schools, and as beneficiaries of family wealth accumulated over several generations, FDR and Grew did not see eye to eye on Japan. Their views on the Soviet Union diverged even more.

In the years before Pearl Harbor, Grew had placed his faith in the good intentions of what he termed the Japanese "moderates," the civilian leaders who had guided Japan through a decade of cooperative diplomacy with the U.S. in the 1920s. As the Japanese government came under the sway of radical militarists, Grew continued to hope that with the aid of the young emperor Hirohito they would eventually regain control and return Japan to a more peaceful role in international affairs. Grew's analysis of Japanese politics suffered from his reliance on Japan's cosmopolitan elite for insights into government activity. The group he and others termed "moderates" were staunchly conservative, even reactionary, in domestic politics. Like the militarists, they also sought Japanese dominance of East Asia, although they hoped it could be accomplished less violently and without antagonizing the United States.

After Japan invaded China in 1937, the men who Grew trusted to steer Japan on a saner course lost any ability to influence policy. Nevertheless, in late 1941, not long before Pearl Harbor, Grew continued to believe that a leaders' meeting between Roosevelt and the Japanese prime minister would avert a final break in relations. Roosevelt disagreed. Grew's perspective was bilateral and constricted by his residence in Tokyo. Roosevelt's was global, considering the interests of allies and potential allies. Grew's desire to avoid conflict was admirable, but Roosevelt had to consider how an eleventh-hour compromise would look to the Chinese or, even more importantly, the Russians, who were reeling from the invasion Hitler launched against them in June 1941. American intelligence showing Japanese preparations for further military advances reinforced Roosevelt's perception of Japanese duplicity and strengthened his inclination to stand with the nations opposing the Axis powers. There would be no leaders' meeting.[32]

Nearly four years later, Grew believed that he would once more be able to prevent a catastrophe by restraining Soviet advances in Asia. The War Department promptly threw cold water on those aspirations. On May 21, Secretary of War Henry Stimson submitted to Grew an analysis prepared by the Army's Strategy and Policy Group (S&P) and approved by General Marshall. The Army's paper concluded that the United States still needed the Red Army to tie down Japanese forces in Manchuria. Moreover, according to the S&P, the Yalta agreements gave to the Russians nothing they could not take by force. Given those circumstances, the Army concluded that there was little point in pressing for a "reconsideration" of the existing agreements, although Grew was welcome to try. After consulting with Admiral King, Forrestal sent Grew a memorandum supporting the Army's view.[33] Grew's plan to limit Soviet expansion fell victim to military necessity.

But what if the war ended before the Russians entered? The Yalta agreements called for Soviet entry into the Pacific War three months after Germany's surrender. Grew wondered whether it would be possible to induce Japan's surrender before then. Its situation was militarily hopeless. Its transportation and productive capacity were collapsing under the weight of massively destructive B-29 attacks that pummeled Japanese cities with impunity. American submarines had annihilated Japan's merchant fleet and isolated the home islands from the empire's resource areas. Surely

Joseph C. Grew. U.S. Library of Congress Print and Photographs Division.

there were leaders in Tokyo who understood the hopelessness of their position. Grew believed there were. He saw the appointment of Suzuki as prime minister as an indication that the tide was turning in Tokyo in favor of the moderates.

He believed, however, that the peace faction in Japan would not succeed unless the United States abandoned its policy of unconditional surrender. The American refusal to discuss the terms created an insuperable obstacle for the moderates. They could not argue for peace if it meant leaving the fate of the emperor and the imperial institution to the mercy of the victors. Grew felt sure that would be unacceptable to all Japanese, not just the militarists. Therefore, the Japanese would need some guarantee that they could preserve the throne and shield Hirohito from punishment before they could consider ending the war. Grew's ten years in Japan had convinced him that the emperor was a peace-loving monarch who regretted the war but had no influence over its direction. The emperor's power was largely symbolic, according to Grew. Paradoxically, the moderates needed imperial approval to succeed. That would not be forthcoming without the desired guarantees from the Americans on the inviolability of the imperial institution.

Grew believed that compromise with Japan offered so many benefits it would amount to diplomatic malpractice to not pursue a negotiated settlement. The most obvious would be the tens of thousands of American lives saved by avoiding an invasion of Japan's home islands. However, Grew could not have separated that outcome from its corollary; an early end to the war would void the Yalta agreements and withdraw American approval for Russian encroachment in northeast Asia. Despite the rebuff from the Army, Grew pushed ahead with his efforts to induce Japan's surrender on conditions less severe than unconditional.

On May 27, American newspapers reported that the latest B-29 raids on Tokyo had sent flames roaring into the imperial compound. Grew was convinced that there was no time to lose. The situation demanded action. Surely, the threat of immolation would concentrate Hirohito's mind on survival and make him more willing to stop the war, providing he survived. On May 28, Grew met with Truman to discuss his thoughts on ending the war. Grew hoped that the president would use his forthcoming address to Congress on the military situation to offer the Japanese a version of unconditional surrender that they would find acceptable. The only way to accomplish that, Grew believed, would be to assure the Japanese that the United States would not destroy the imperial institution. That seemed a minor concession, Grew believed, since the Japanese would eventually restore the monarchy once the Americans left. Preservation of the imperial institution also made sense because the most that one could hope for in Japan was a constitutional monarchy, given that experience showed that democracy there "would never work."

Grew pressed his case by lecturing the president on Japanese history. Drawing on his decade of experience in Japan, the former ambassador asserted that the American critics of Japan's monarchy misunderstood its past. For much of its history, Japan's emperors were confined to Kyoto and kept poor and powerless while the Shoguns, predecessors of the modern militarists, ruled the country and made war on its neighbors. The Meiji restoration in 1868 changed all that. The Meiji emperor, Grew explained, was "a strong man who overcame the militaristic Shoguns and who started Japan on a moderate peaceful course." Unfortunately, Emperor Meiji's successors, Hirohito and his father, were not as strong and the militarists stormed back into power. Hirohito and his advisors wanted peace, but they were overwhelmed by the militarists. "The foregoing facts," Grew added, "indicate clearly that Japan does not need an Emperor to be militaristic nor are the Japanese militaristic because they have an Emperor." The military clique that seized control of the government rendered Hirohito and his peace-minded advisors powerless. That did not exonerate Hirohito from responsibility for signing the war declaration, Grew admitted, but once the militarists were deposed, the throne could be used as a cornerstone by the long-suppressed moderates to build a new government.[34]

Grew's recitation of Japanese history contained glaring inaccuracies and was open to question as to its logic. For example, it is unclear as to what he was referring when he asserted that experience had shown the Japanese unsuited for democracy. More troubling was his depiction of the Meiji era, in which Japan fought China and Russia, colonized Taiwan, and exerted dominion over Korea, as one of moderation and peace. Japan may have been at peace with the U.S. but not with Asia. Grew's view of Japanese history as oscillating between moderation and militarism glossed over how the militarists came to power and what role they played.[35] His analysis did not address whether they were anomalous or a constant presence in Japanese life, a dormant virus that was activated when the body politic came under stress. Perhaps he thought it was not that important. The postwar era would belong to the moderates and their constitutional monarchy.

Regarding the emperor, the undersecretary's conclusions were distorted. The Meiji emperor did not subdue the Shogun; the oligarchs who engineered the restoration did. They built on that success by embarking on a nation-building program that emphasized Japanese uniqueness. Grew was correct that in 1937 the militarists had seized the throne for their own uses. But the modern imperial institution had not been the benign force in Japanese life that he claimed it was. The Meiji Constitution (1889), which borrowed heavily from the Prussian Constitution, was a gift from the emperor to the Japanese people and sovereignty resided in the emperor. It was an authoritarian system meant to ensure the supremacy of the state. In the new nation, the emperor was the source of all governmental authority. He was also supreme military commander. In practical terms, the oligarchs ruled in the emperor's name and used his authority to build the militarily powerful state that joined the ranks of the great powers in the early twentieth century.[36]

Propagandists worked tirelessly to inculcate a spirit of selfless loyalty to the emperor, who presided as head of the national family. That made him indispensable as the embodiment of *kokutai*, which is usually translated as "national structure" or "national polity." The authority vested in the monarchy made it a bulwark against reform from below. Subjects had many obligations but few rights under the constitution. Dissent was equated to disloyalty. In 1937, ultranationalists took the imperial idea to its extreme conclusion and declared the emperor divine. That was the system that survived into the war.[37]

Truman did not question Grew's analysis. If he had any doubts, he kept them to himself. Instead, the president said he was interested in what Grew had said because his thoughts "had been following the same line." Truman was almost certainly humoring Grew at this point. In any case, despite his supposed sympathy for Grew's views, Truman asked Grew to solicit the opinions of the Joint Chiefs of Staff and the secretaries of the War and Navy Departments on the subject. Shortly after he left the White House, Grew arranged to meet with Stimson, Forrestal, Marshall, and Chief of Naval Operations Admiral Ernest King in Stimson's Pentagon office at 11:00 a.m. the next day.[38] It is not surprising that Truman directed Grew to consult with the military on his proposal. After all, Grew was asking the president to drastically alter policy on Japan. As it turned out, the leaders of the armed services had been reviewing the policy of unconditional surrender, especially in connection to the status of the emperor, for several months.

By January 1945, staff officers in the U.S. Army and Navy were dealing with two related contingencies. The first was that Japan might seek to end the war soon after Germany was defeated, which was expected by early summer.[39] The second was that the Japanese would fight on and make an invasion necessary. The second contingency was meeting resistance from the Navy, which argued that blockade and bombardment would bring Japan to its knees. General Marshall and his staff believed that a strategy of siege would lengthen the war, sap American morale, and result in an undesirable negotiated settlement. He instructed his planners to think about the how the U.S. would respond to the first contingency while they also made certain that plans went forward for an invasion.

By early April, staff officers from the Army, Navy, and Army Air Force were working together under the auspices of the Joint Chiefs of Staff to estimate under what circumstances the Japanese would recognize they were defeated and surrender. The planners could only guess as to the timing. Further speculation produced a range of possibilities regarding the condition of the government in Japan that would eventually agree to surrender and its ability to command its armed forces to lay down their arms. The staff officers were more certain about when the Japanese would know they were defeated. In fact, it was clear that some members of the Japanese government already realized the inevitability of defeat. Others would reach that conclusion during the coming months, when the American bombardment reached its crescendo. The holdouts would finally accept reality when the Russians entered the war.

The planners cautioned, however, that a realization of defeat would not automatically lead to surrender. The problem was the policy of unconditionality. According to the Joint Intelligence Staff, "The literal meaning of unconditional surrender is a term which is unknown to the Japanese." This obstacle might be overcome if the Americans could explain to the Japanese government that it did not mean "annihilation or national suicide." In the meantime, the authors of the report added, by midsummer the Japanese government would seek ways to "surrender without the stigma of admitting it is 'unconditional surrender.'"[40]

The Joint Intelligence Staff's analysis of a military problem—the possibility of an early Japanese surrender and the conditions under which that might occur—had led it into a political minefield. The staff officers asserted that the policy of unconditional surrender was an obstacle to peace. To obtain their war aims, the Allies would need to clarify the policy's meaning, preferably in a form that removed its alleged stigma. Roosevelt, on the other hand, had no desire to remove whatever stigma attached to the policy. He had already said publicly on several occasions that it did not mean the enslavement of the Germans or Japanese. Beyond that, he was not prepared to go. Evidence of the atrocious treatment of American prisoners only strengthened the president's commitment. Speaking to reporters in July 1944, Roosevelt said, "Practically all Germans deny the fact that they surrendered during the last war, but this time they are going to know it. And so are the Japs."[41]

The Joint Intelligence Staff's assertion that unconditional surrender did not translate into Japanese was also suspect.[42] The meaning of the term was not lost in translation. The Japanese objected to the policy because they knew precisely what it meant: that the Allies would control their nation and reform its social and political structure. The whole point of it was to end the war in such a way that the Allies would be free to make the changes they found necessary. The extent of those changes would be determined by the circumstances of surrender. Japanese troops, supported by the government in Tokyo, had been on a rampage through Asia for almost fifteen years. They had plundered the areas they conquered and mercilessly subjected millions of people to violence and starvation. How could anyone be certain what steps were needed to bring the perpetrators to justice and ensure that the institutions that made that devastation possible were eliminated? Roosevelt refused to commit the Allies to any policies that would limit their options until the Japanese laid down their arms.

Members of the Joint Intelligence Staff were not alone in struggling with the issue of an early surrender. By early May, Army and Navy planners couldn't agree on how conditions on the battle fronts—both in Germany and the Pacific—affected the possibility. The Army officers believed that the German collapse was likely to compel the Japanese to seek a way out of the war. The Japanese were isolated and anxious about what the Russians would do. They also would do almost anything to keep the emperor and his family out of the hands of a foreign invader. The Army report's authors optimistically added that the recent installation of the "moderate" Suzuki as prime minister meant "that the formerly strong extremist group is no longer dominate in Japan." These circumstances made a Japanese peace offer likely. It was equally likely that the offer would contain conditions that the Allies would find unacceptable such as no occupation of the home is-lands. Nevertheless, growing war weariness on the American home front might make such an offer difficult to refuse. The alternative would be to launch an invasion. To avoid having to face that dilemma, the staff officers recommended that the United States issue a demand for Japan's imme-diate unconditional surrender. The attached draft of the demand warned the Japanese that they faced the same fate as Germany and that the emperor and imperial family would either be killed during the invasion or taken captive by the Allies.[43]

The Army's paper was noteworthy for suggesting that the Allies would need to assure the Japanese that the imperial family and by extension the monarchy would remain intact after a surrender. Over the next three months the debate over modification of unconditional surrender would turn on the question of what was to be done with the emperor and the monarchy. Already there was disagreement on that score. When transmitting the draft demand up the chain of command, the Army's assistant chief of staff explained that regarding the emperor, "there are major differences of opinion."

That was not the only source of disagreement. Navy representatives on the joint staff objected to linking the demand for unconditional surrender to Germany's defeat. The battle for Okinawa was a little over a month old and after a promising start had become a brutal campaign of attrition. The Navy, under whose direction the campaign was waged, was suffering heavy casualties from kamikaze attacks on ships supporting the land forces. The Army predicted that the Japanese would be demoralized by Germany's surrender. The Navy worried that the Japanese would feel emboldened by the heavy toll they exacted from the Americans on Okinawa. A demand for Japan's surrender had to be made from a position of strength, otherwise the Japanese high command would view it as evidence of weakening American morale. Rather than send the Army's paper to the Joint Chiefs where it would face certain rejection by the Navy, it was shunted off to a subcommittee in the faint hope that some compromise could be found.[44]

The staff officers struggling to make projections about Japan's future actions had veered into speculating about what steps the United States could take to encourage a timely Japanese surrender. On occasion they wriggled out of the constraints imposed by the unconditional surrender policy, only to find their efforts stymied by internal disagreement over the fate of the emperor and the timing of a warning. Undaunted, they continued to seek compromise on a statement demanding Japan's surrender. The least controversial of the proposals they had recommended involved a clarification of the assurance to Japanese subjects that the policy did not mean their destruction or enslavement. As noted, FDR had already made several statements in that vein. Truman reiterated them on May 8 in his public announcement of Germany's surrender. In that speech, the president threatened the Japanese with the same level of destruction the Allies had brought to bear on Germany if they did not surrender unconditionally. He then explained that this meant the end of the war as well as of the influence of Japan's militaristic leaders. It also meant "provision for the return of soldiers and sailors to their farms, families, jobs." "Unconditional surrender" he continued, echoing his predecessor, "does not mean the extermination or enslavement of the Japanese people."[45]

Truman's assurance made little impact on the Japanese government's commitment to carry on with the war. Nor, as it turned out, did Germany's surrender—despite the efforts of Foreign Minister Togo to seize the moment for a reappraisal of Japan's situation. Between May 11 and May 14, Togo arranged for a series of meetings of the Supreme Council for the

Direction of the War that restricted attendance to the Big Six, the foreign minister, Army and Navy chiefs of staff, Army and navy ministers, and the minister of foreign affairs. Togo's intention was to exclude the subcabinet officials and midlevel officers who normally produced the policies approved by their superiors. Most of these lesser officials were fire-breathing bitterenders who would rather see Japan's hundred million souls die in defense of the sacred homeland than endure the humiliation of surrender. Togo hoped that the absence of these apocalyptically inclined officials would encourage the Big Six to speak more freely and discuss alternatives to ending the war that did not include the obliteration of the nation.

After much discussion, the meetings yielded a three-point plan of action, all of which centered on the Soviet Union. The product of compromise, as opposed to firm agreement, the plan sought to obtain the Soviet Union's pledge to stay out of the Pacific War. The Japanese would also seek to persuade the Soviets to adopt a friendly attitude toward Japan. To gain Russia's friendship, Tokyo would be willing to swap economic and territorial concessions, including the fruits of Japan's victory over Russia in 1905, in exchange for oil and other war materials. If the Japanese failed to secure the objectives of the first two points, they would, as a last resort, seek Russia's good offices in mediating an end to the conflict on terms favorable to Japan.[46]

Following the meetings, the Big Six decided that an emissary would be dispatched to meet with the Soviet ambassador. Togo regarded the assignment as doomed from the start. He tried but failed to convince his colleagues that the Russians had already made their own bargain with the Americans and British at Japan's expense. Togo's handpicked envoy eventually arranged to meet with the Soviet ambassador in Hakone, outside Tokyo. The discussions on improving Japan-Soviet relations began on June 3, nearly three weeks after the Big Six meetings ended. The Soviet ambassador, Jacob Malik, dragged out these preliminary conversations by explaining that he needed instructions from Moscow.[47] As Malik waited, the situation worsened for Japan.

While the Japanese pursued a rapprochement with the Russians, the Americans continued to evaluate the desirability of issuing a warning to the Japanese that time was running out. Toward that end, the Joint Intelligence Staff continued to labor on a paper that could be approved by the Joint Chiefs and forwarded to the State Department. It would then be up to the State Department to decide how to handle their proposals, but the staff officers hoped that their demand for unconditional surrender would be presented to the Japanese government through diplomatic channels. Those hopes were frustrated by continued disagreement among the staff officers, leading to the deletion of some of the main justifications for issuing a demand for Japan's surrender. As the paper neared completion, the reference to the supposedly moderate cast of the Suzuki cabinet was stricken. So, too, was any mention of the emperor. What was left was a demand for unconditional surrender that did not go beyond the president's May 8 statement. Even those changes were not enough to overcome the chief obstacle to its release. On May 20, Assistant Secretary of War John J. McCloy advised General Marshall that the secretary of war opposed issuing the demand for unconditional surrender until after the battle for Okinawa was won.[48]

This was the third time in recent weeks that Stimson had swatted away proposed changes in established policy. Earlier, he had advised Truman against confronting the Soviets over Poland and quashed Grew's attempt to revisit the Yalta agreements on Asia. Various officials, most notably Grew and Ambassador Harriman, had taken advantage of the change of leadership in the White House to recommend to the new president policies that struck Stimson as recklessly provocative. Stimson did not believe that Poland was important enough to risk a breach with the Russians, especially when the Red Army was needed to drive the Japanese out of Manchuria. Circumstances demanded attention to timing and a careful balancing of means and ends. Harriman and Churchill wanted Truman to arrange an early meeting with Stalin, but Stimson counseled delay. "We shall prob ably hold more cards in our hands later than now," he explained. The cards Stimson referred to were the Russians' need for American assistance in rebuilding their industries and Anglo-American development of an atomic weapon. Stimson confidently predicted that America's commanding economic position and its impending possession of this weapon would amount to "a royal straight flush," an unbeatable hand, provided that the United States bided its time.[49]

Though it wasn't directed at him, Truman would have had little difficulty understanding that Stimson's poker metaphor was a disguised reference to the atomic bomb. Stimson had informed Truman about its existence after the first cabinet meeting on the night of April 12. On April 25, Stimson gave the new president a full briefing. Also present was Major General Leslie Groves, the commander of the Manhattan Engineering District, the code name for the atomic bomb project. Groves had prepared a memorandum on the weapon's development and current status. Stimson also presented a memorandum. "Within four months," it began, "we shall have in all probability completed the most terrible weapon ever known in human history, one bomb of which could destroy a whole city."[50] The remainder of Stimson's memo explained Great Britain's role in the development of the bomb and discussed in broad terms the problems that would arise once the secret of the atomic bomb was revealed to the world. It also described the history of the project and explained that the bomb would be ready by August 1 and that a second would be ready by the end of the year. The project scientists were working on a second type of bomb, an implosion device, but, Groves explained, they had run into problems. If they were able to solve those problems, an implosion device would be ready by the end of August and subsequent bombs would be ready every ten days after that. The bomb would be dropped by a specially organized unit of the Twentieth Air Force, which was about to move overseas for more training.[51]

Armed with this new knowledge, Truman could hope that the bomb would compel Japan's surrender without an invasion, but he could not count on it. A lot could happen in four months to upset the timetable Groves had presented. Success was tantalizingly close but still out of reach. Stimson made sure that the new president understood that.

In advising the president, the seventy-seven-year-old Stimson drew on the wisdom he had acquired during a long, distinguished career of public service. A graduate of Yale and of Harvard Law School, Stimson had entered the business world as a clerk in the prestigious Wall Street firm of Root and Clarke. Within two years, he became a partner in the firm and a protégé of Elihu Root, a prominent Republican statesman. Over the next five decades, Stimson, like Root, moved easily between the worlds of corporate law and government service. He entered the public realm in 1906 with an appointment as U.S. attorney general in the Southern District of New York, a position once held by his mentor. Stimson subsequently lost a bid to become governor of New York but continued his climb. He became secretary of war under William Howard Taft, and then served as an artillery officer in France during the Great War. After the war, Stimson acquired valuable experience in Asia as governor-general of the Philippines and subsequently became secretary of state for Herbert Hoover just before Japan commenced a decade of violent expansion in Asia that would lead to Pearl Harbor. In 1940, as war engulfed Europe, FDR appointed the internationalist-minded

Stimson secretary of war to build bipartisan support for a more activist foreign policy. During his service as colonial proconsul and the nation's top diplomat, Stimson (like Grew) developed an appreciation for Japan's moderate leaders during the relatively quiescent 1920s. That appreciation was tested when the cooperative diplomacy of the 1920s was disrupted by Japan's nationalistic drive for self-sufficiency in Asia. When the Japanese Army broke free of Tokyo's constraints and seized Manchuria in northeast China in 1931, Stimson sought to haul Japan before the court of public opinion, but his efforts were undercut by President Hoover. With the United States mired in depression, Hoover saw no reason to antagonize Japan over control of an area of relative unimportance to the U.S., especially since he thought Japanese colonialism might impose order on the chaos that seemed to perpetually envelop China. Stimson remained confident in the moral superiority of his cause, but some, including Hoover, criticized him for sticking pins in a tiger. What seemed like Stimson's last chance at public service degenerated into an education in the frustrations of conducting diplomacy unsupported by the threat of force.[52]

In 1931, Stimson had hoped to strengthen the moderates in Tokyo by opposing Japanese aggression in Manchuria. In 1945, he was once again hoping to tip the balance in favor of the suppressed peace faction believed to be aligned with the emperor. The situation demanded caution. A wrong step could play into the hands of the militarists. This was not the time for diplomatic initiatives. Eight weeks after they had come ashore on Okinawa, the Americans had yet to pierce the Imperial Japanese Army's main defensive line. A banner headline in the *Washington Post* drove the point home. "Okinawa Struggle in Bloody Deadlock: Nine Costly Charges by Yanks Win One Height," it read. The article went on to describe the valiant charges made by Marines over seven days to take the 150-foot-high Sugar Loaf Hill. The Marines, their ranks thinned by casualties, seized the rise on the seventh day, but Japanese snipers remained dug into caves and tunnels on the hill where they continued to make control of the capital city of Naha untenable for the Americans.[53] The Japanese were destined to lose, of course, but Colonel Yahara's strategy of attrition was paying off.

Stimson's unwillingness to engage in diplomacy from a position of apparent weakness momentarily put the brakes on staff officers' efforts to issue a warning to Japan, regardless of its specific contents. A week later, he rebuffed Grew's statement with its concessions on the emperor for the same reason. The May 29 meeting of the secretaries of state, war, and Navy, along with the service chiefs lasted about an hour. It began with Grew explaining his discussion with the president the previous day. He then presented a draft of the text he hoped to add to Truman's forthcoming address to Congress. Grew explained in his memo on the meeting that he hoped the president would "indicate to the Japanese that we have no intention of determining Japan's future political structure, which should be left to themselves." By Japan's "political structure," Grew of course meant the monarchy. According to Secretary of the Navy Forrestal, Grew proposed having the president say that American objectives did not include the destruction of Japan's "political concepts, of their religion, and particularly of the Emperor as a symbol of their religion." Stimson supported modification of unconditional surrender but continued to believe that this was not the time. For his part, Elmer Davis, the director of the Office of War Information, strongly opposed any attempt to modify unconditional surrender. Forrestal asked Grew if it would suffice to assure the Japanese that unconditional surrender did not mean their annihilation. According to Forrestal, Eugene Dooman, a Japan specialist and Grew's former counselor of embassy in Tokyo, replied, "If the Japanese became imbued with the idea that the United States was set on the destruction of their philosophy of government and of their religion we would face a truly national suicidal defense."[54]

Neither Grew nor Dooman thought it necessary to mention that they had encountered strong opposition to the proposed modification of unconditional surrender within the State Department. Leading the opposition to Grew's "clarification" of the policy were Assistant Secretary of State for Legislative Affairs Dean Acheson and Assistant Secretary of State for Public Affairs Archibald MacLeish. Acheson, described by left-wing journalist I. F. Stone as a "progressive and intelligent specimen of the corporate lawyer," thought the whole system needed to be pulled out by the roots, starting with the imperial institution. In private, Acheson referred to Grew as the "prince of appeasers."[55] MacLeish moved to the State Department because of his impeccable credentials as a spokesman for liberal internationalists. In December 1944, he had left his position as librarian of Congress at FDR's urging to become assistant secretary of state for public affairs. (When he accepted the appointment, FDR congratulated him on moving from one mausoleum to another.)[56]

Acheson and MacLeish questioned the desirability of exempting the emperor from punishment and permitting the Japanese to preserve an institution that was so easily exploited by the militarists.[57] That was a view held by Owen Lattimore, a China scholar and advisor in the Pacific section of the Office of War Information. Lattimore published his thoughts on reconstructing Japan in February 1945 in a slim volume titled *Solution in Asia*. Lattimore argued that democratization was possible in Japan, but first the Allies had to "puncture the myth of the divinity of the Mikado." The best way to do that, he advised, was to exile Hirohito and all males eligible for the throne to China under United Nations supervision.[58]

Grew and Dooman regarded such criticisms as fueled by blind prejudice and general ignorance of Japanese history and culture. Dooman—who had been born in Japan, spoke Japanese fluently, and had attended the elite Peers School before finishing his education in the United States—could claim even more intimate knowledge of Japan than Grew. Neither man lacked for self-confidence in claiming expertise on Japan. They knew that critics were already calling them appeasers because of their views of the emperor. Nevertheless, in the weeks ahead they would continue to advocate preserving the monarchy.

The meeting in Stimson's office ended with the secretaries agreeing to postpone issuing a statement. The capture of Okinawa, which would not be completed until June 22, no longer seemed likely to shock the Japanese into surrendering. Whatever advantage might have been gained by pairing a surrender demand with the invasion of Japanese territory had vanished. Some other demonstration of power would be needed for that purpose. Stimson, Grew, Forrestal, and the service chiefs knew that meant the atomic bomb, but were not free to speak openly in front of their junior colleagues. Grew was disappointed with the outcome of the meeting but his memorandum of conversation put the best face on the proceedings. He omitted Davis's objections and emphasized that the meeting reached consensus on the advisability of issuing the proposed warning at some point. For the time being, however, the warning, with its "clarification" of unconditional surrender, would have to wait.

On June 1, Truman issued a lengthy Memorial Day message to Congress celebrating American achievements in the war and laying out the work that remained to defeat Japan. The message contained no references to the emperor and no clarification of what surrender meant beyond the now-standard assurance "We have no desire or intention to destroy or enslave the Japanese people." Even more discouraging for Grew was Truman's warning that the Japanese were counting on American war weariness to "force us to settle for some compromise short of unconditional surrender."[59] The president assured Congress that would not happen. Grew could be excused if he thought Truman was speaking to him. Nevertheless, he was not ready to give up, especially when he knew what was in store for Japan.

In the months leading up to the Memorial Day message, the possibility of coaxing Japan's surrender without an invasion had been widely studied and discussed in the government. The bureaucratic axiom that where you stand depends on where you sit helps explain the timing and tenor of these discussions. Administration officials who had to deal with Soviet recalcitrance in Eastern Europe were among the first to see the advantage of modifying unconditional surrender in terms of how it would affect postwar relations with the Soviet Union. Mid-level military planners were less overtly political in their inquiries. They were primarily concerned with ending the war with a minimum loss of American lives. The impending entry of the Soviet Union into the Pacific War did not cast such a dark shadow over their deliberations.

Nevertheless, it was a short leap from thinking about how modification of unconditional surrender would save American lives to considering the geopolitical benefits of an early surrender. It is not surprising that Admirals Cooke and Richards took that leap. The Navy's support for unconditional surrender had always been lukewarm at best. It cooled considerably once the Imperial Japanese Navy was destroyed, given that it made blockade seem a reasonable policy to pursue. Admiral King supported unconditional surrender when it served to rally the home front, but Navy plans always assumed that the destruction of Japan's navy would be the final major operation in the war. Victory at sea, according to King, would be followed by strangulation of Japan's economy. Navy planners expected that at some point in the siege, Japan's warlords would surrender. It would be an unspectacular finish to the war but also a low-risk one.

Cooke and Richards thought that Japan was already on the verge of collapse and that the only obstacle preventing Japan's militarists from accepting the inevitability of defeat was the policy of unconditional surrender. The U.S. could remove that obstacle and induce Japan to surrender by modifying it. The war would not end with the total defeat of Japan's forces that FDR sought, but that would not matter because the destruction of Japan's navy already made it impossible for the resource-poor island nation to pose any danger to the United States. From the Navy's perspective, the benefits to be gained from a modest change in policy were irresistible. An early surrender would save thousands of American lives, preempt a Soviet invasion of northeast Asia, and confirm the role of sea power as the decisive factor in the victory.

General Marshall and members of his staff did not share the Navy's confidence in a strategy of siege. They believed that anything that delayed the outcome of the war favored the Japanese. A siege was a strategy for protracted war. To conduct an effective siege, the Navy would need to seize bases near Japan. Army staff officers worried that those peripheral operations would squander American resources without producing a swift victory. That would leave the U.S. in the undesirable position of having to maintain a blockade for an extended period. The longer the war lasted, the greater the risk of losing the American public's support for the campaign against Japan. If Japan did not yield, the U.S. would be faced with having to mobilize again for an invasion or negotiate with Japan's militarists. The first option was politically unfeasible, the second politically and militarily unthinkable.[60]

The views of Army staff officers differed in other ways from those of their Navy partners. The Army's representatives on the Joint Staff committees doubted that Japan could be induced to surrender before the Soviet Union entered the war. They also doubted that Japan could be coaxed into surrendering through a modification of unconditional surrender. But they were not opposed to trying, so long as the results produced the complete victory that they thought essential to preventing a resurgence of Japanese power. There was still time to refine the wording of a statement to Japan that would serve as both a warning and an offer of more acceptable terms. The invasion of Kyushu was not slated to begin until November.

Everyone agreed that the success of any overture depended on the ability of the U.S. to maintain unrelenting pressure on Japan. Toward that end, the Navy preyed on shipping in Japan's narrow seas, carrier-based aircraft struck at enemy airfields in the home islands, and B-29s continued their relentless bombardment of Japanese cities.[61] Several hundred miles to the south, the campaign on Okinawa entered its third month.

# 2

# "We Do Not Exclude a Constitutional Monarch Under the Present Dynasty"

During the first week of June, Japanese forces began an orderly retreat from the Shuri line to the Kiyan Peninsula, located at the southernmost part of Okinawa. North and west of Kiyan, units of the Imperial Navy dug in for the defense of Oroku Peninsula below Naha on the East China Sea. On June 5, Admiral Ota Minoru radioed what he thought would be a final message to the head of the Thirty-Second Army. After expressing gratitude for the opportunity to serve in the defense of Okinawa, Ota signed off, "Though I die on the desolate battlefield of Okinawa, I will continue to protect the great spirit of Japan." General Ushijima Mitsuru, the head of the Thirty-Second Army, urged Ota to withdraw, if possible, but he did not command the admiral to do so. Ota declined the invitation to die with the Army forces gathering in the south and elected instead to perish in the underground warren of tunnels his staff was using as a headquarters.

Elements from the Sixth Marine Division began the assault on the Oroku positions on June 4. They were soon joined by the First Marine Division. Several days into operation, the Marines found that the only way to safely reinforce their tenuously held positions was by delivering men in tanks who would drop out of the bottom hatch and crawl to safety when they reached their destination. The Marines subsequently learned that much of the enemy's firepower came from machine guns and cannons taken from damaged aircraft and converted for use against the attackers. The battle took ten days to complete. By the time it ended, on June 14, five thousand Japanese, nearly all the defenders, were dead. Several hundred naval personnel died in a futile counterattack, while others blew themselves up with satchel charges.

Admiral Ota and five members of his staff were found dead in their head-quarters, their throats cut and their bodies arranged neatly on a raised mattress. The Marines found two hundred more bodies scattered through the tunnels. During the battle the Marines suffered 1,068 casualties (killed and wounded), a number proportionately higher than the casualty rate for the capture of Shuri. Perhaps most disturbing was that the Marines had faced a poorly trained and ill-equipped force pressed into service to defend ground they had no hope of holding. Nevertheless, the enemy had fought with remarkable tenacity. Farther to the south, the battle for Okinawa continued.[1]

By the time that Admiral Ota was making his last stand in early June, communication between Okinawa and Imperial General Headquarters (IGHQ) was sporadic at best. Assuming the imminent end of resistance on the island, IGHQ reassessed its approach to defending the homeland. The strategy of attrition through protracted warfare had worked as well as could be expected on Iwo Jima and Okinawa. The Americans had paid dearly for their victories. But they had still managed to seize their objectives. That result would not be acceptable when the battleground was the sacred homeland.

On June 6, IGHQ issued a new field manual explaining its revised tactical doctrine. Rather than allow the Americans to establish themselves ashore, the Army now planned to attack the invaders before they could secure a lodgment on the beachheads. By having the defenders close to the invaders at the water's edge, the Japanese hoped to negate the Americans' advantage in artillery and naval gunfire. Other aspects of *Ketsu-Go* remained intact. The Japanese counted on "special attack" forces (suicide planes, small boats, and frogmen) to sow confusion among the invaders and reduce the size of the landing force by as much as 50 percent, although most field commanders thought that percentage wildly optimistic. Ultimately, however, IGHQ viewed all the defenders as "special attack" forces. That expectation was subsequently made clear through orders instructing the defenders on Kyushu to force American tanks onto rugged terrain, where they could be attacked by suicide units. "Tokyo is ordering all officers and men," read the directive, "regardless of branch of service, to execute such suicide attacks."[2]

IGHQ's new doctrine coincided with a decision reached at a meeting of the Supreme Council for the Direction of the War, also on June 6, one that reaffirmed Japan's commitment to waging the decisive battle on the home islands. This meeting was arranged at short notice by the Army for the main purpose of ramming through a hastily prepared paper titled "Fundamental

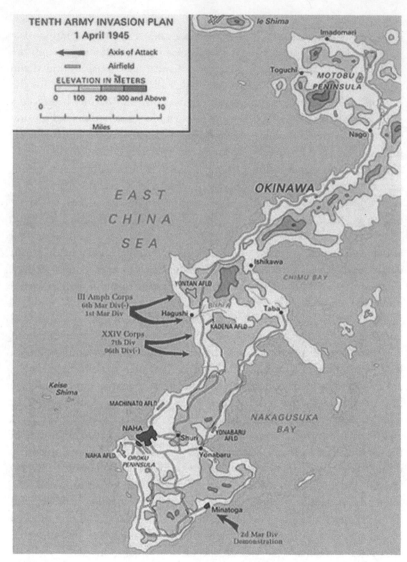

Okinawa: Tenth Army Invasion Plan. U.S. Army Campaigns of World War II: Ryukyus. Center for Military History.

Policy to Be Followed Henceforth in the Conduct of the War." It asserted that the United States was confronted with numerous problems. These included the death of FDR, mounting casualties, and war fatigue since V-E Day. The Americans remained committed to prosecuting the war vigorously, the report added. However, there were other factors in Japan's favor, including the growing friction among the Allies over European issues and Chiang Kai-shek's concerns about his Communist rivals. An immediate break in the alliance was doubtful but time was on Japan's side. "Should Japan resolutely continue the war and force heavy enemy attrition until the latter part of this year, it may be possible to diminish considerably the enemy's will to continue the war."[3]

Unlike the earlier meetings that Togo had arranged in May, all of the Big Six's subordinates were in attendance. That made the outcome a foregone conclusion even though the gathering had before it ample evidence of Japan's grim prospects. This evidence was made available in two reports—"Estimate of the World Situation" and "The Present State of National Power"—both of which had been requested by Togo as a condition of his joining the cabinet in April, meaning that it had taken two precious months to complete the reports. Nonetheless, the information they contained unambiguously illustrated the hopelessness of Japan's situation. "The Present State of National Power" was the more damning. "It has become increasingly difficult," the report stated, "to meet the requirements of total war." The report revealed that Japan's industrial capacity had shriveled due to lack of coal, oil, and industrial salts. The Navy's surface fleet had all but vanished, and the Army was unable to equip the forces it was raising for homeland defense. Communications with other areas of the empire were severed and food supplies at home were dangerously low.

Togo had expected as much. His aim all along had been to force Prime Minister Suzuki to abandon the military's doomed strategy and begin negotiations for Japan's surrender. Unfortunately for Togo, the venue in which the two reports were presented did not allow for a forthright discussion of their contents. Despite the evidence staring themselves in the face, everyone present, except for Togo, supported the Army's "Fundamental Policy" or remained silent, which amounted to the same thing. Suzuki, to Togo's dismay, supported the Army.[4]

The following day, the full cabinet met and ceremoniously applied its rubber stamp to the Army's policy. On June 8, the same group assembled before the emperor. The purpose of this imperial conference was to sanctify the approval of the Army's policy by presenting it to his majesty. Tradition did not require any action by the emperor. His silence was expected. The emperor dutifully fulfilled his responsibility by not uttering a word. In the ensuing discussion only Togo registered any reservations about the Army's policy. Then Suzuki twice polled those present asking first if they disapproved and then if they approved. When no one spoke either time, he declared the policy approved.[5]

Years after the meeting, Marquis Kido Koichi, Lord Keeper of the Privy Seal, recalled that he saw a look of consternation on the emperor's face during the discussion of the Fundamental Policy. Kido may have been indulging in fanciful retrospection, but there is no doubt that he was dismayed by what he heard at the meeting. His Gilbert and Sullivan–sounding title notwithstanding, Kido played an important role as political advisor to the emperor and liaison between the throne and cabinet. His main allegiance was to the throne and his primary goal was preserving the institution of the monarchy. Kido worried that the greater the hardships the government expected the

Shigenori Tōgō.

Japanese people to endure, the more susceptible they would be to communist propaganda. Civil unrest could topple the imperial system, and with it
the main bulwark against social chaos in Japan.[6]

Over the next several days, Kido drafted a plan for ending the war, en-
listed the support of several confidants, gained the emperor's approval to put
the plan into action, and, with some additional effort, gained the indecisive
Suzuki's cooperation.[7] Under the circumstances, any deviation from the
military's plan to die in the last ditch was noteworthy, but Kido's proposal
had little chance of producing the results he desired. It called for Japan's
withdrawal from the European colonies it had conquered, providing they
were granted their independence. Japan would also disarm itself and accept
limits imposed on its defense establishment. There would be no occupation
of the homeland. Kido did not mention the status of the emperor because
the entire proposal was designed to preserve Japan's governing system, including the court, in its present form. To execute this plan, Kido advised
the emperor to seek Soviet assistance as a mediator between Japan and the
Allies.

The fact that Kido's plan was considered daring at the time speaks volumes
about Japanese leaders' unwillingness to pursue a diplomatic strategy that
reflected the situation on the battlefield. It also revealed considerable confusion within the government. Hirohito did not know that a month earlier
the Big Six had devised a three point plan and approved negotiations with
the Russians. Suzuki had somehow neglected to mention that to the emperor. That bureaucratic confusion was accompanied by collective wishful
thinking, as illustrated in the reliance on the Soviet Union's good offices.
Kido later explained that he turned to the Russians because they were the
only neutral great power capable of standing between Japan and its enemies.
The lesser countries, Switzerland and Sweden for example, would be easily
bullied by the Allies into steering the negotiations toward unconditional
surrender. That was to be avoided at all costs.

What Kido and his supporters, including the emperor, sought was peace,
not surrender, and certainly not unconditional surrender. The Russians, of
course, had little interest in sparing Japan from humiliation. Kido's proposed
liberation of Europe's Asian colonies would also be unacceptable to the
Allies, none of which wanted to recast Japan's aggression as a self-sacrificing
crusade against white hegemony in Asia. On the other hand, Kido's explicit proposals regarding the military, self-disarmament, and no occupation might seem unrealistic from today's perspective, but they were not out

of the realm of possibility when he drafted them. There were American officials who questioned the need to occupy Japan after the war. And, of course, there were also some officials in the Truman administration, particularly Joseph Grew and Eugene Dooman, who believed that the preservation of the monarchy would end the war early and maintain stability in postwar Japanese society. Kido would not have disagreed.

Suzuki brought Kido's proposal to the Big Six for consideration on June 18. To his surprise and relief, the Army and Navy ministers did not reject it out of hand. They did, however, insist that any diplomatic initiative would have to come after Japan had strengthened its bargaining position by winning a battle over the Americans. That was an unwelcome restriction. On the other hand, the leaders did agree that when the overture was made, it should be with the aim of obtaining Soviet aid in ending the war. The leaders were at least willing to realize that there was little hope for negotiation of a nonaggression pact or renewal of the neutrality treaty. That was a start. However, the outcome of the meeting still fell short of fulfilling Kido's and Hirohito's desire for an immediate overture to Moscow. When Kido received the news, he advised the emperor to summon the Big Six to another imperial conference.

The conference met four days later. Breaking with common practice, the emperor opened the session by asking with his customary indirectness if his subjects had considered other methods of dealing with the present crisis apart from the previous agreement on the Fundamental Policy. Togo responded by repeating his previous endorsement of diplomatic negotiations. In response to the emperor's query about timing, he explained that Japanese emissaries would have to arrive in Moscow before Stalin departed for the Allied conference in Potsdam in mid-July. He also emphasized the need for Japan to offer to make peace while it still retained some semblance of military strength. The Army's representatives countered by recommending a more cautious approach to any diplomatic undertaking. Hirohito weighed in again, asking if it was not possible to miss an opportunity by being too cautious. Army Chief of Staff Umezu Yoshijiro reversed himself and agreed that negotiations should begin immediately. With that, the emperor left the room. The Japanese would seek Soviet aid in negotiating an end to the war. No one mentioned the word "surrender."[8]

It had taken the head of state, the emperor, and the head of government, Suzuki, nearly three months to arrive at the same conclusion about Japan's situation. Suzuki, Hirohito, and Kido had separated themselves from the military and were now committed to finding a peaceful end to the war, one that would preserve the monarchy and save Japan from the annihilation or revolution that was sure to follow if the war continued. While Kido's plan went forward with the emperor's blessing, American officials were also exploring ways to end the war without fighting the decisive battle longed for by IGHQ. As Truman was learning, there was no shortage of people willing to give him advice on how to do that, whether he asked for it or not.

The war with Japan was not on the agenda when Truman invited former president Herbert Hoover to the White House on May 28, but Hoover managed to make it a major point of discussion anyway. Truman liked to portray his invitation to Hoover as a courtesy and a sign of respect from one president to his predecessor. The documentary record shows otherwise. Hoover went to considerable lengths to wrangle an invitation to the White House on his terms. For his part, Truman hoped his bipartisan gesture would warm a few Republican hearts in Congress.[9]

Ostensibly, Truman sought Hoover's counsel on managing postwar relief programs in Europe, but "the Great Humanitarian" was not shy about offering his views on the steps that were needed to clean up what he regarded as the deplorable state of food policy at home. Not surprisingly, Hoover's point of reference was his own management of domestic food policy during World War I, which he deemed an unalloyed success. Equally unsurprising, he recommended that food pricing be taken out of the hands of the Office of Price Administration (OPA), a New Deal–style agency that intervened in the lives of most citizens by setting prices on consumer goods and issuing rationing coupons.[10]

In the course of their meeting, however, Hoover also offered his assessment of the political and military conditions in Europe and Asia and advised Truman on how to end the war with Japan. Hoover, of course, had been the first president to cope with Japanese expansion in the early 1930s. At that time he avoided direct confrontation and settled on a policy of nonrecognition of Japanese territorial aggrandizement, the so-called Hoover–Stimson Doctrine. In Hoover's assessment, Japan's invasion of Manchuria did not threaten American vital interests. When he left office in 1933 he continued to believe that the moderate politicians who had guided Japanese diplomacy in the 1920s would eventually regain power and steer the country toward cooperation with the U.S.[11] As Hoover saw it, his reasoned policy had been obliterated when Roosevelt provoked Japan into attacking the United States. Now Hoover's worst fears were being realized at home and abroad.[12] FDR had used the war to enlarge the powers of the president and enacted unprecedented government regulation of the economy. In Asia, a shattered Japan and enfeebled China left the way open for Soviet expansion. The prospects grew bleaker by the hour, but Hoover thought there was still time to save the situation.

Hoover's first visit to the White House since leaving office twelve years earlier offered the former president a chance at vindication. He was not about to pass up that opportunity. After discussing the relief situation, Hoover turned to the problem of Asia. Hoover's recommendations on ending the war were bracketed by observations critical of the Soviet Union, leaving little doubt that he saw a negotiated surrender as key to preventing Soviet domination of East Asia. According to a memorandum he prepared after his meeting, Hoover began by cautioning Truman that the "Asiatic" nature of the Russians made them untrustworthy. Hoover then warned the president that an invasion of Japan could cost upward of five hundred thousand American lives. To avoid such a bloodbath, Truman should ignore "the excited minority of our people" bent on vengeance and modify unconditional surrender by letting the Japanese know that they could keep the emperor.[13] Hoover also thought that it was advisable to let Japan maintain control over Korea and Formosa, areas he considered to have been much improved by Japanese colonialism. He ended by reminding Truman that the Soviets would only enter the war with Japan during the "last five minutes."[14]

Hoover's memorandum of the meeting presents it as a lengthy monologue interrupted by only occasional queries from Truman. If the president said anything of substance to Hoover, the latter failed to note it. For his part, Truman gave it only cursory mention in the diary he kept during the period. "Saw Herbert Hoover day before yesterday," Truman wrote on June 1, three days later, "and had pleasant and constructive conversation on food and the general troubles of U.S. presidents—two in particular." In addition to getting the date of the meeting wrong, Truman recalled that he and Hoover had talked "about our prima donnas and wondered what makes 'em"—apparently a matter of some importance to the president, but which Hoover thought not worth recording. Truman did not mention his discussion with Hoover about ending the war.[15] It is difficult to know how to interpret Truman's notes. They were usually written in haste and frequently appear to have been drafted in anticipation that they would be read by others. One can speculate about the reasons for important omissions but be certain, as will be seen again later, only that the president's supposedly frank notes could be incomplete and inaccurate.

Hoover had hoped that the meeting would result in his being appointed to an administrative position. When that did not happen, he concluded that his invitation to the White House had been for show.[16] Certainly, Hoover expected too much from the meeting. It is also clear that Truman hoped to gain some political advantage from hosting the titular leader of the opposition at the White House. Indeed, Hoover fed that expectation after the meeting by informing Truman through intermediaries that he would be willing to encourage Republicans in Congress to cooperate with the president.[17] Nevertheless, Hoover overreacted when he dismissed the meeting as a publicity stunt. As far as Hoover was concerned, he was the man for the job of organizing food distribution. Truman's failure to see that proved he was not serious about addressing the issue. It does not seem to have occurred to the former president that Truman, or anyone else for that matter, might genuinely disagree with anything he said, or that he might find Hoover's explicit and implicit criticisms of Roosevelt offensive in light of the circumstances that brought Truman to the presidency.

Hoover's recommendations to Truman on the Pacific War strategy were in a category by themselves. Following the meeting, Hoover, at Truman's request, submitted a typed copy of his recommendations titled "Memorandum on Ending the Japanese War." As noted, Hoover strongly urged the president to offer the Japanese a way out by allowing them to retain the emperor and a portion of their empire. Hoover believed that a negotiated surrender would save between five hundred thousand and one million American lives and that it might also preempt Soviet entry into the war, thereby limiting Russian gains in Asia. The former president also thought the United States should make it clear that it had no intention "to interference [sic] in the Japanese way of life," thereby ruling out any long-term occupation of Japan. Hoover later insisted that Truman had promised to make a public announcement to the Japanese offering them a chance to keep the emperor, though he made no mention of that pledge in his memorandum of the meeting.[18]

Hoover's meeting with Truman suggested how difficult it was to disentangle domestic and foreign policies. In making his pitch to the president, Hoover was essentially asking Truman to approve the emerging Republican agenda, not just strategies about price controls and food distribution. Several days after his White House visit, Hoover met with nine Republican senators at the home of William R. Castle, formerly Hoover's undersecretary of

Herbert Clark Hoover. Harris and Ewing Collection, Library of Congress.

state and, briefly, ambassador to Japan. According to Castle, Hoover's advocacy of a negotiated settlement with Japan was well received by the senators. Shortly afterward, Castle discussed the matter with Hugh Wilson, another former diplomat who was serving as foreign policy advisor to the Republican Party. Wilson welcomed Hoover's recommendations on Japan, calling them "an opportunity for the minority party to take the lead." Wilson recognized, however, that the subject had to be approached cautiously to avoid accusations of appeasement.[19]

Circumstances seemed to favor the adoption of Republican policies, such as the ones that Hoover brought to the Truman White House. Republicans felt that "the atmosphere in Washington [was] infinitely better since Roosevelt's death," as Castle wrote Hoover, and they dared hope that Truman would steer toward a more conservative course in the months ahead.[20] Supporting this view was John Callan O'Laughlin, a former member of the Republican National Committee and a Hoover confidant. O'Laughlin published the *Army and Navy Journal* and authored a personal newsletter filled with insider's information on classified military matters and political gossip. Among his recipients was Hoover, whom O'Laughlin addressed as "Chief." Reporting on the Washington scene, O'Laughlin noted as a hopeful sign the recently submitted report by Fred Vinson, director of the Office of War Mobilization and Reconversion. "There is nothing New Deal about the report," he wrote. "Conspicuous by its absence is the Roosevelt plan to provide 80 million post-war jobs."[21] O'Laughlin, like other observers, appears to have mistaken Truman's plain speaking and the departure of Roosevelt loyalists from the cabinet as indications that the new president was rejecting his predecessor's policies.[22] That was hardly the case. Truman had supported New Deal programs in Congress and accumulated a voting record that, if anything, put him on the left wing of the congressional Democrats. As journalist and historian Robert Donovan put it, Truman was "a vote for the New Deal, not a voice."[23] By the time FDR picked him for the vice presidency, Truman had shed his identification with the more conservative congressional Democrats and aligned himself with the liberal wing of the party that still controlled the nomination process.[24]

Republicans misread Truman's affiliation, but they accurately judged the political environment he was entering. By the time he joined FDR on the national ticket, the New Deal was in retreat. Following the 1942 congressional election in which the Democrats lost forty-five House seats and nine Senate seats, Fortune magazine celebrated the return of "normalcy" men to Congress. The Democrats held slim majorities in both houses, but southern conservative Democrats usually sided with Republicans on social and economic measures. By 1944, liberal poet and essayist and soon-to-be assistant secretary of state Archibald MacLeish observed bitterly, "It is no longer feared, it is assumed that the country is headed back to normalcy, that Harding is just around the corner, that the twenties will repeat themselves.[25]

The administration Truman joined was much different from the one that had produced the signal legislation of the New Deal in 1933. Liberals still held key positions, but they shared power with the more conservative element in Congress. In response to the global crisis beginning in the late 1930s, FDR had created something akin to a coalition government, bringing Republicans like Secretary of War Henry Stimson and Navy Secretary Frank Knox into the administration to manage the wartime economy and oversee military production. Often during the war, they had circumvented New Deal policies in the name of efficiency. As Stimson explained, "If you are going to go to war in a capitalist country you have to let business make money out of the process or business won't work."[26]

A host of Republicans would have agreed. Instead of regulating business and supervising its actions, the federal government became the principal underwriter of business expansion and windfall profits. When it came to war contracts, big business was the big winner. In 1940, as the defense program got under way, 175,000 companies were providing 70 percent of the U.S. manufacturing output and one hundred companies provided the other 30 percent. By 1943, the ratio had flipped, one hundred companies held 70 percent of war and civilian contracts.[27]

The close collaboration between government and business, as well as the impressive output of America's industries during wartime, helped to redeem the shattered image of business and restore the shaken confidence of industry leaders. Nevertheless, by war's end, conservative business leaders feared that the continued popularity of New Deal liberalism at home and the spread of socialism abroad foreshadowed major and unwelcome changes in the U.S. economy.[28]

With the war nearing its conclusion, national business organizations mobilized their resources for a campaign against the revival or extension of New Deal programs.[29] One of their first targets was the Office of Price Administration. In late spring 1945, as the war in Europe ended, OPA came under intensified criticism from producers who called for a return to market principles in setting prices. Consumers and labor organizations rallied against attempts to limit OPA's power. On May 27, the day before Hoover advised Truman to strip OPA of its control over food prices, twenty-two national consumer groups issued a call in Washington to block an attempt by Senator Robert Taft to weaken OPA. Employing wartime rhetoric, OPA's defenders insisted that "there should be no 'negotiated peace' with inflation. There must be no compromise with black markets. Rationing must continue to assure fair sharing and to enable us to prevent starvation of liberated peoples."[30]

Given OPA's support among key Democratic groups, it is not surprising that Truman did not act upon Hoover's proposal to take food pricing away from the agency. Nor is it surprising that Truman did not heed Hoover's advice to disregard the supposedly "excited minority" who insisted on unconditional surrender without modification, especially on the emperor. Truman respected Hoover's administrative abilities, but it is doubtful that he had much regard for the former president's political acumen, especially when it came to public opinion. For the time being, Truman held to the New Deal program at home and abroad.

That stance was becoming increasingly difficult, however. Hoover and other Republicans opposed the New Deal at home and abroad. The question was what the members of the New Deal coalition desired. Consumers might demand inflation's unconditional surrender, but would they oppose a negotiated peace with Japan if it would end the war quickly and bring loved ones home safely? Truman's handling of Hoover's memo on ending the war suggests that the president thought first of the economic and domestic political implications of modifying unconditional surrender. When Truman received the memorandum, he turned it over to Fred Vinson, a former federal judge, congressman, and, at that moment, the director of the Office of War Mobilization and Reconversion. [31] A key congressional supporter of the New Deal, Vinson quickly gained Truman's confidence as "a straight shooter" who knew Congress and was "a man to trust." [32]

After holding the Hoover memorandum for almost a week, Vinson returned it to Truman with the recommendation that the president submit it to the secretaries of state and war, and, significantly, that he also seek the advice of Cordell Hull, who had been Roosevelt's secretary of state for eleven years. Vinson's cover letter returning the memo gives no indication of his thoughts on the topic, nor do we have any other information on what he might have recommended to Truman besides giving the memo wider circulation. Truman followed that advice and sent copies to Stimson, Acting Secretary of State Grew, and Cordell Hull. [33]

On June 9, when Stimson received a copy of Hoover's memorandum from the White House, he already had read a less detailed version of that document that Hoover had presented to him in mid-May. Stimson had in turn asked for the views of the staff officers in the Strategy and Policy Group (S&P) of the Operations and Plans Division, saying only that it had been composed by an anonymous "economist" rather than by a former president. S&P's response, which was sent to Stimson on June 7, more than a week after Hoover's visit with Truman, cast doubt on the geopolitical basis of Hoover's memorandum. The staff officers did not believe an early peace, which they thought unlikely under any circumstances, would prevent the Soviet Union from entering the war and becoming the major power in northeast Asia. They added that the Russians would "with some justice" view a compromise peace from which they were excluded as a breach of the agreements made at Yalta. Regarding Hoover's warnings about the economic effects of a prolonged war, the officers conceded that "this was an economic matter requiring further investigation, but it appears doubtful that the U.S. economy would be 'prostrate' in 'eighteen months.'" The staff officers categorically dismissed Hoover's prediction of more than five hundred thousand casualties in an invasion of the home islands of Japan as "entirely too high." They also thought it unwise to allow Japan to retain Formosa and Korea, given that the allies were committed through the 1943 Cairo Declaration to an independent Korea and the restoration of Formosa to China. They did, however, agree that it would be advisable to issue a warning to Japan that specified the meaning of unconditional surrender using terms that would lead to the achievement of American war aims.[34]

Stimson therefore already had S&P's comments in hand when he received Truman's request to comment on the memorandum that Hoover wrote after his meeting with the president. Stimson promptly submitted this newer version to S&P for comment, noting only that it was written by the same anonymous "economist" who had written the previous memorandum. On June 15, Marshall submitted S&P's comments to Stimson with the observation that he was "in substantial agreement" with its contents. For the most part, S&P repeated its earlier assessment. The staff officers again agreed in principle with Hoover's recommendation that the United States, either alone or in conjunction with its allies, issue a warning to Japan specifying the meaning of unconditional surrender in a manner that was consistent with previous public declarations. That ruled out any proposal to let Japan keep either Formosa or Korea, which they deemed unwise in any case. The officers in S&P also stressed the importance of cooperation with the Soviet Union and emphasized that the U.S. would not be able to challenge the Russians on the mainland of northeast Asia. Once again, the staff officers dismissed the estimate of five hundred thousand to one million deaths as entirely too high. Unlike Hoover, S&P believed that an occupation of at least selected points in Japan would be necessary to disarm Japan. They also rejected the contention that the establishment of a military government in Japan would be "an impossible task."

Regarding the American home front, the staff officers repeated their earlier belief that there was little chance of the U.S. exhausting its resources in fighting Japan. They even more firmly rejected Hoover's analysis of the political situation in Japan. Citing input from Army intelligence, the staff officers said that there was little difference between Prime Minister Suzuki and the militarists controlling the government in Tokyo. They also discounted the significance of a "liberal minded" peace faction in Japan's middle classes. According to Army intelligence, the "liberals" were few and hardly deserved the name. They sought the same ends as the militarists, domination of Asia, though greater exposure to the world outside of Japan had given them a healthier regard for American power.[35]

On June 16 Stimson sent S&P's comments to Truman under a cover letter that contained his own thoughts on Hoover's memorandum.[36] Like Hoover, Stimson stressed the perils of invading Japan and the difficulty of occupying and governing Japan through military government. He also agreed with Hoover on the potential advantages of softening the peace terms by allowing Japan to maintain the emperor on the throne if the Japanese people so desired. Drawing on his prewar experience with Japan, Stimson continued to believe that there was in Japan a sizeable group of what he described as moderate politicians who were working secretly to bring the war to an end. This peace faction, Stimson believed, was forming around the throne, seeking to use the emperor's immense influence to challenge the militarists when the time was right. A public declaration guaranteeing the safety of the emperor and preservation of the imperial institution might just give the peace faction the leverage it needed to gain control of the government and end the war.[37]

Grew had made the same point when he met with Truman on May 28, the same day the president met with Hoover. Although he had failed to gain the president's approval, Grew remained adamant about the need to issue a prompt warning to Japan that would clarify but also modify the meaning of unconditional surrender. Hoover's memorandum gave him a second chance to drive that point home. On Friday, June 15, the acting secretary of state went to the White House to deliver his evaluation of Hoover's memorandum and a draft statement clarifying unconditional surrender that he hoped the president would issue. Truman replied with his now-standard bland assurance that he was happy to have the material. He added that he would be meeting with the Joint Chiefs on Monday to discuss the war against Japan but that it would be a primarily a military discussion. Assistant Secretary of State Julius Holmes, who had accompanied Grew, observed that those military discussions were bound to be intertwined with political matters. Truman invited Grew to attend the meeting. Grew replied by asking if he could bring Dooman, whom he called the department's foremost expert on Japan, and Truman agreed.[38]

The report that Grew left with Truman took issue with several aspects of the Hoover memorandum. Like the staff officers in

S&P, Grew thought that the Cairo Declaration overrode Hoover's recommendations regarding Korea and Taiwan. He also believed that the U.S. would have to occupy Japan and control it in the immediate postwar period through some form of military government. Japan could not be safely demilitarized unless the U.S. enacted social and political reforms (for example, freedom of speech, religious freedom) that would foster democratic government. In short, Grew thought that Hoover's recommendations let Japan off too easily and would not tear out the root causes of Japanese militarism.

About the emperor, however, Grew and Hoover were of the same mind. Truman's request for input from the secretary of state had given Grew an opportunity to ignore the criticisms of his subordinates and speak his mind on the subject. The former ambassador once again explained that all available evidence strongly indicated the "non-molestation of the person of the present emperor and the preservation of the institution of the throne comprise irreducible Japanese terms." Japanese devotion to the throne made it expedient for the United States to compromise on the fate of the emperor. If the United States guaranteed that the emperor would not be harmed and the imperial institution would not be destroyed, the United States would save thousands of lives and the Japanese would be willing to undergo "drastic privations so long as these irreducible terms were met." Conversely, the Americans could expect "prolonged resistance" if Washington insisted on destroying the imperial institution and trying the emperor as a war criminal.[39]

The attached four-and-a-half-page draft statement that Grew left on this visit was written by Dooman. It began by describing Japan's desperate situation and threatened that worse was yet to come. It also declared that it would be occupied after the war and that the Japanese would have to travel a "road of hardships" before they reentered the international community. The tone was stern and unyielding throughout, so much so that the statement hardly seemed an attempt to entice Japan into surrendering. On the future of the monarchy, the draft statement was mute. Instead of forthrightly promising that the Japanese would be able to maintain the imperial system, it only hinted at that possibility by quoting a public announcement that had been made by Chiang Kai-shek on New Year's Day, 1944. In that radio address, Chiang had said that he believed that "all the Japanese militarists must be wiped out and the Japanese political system must be purged of every vestige of aggressive elements." Regarding Japan's government after the occupation, Chiang said only that he would leave that to be decided by "the awakened and repentant Japanese people."[40]

It is not clear why Grew or Dooman thought that the Japanese would find Chiang's announcement reassuring. The Chinese counted Hirohito among the militarists and saw the monarchy as an aggressive element to be purged.[41] Opposition within the State Department and fear of a public backlash had caused Grew and Dooman to become evasive, and to use the pronouncements of a foreign leader to make their case. The Japanese would have to be clairvoyant to know that the proposed statement contained a pledge to preserve the imperial system.

Grew had pulled his punches. Still, over the next few days he continued to press the case for promptly issuing a warning to Japan. On June 16, he returned to the White House with a memorandum addressed to Judge Samuel Rosenman, the president's counselor, recommending that several provisions be added to his proposed statement to the Japanese. Grew's latest memo began by asserting that the impending conclusion of the Okinawa campaign—it was roughly a week away—would provide a good opportunity to issue a statement to the Japanese clarifying unconditional surrender. He emphasized the need for tough language to make the Japanese know that the U.S. was serious about cutting out "the cancer of militarism." But he also thought it necessary to tell the Japanese that they would be free to choose their own form of government. Grew felt certain that "the intelligent element in our press and public" would recognize that it was "plain common sense" to try to save tens of thousands of American lives by bringing the Japanese to unconditional surrender as soon as possible. He also included in his latest memo several additions to Dooman's draft statement. Grew thought it would be useful if Truman discussed these with the Joint Chiefs when they met on June 18. The several additions he referred to proclaimed that the U.S. would encourage free speech and freedom of religion in Japan, permit the Japanese to reestablish themselves as "honorable neighbors," and eventually give Japan an opportunity to participate in the world economy.[42] Once again, Grew failed to address head-on the one issue that he had formerly insisted concerned all Japanese: the fate of the monarchy.

Grew's memo assured Rosenman that Secretary of State Stettinius approved the additions contained in his most recent memorandum. However, it neglected to say that Stettinius also recommended that the president put the subject of a warning to Japan on the agenda of the forthcoming conference at Potsdam so that it could be coordinated with the Allies, including Russia. Grew wanted the U.S. to issue it as soon as possible, ideally without Soviet approval. Instead of revising his new memo to reflect fully Stettinius's recommendation, Grew handed Truman Stettinius's message knowing that it contradicted the advice contained in his own memorandum. It was a surprisingly clumsy performance by such a seasoned diplomat.[43]

Grew met again with Truman on Monday, June 18, the same day that the president's military advisors were scheduled to discuss strategy in the Pacific War. This was Grew's fourth meeting at the White House on the subject of unconditional surrender. In their first meeting on the subject on May 28 Grew had left the president an essay explaining how Japan could be enticed into surrendering. Two weeks later, he delivered to the president an evaluation of Hoover's memorandum and a draft of a warning to Japan that clarified the meaning of unconditional surrender. The next day, June 16, he met with Truman again to deliver a second memorandum reinforcing the previous one. Throughout it all, the president had offered only the most tepid encouragement while pointedly declining to approve Grew's proposed statement. On June 18 Truman informed him that after considering Grew's recommendation, he had decided to postpone action until the meeting of the Big Three at Potsdam—in other words, that he would follow Stettinius's counsel. A dejected Grew noted only that Truman had asked him to put the subject on the agenda of the forthcoming meeting.[44]

Grew did not know at the time, but his effort had been thwarted even before Truman received Stettinius's message. On June 12, the president had received similar advice from Cordell Hull, who had served as FDR's secretary of state for eleven years (1933–1944) before he was forced to resign because of ill health. It was only natural that Truman would seek his advice about a policy so closely linked to Roosevelt. When he sent him the copy of the Hoover memo, his cover note opened with the salutation "Dear Cordell" and was signed "Harry." Hull's reply spared Truman yet another lecture on Japanese culture and got right to the point. He saw little reason to compromise with Japan. Truman's Memorial Day address had served notice to the Japanese, and that was enough. Hull conceded that Hoover had raised numerous questions concerning the best methods for eliminating Japanese militarism that would "raise broadly the question of what to do with the Emperor, etc. etc." But Hull doubted that it would be useful for him to "discuss any of these questions to which Mr. Hoover refers in his appeasement proposal."[45] Truman could hardly miss the significance of the end of that sentence. Hoover, and by extension Grew and Stimson, were promoting a policy of appeasement. Hull carried the day. For the moment there would be no modification of unconditional surrender.

On June 18, the same day that he informed Grew of his decision to postpone issuing a statement, Truman met with Stimson, Forrestal, and the Joint Chiefs to discuss Pacific War strategy. The meeting established a date for the invasion of Kyushu, the first operation in the assault on Japan's home islands. Beforehand Truman had recorded his concerns about the casualties American forces would suffer in any invasion. He pursued that matter at length during the meeting itself. The discussion of casualty estimates provided several of those present an opportunity to raise the question of unconditional surrender. Stimson approached obliquely. He agreed with the Joint Chiefs that militarily there was no choice but to plan for the attack on Kyushu, but felt responsible for raising political considerations. Something should be done to encourage what he termed the "submerged class" in Japan that desired peace. Truman replied that such a possibility was being worked on all the time. Prompted by the president, Forrestal concurred with the decision to invade Kyushu, which he deemed necessary even if the Joint Chiefs later opted for a blockade of Honshu. Assistant Secretary of War McCloy spoke next. He declared that the time was propitious "to study all possible means possible for bringing out the influence of the submerged group in Japan which had been referred to by Mr. Stimson."

According to the minutes of this June 18 meeting, Truman switched the subject to Russian entry into the war. The president stated that when he went to Potsdam it would be with the intention of obtaining the maximum assistance against Japan. To that end, he wanted to know from those present what he needed to do to be in the strongest possible position in his discussions with the Russians. Speaking next, and rather than addressing Truman's question directly, Admiral Leahy launched an attack on the policy of unconditional surrender. Leahy said that even without unconditional surrender he "feared no menace from Japan in the foreseeable future." An insistence on it would unnecessarily increase American casualties. Faced with a point-blank challenge to the policy, Truman passed the buck. He replied that it was with Leahy's thoughts in mind that he had "left the door open to Congress to take appropriate action with reference to unconditional surrender," but that he did not feel that he could do anything at the moment to change public opinion.[46]

What occurred next is a matter of some disagreement. The official record of the meeting reads that the discussion turned to "certain other matters," which historians have generally agreed was a reference to an off-the-record discussion of the atomic bomb.[47] The minutes then note that Truman approved a memo that Leahy read recommending the reinstatement of Lend Lease supplies to the French. Truman closed the meeting by expressing his thanks to the Joint Chiefs and saying that he now felt "satisfied and reassured" about operation OLYMPIC, as the invasion of the home islands was being called.[48]

McCloy recalled things ending differently. In March 1947, he told Forrestal that as the meeting broke up, he addressed the group, saying that although he had not been asked his opinion, he wanted to state his views. According to McCloy, he advocated warning the Japanese about the atomic bomb but also assuring them that they could retain the emperor and a form of government of their own choosing.[49] McCloy told Forrestal that the military officers present had been annoyed by his meddling in their business but that Truman welcomed it and ordered "such a political offensive to be set in motion."[50] It was a story that McCloy would tell many times afterward—with some variation.

There are several reasons to doubt the accuracy of McCloy's account. First, the official record shows that McCloy did not remain silent until the end of the meeting. He spoke in support of Stimson's proposal to pursue a diplomatic solution by strengthening the "submerged" group of Japanese leaders who favored peace. Second, none of those at the meeting left any record that supported McCloy's version.[51]

There are other inconsistencies in McCloy's story and the later versions of it that he gave to journalists and historians. McCloy had told Forrestal that he insisted on speaking his mind at the end of the meeting because he had not spoken previously. In a later version, McCloy maintained that Truman had told him that he could not leave without giving his opinion.[52] Nevertheless, despite its inconsistencies, and despite the absence of contemporary supporting evidence, McCloy's story is often cited by historians.[53] That, in turn, has led to an important misunderstanding in how the warning to Japan known as the Potsdam Declaration was written.

As noted, McCloy ended his story by saying that Truman approved his recommendation and ordered "a political offensive to be put in motion." There is ample reason to believe that Truman did no such thing. Earlier that day he had, as noted, told Grew to put the subject of a warning to

Japan on the agenda for the Potsdam conference, which was a month away. He did not commit the U.S. to making a statement or approve the draft that Grew gave him; indeed, he did the opposite. Nor did he ask Grew to pursue the matter further. Moreover, the official minutes from the meeting with the Joint Chiefs show that Truman was evasive whenever someone recommended that the U.S. try to encourage the peace party in Japan. In reply to Stimson's suggestion, he said the "possibility was being worked on all the time." When Leahy suggested that the U.S. ditch the policy of unconditional surrender, the president said only that he would leave the door open for Congress to do something, and that he could not change public opinion at this time. These are determinedly noncommittal.

What is clear is that despite Truman's reticence, Stimson, Grew, and Forrestal—the so-called Committee of Three, consisting of the secretaries of Navy, state, and war—remained convinced that the U.S. should issue a warning to the Japanese that would clarify the meaning of unconditional surrender and assure them that they could preserve the monarchy. Over the next several weeks they took it upon themselves to prepare a statement for the president to issue. There is no indication that the president instructed them to do so, as McCloy later alleged, or that they apprised the president of what they were up to. They began slowly, but the work went quickly once they decided to draft a warning.

The day after the June 18 White House meeting, the three met in Stimson's Pentagon office. Forrestal was on Capitol Hill, so Undersecretary of the Navy Artemus Gates took his place. McCloy was present as the recorder. They agreed that the U.S. should issue a warning to Japan that would clarify the meaning of unconditional surrender in such a way as to entice Japan into ending hostilities. Stimson opened the meeting by asking how the U.S. could achieve its objectives in the war without waging a cave-to-cave campaign. The key would be enlisting the support of Japan's moderates. Stimson noted that the moderates in Japan had been willing to cooperate with the West until the hardship caused by the Great Depression gave the militarists the upper hand. Grew supplemented Stimson's analysis by explaining that the Americans needed to ignore Japanese bluster about fighting to the last man. As he had told Truman earlier, to prove he wasn't seeking appeasement, Grew added that the U.S. would have to occupy Tokyo and root out Japanese militarism. There could be no compromise peace. Without any sense of contradiction, Grew added that he thought the Japanese should be permitted to retain the monarchy, although he conceded that there were others in the State Department who wanted to eliminate the institution.

Stimson subsequently recorded in his office diary that, he, Grew, and Forrestal agreed that the U.S. should issue a statement on its policy of unconditional surrender. He also noted that Truman opposed doing anything before meeting with Churchill and Stalin at Potsdam. That did not bother Stimson in the way it had Grew. He thought it best to back up any warning with a demonstration of U.S. power, by which he meant an escalation in B-29 bombings, or the use of the atomic bomb. No one mentioned that the president had wanted the Committee of Three to prepare the warning to Japan. If, as McCloy said, Truman had agreed with him about warning the Japanese, surely this would have been the time for him to inform his cabinet. McCloy remained silent on the issue. In fact, the meeting ended without the committee taking any action to draft the warning they all nonetheless believed should be issued.[54]

In the week after this June 19 meeting, leadership on the issue passed from Grew to Stimson. When the Committee of Three met on June 26, Stimson began by promptly addressing "the subject of trying to get Japan to surrender by giving her a warning after she had been sufficiently pounded possibly with S-1 [the atomic bomb]." He then read the draft of a letter he planned to give to Truman. In the lively discussion that followed, all agreed that a warning should be made before the U.S. invaded Japan in November. The members acknowledged that while the warning might not achieve its desired aim, it would still be beneficial. If the Japanese refused to surrender, their negative response would "check in the U.S. the deterioration of will to complete the defeat of Japan" and make clear to the American public the necessity of the fullest efforts to finish the job. Following their discussion, the members appointed a subcommittee to draft the warning. McCloy chaired the group; Dooman and Joseph Ballantine, another Japan specialist, represented State; and Captain Matthias Correa represented the Navy.[55]

The subcommittee met the next day, June 27, and, at McCloy's urging, endeavored to complete a draft warning for Stimson's use when he met with Truman the following Monday, July 2. It quickly became clear that the bulk of the work would be done by a group of staff officers from the Army's Strategy and Policy Group (S&P) and Army intelligence (G-2). McCloy stacked the first meeting with five staff officers. Captain Correa, the Navy's representative, did not attend. Dooman was also absent. Ballantine was the lone representative from the State Department, though he brought with him a copy of Dooman's warning to Japan. The Army representatives quickly deemed it so vague as to be practically useless.[56]

At a meeting on June 28, Dooman attended in place of Ballantine, but the Army's members had already privately concluded that he was more hindrance than help. Brigadier General George Lincoln, the head of S&P, complained to Assistant Chief of Staff General John E. Hull that while Stimson was searching for terms that would be acceptable to Japan and still satisfactory to the U.S., Dooman "apparently has so little hope of Japanese acceptance that he is trying really only to insure that the terms will *cause no criticism* in the U.S." Lincoln determined that a choice had to be made. "Shall we state a flat intention to allow the Japanese to retain the structure of a constitutional monarchy, and tempt the Japanese public, or state the opposite intention and please (again in theory) the U.S. public, or leave the matter vague and impress neither side, probably?"[57]

While the subcommittee hammered out the terms for the warning, the Army's staff officers were also preparing a recommendation for the best time to issue the warning and the means. The State Department's contribution to the finished products was negligible. The Army's staff officers had more than numbers on their side. The officers of S&P were a tight-knit, politically astute group. Their job required them to think in terms of contingencies and anticipate the political implications of military policies. They wrote in the crisp, declarative prose of men trained to write orders that would not be susceptible to misinterpretation. The State Department's main disadvantage was that its representatives on the subcommittee knew that they did not speak for the entire department. Dooman and Ballantine knew that Acheson and MacLeish disapproved of any change to the policy of unconditional surrender. They also knew that some members of Congress suspected Grew of sympathy for the Japanese monarchy. Given those conditions, they trod warily, letting the War Department take point.

The warning, accompanying papers, and a brief cover letter from McCloy were ready on Friday, June 29, and delivered by courier to Stimson at his home on Long Island, where he had been since Wednesday. McCloy flew up the next day to review the documents with the secretary of war.[58] In his cover letter, McCloy noted that because the Army's planners were unaware of the atomic bomb, they had not included its use into their recommended timing for the warning. He added that the subcommittee's members agreed that rather than transmit the warning through diplomatic channels, it should be issued as a "declaration with all the usual propaganda following it up."

The most controversial part of the draft warning was its assurance that following the occupation, the Japanese would be able to have a constitutional monarchy under the present dynasty if they desired it. McCloy noted the divided opinion in the State Department on this issue and the possibility that preservation of the monarchy would cause repercussions at home, "but without it those who seem to know most about Japan feel there would be very little likelihood of acceptance."[59]

Stimson was generally satisfied with the documents despite the fact they had been written without crucial information about the atomic bomb. The subcommittee advised that the best time to issue a warning would be late August or early September, when the pressure on Japan would be at its peak. OLYMPIC was to begin in November, and a long-awaited Chinese offensive aimed at eventually retaking Hong Kong would be underway, as would a British-led operation against the Swettenham–Port Dickson area on the west coast of the Malay Peninsula. The American air campaign against Japan would also be reaching its zenith with eight additional heavy bombardment groups moving onto Okinawa.

Finally, the Soviets would also be in the war by then. The officers in S&P assumed that they would enter the war sometime between the middle of August and early September. They thought that when Truman, Stalin, and Churchill met at Potsdam, the U.S. should obtain from the Russians a specific date they would enter the war so that the warning could be timed. They also predicted that it would take the Red Army about thirty days before it began to make headway against the Japanese. That would give the Japanese time to weigh the attractiveness of terms contained in the Allied warning before the inevitable rout of their forces in Manchuria commenced. Further, it would allow the Americans more time to redeploy troops to the Pacific so that they would be able to occupy Japan quickly following surrender. Until then, the Americans would need to regroup and replenish the battle-weary forces they had scattered through the Philippines and on Okinawa.[60]

S&P's recommendation on timing reflected a strategic view based on assumptions about the continuing tenacity of Japanese resistance and American dependence on Soviet assistance. In seeking Japan's unconditional surrender, the Army approached its objectives sequentially. The defeat and occupation of Japan came first; all other objectives were secondary. Army planners understood that American national policy supported a strong China, and they acknowledged that Russian entry into the war might undermine that goal, but they calculated that there was little they could do to alter the situation until Japan was occupied. In any case, Russian control of Manchuria would not imperil America's postwar security if the United States held Japan. With Germany defeated, American power appeared to be reaching its height. Paradoxically, the Army's strategists thought in terms of limits and restraints.

What the Army was recommending was dramatically different from what Grew, Forrestal, and Hoover were thinking of when they recommended modifying unconditional surrender. Their hopes of preventing Soviet entry into the war by inducing Japan's surrender had been superseded by the Army's decision to link the warning to a Soviet attack on Japanese forces. The Army's recommendation ignored concerns about the Soviet Union but reflected Stimson's belief that any warning had to be coupled with a demonstration of overwhelming force. The convergence of Allied efforts, including the start of a Soviet campaign in northeast Asia, satisfied that requirement more than any other option—at least that the officers in S&P were aware of.

Stimson returned to Washington on Sunday, July 1, and met with Truman the following day to both discuss the warning to Japan and brief the president on the most recent information regarding the atomic bomb. The secretary of war began by handing Truman a memorandum titled "Proposed Program for Japan," which the president read in Stimson's presence. Stimson wrote that he had visited the areas where the invasion forces would be fighting, and that the terrain favored a last-ditch defense much like the Americans had faced on Iwo Jima and Okinawa. Fortunately, the U.S. would not have to replay those battles on a larger scale. The Japanese were militarily and politically isolated, dreading imminent Soviet entry into the war. Moreover, the United States could draw on nearly inexhaustible resources to wage its campaign.

The secretary of war believed the Japanese understood the hopelessness of their situation and would be amenable to reason in ending the war. "Japan is not a nation composed entirely of mad fanatics of an entirely different mentality than ours," he wrote. In a brief matter of six or seven decades, the Japanese had abandoned their feudal past and adopted Western technology, culture, and social ideas. "She has not only built powerful armies and navies. She has maintained an honest and effective finance and respected position in many of the sciences in which we pride ourselves." Moreover, for the ten years before the militarists seized power, Japan had "lived a reasonably

responsible and respectable international life." Fortunately, there were
enough liberal leaders in Japan who could rebuild the country and bring
it back into the family of nations once the war was over. Stimson believed
that Japan's liberals could be counted on more readily than Germany's had
been.[61] Japan's history gave Stimson hope that an Allied warning would
tip the balance in favor of the liberals. The warning would have to specify
the penalties Japan would pay as the price of its aggression, but it would
also promise the Japanese a hopeful future, including a representative government, if they cooperated in purging militaristic influences from their
society. "I personally think," he added, "that if in saying this we should add
we do not exclude a constitutional monarch under the present dynasty, it
would substantially add to the chances of acceptance."[62]

Stimson's reference to Japan's fiscal probity before the Great Depression
sounded an odd note in his memorandum. While it might have mattered to
a conservative lawyer from a white-shoe firm, it seems difficult to imagine
how Japan's ability to balance its books would outweigh fifteen years of
aggression throughout Asia. Apart from that, however, Stimson's "Proposed
Program for Japan" reprised several themes that had become talking points
in the repertoire of those arguing for modification of unconditional surrender. Japan's unprecedented transformation from feudalism to modernity;
the Japanese government's cooperation with the West, especially during the
1920s; and, of course, the presence of a submerged group of moderates
provided sufficient reason to be hopeful that Japan could be persuaded to
surrender and submit to international norms. Another recurring feature of
this argument was the disparaging of opponents of the monarchy for their
ignorance of Japanese history and their substitution of emotion and prejudice for cool, dispassionate reason.

Following their discussion of the "Proposed Program," Stimson and
Truman reviewed the draft warning that contained the assurance that Japan
would be permitted to keep a constitutional monarchy under the present
dynasty. They also discussed a statement drafted by the Interim Committee,
a group comprised of scientists and civilian advisors organized by Stimson
to advise Truman on the use of the atomic bomb, that the president would
issue after the new weapon was used. Stimson also presented the Interim
Committee's recommendation on how the president should approach
Russia with information about the bomb. It was a lot to digest in one session. Truman, not wanting to rush through such serious matters, asked the
secretary to come back the next day.

That night, Stimson confided to his diary that the shortening of the war with Japan by a surrender and the "proper handling of Germany so as not to create such harshness in seeking vengeance as to make it impossible to lay the foundations of a new Germany" had become his two tasks for the foreseeable future. The secretary lamented that in the first instance he had to deal with the "zeal of the soldier," and in the second, the "zeal of the Jewish American statesman seeking for vengeance." In both cases he felt forced to confront the "feeling of war passion and hysteria" that gripped the American people when they went to war. He added that thus far, Truman struck him as someone trying to keep his balance in this difficult situation and that the president had "certainly been receptive to all my efforts in these directions."[63]

Although Truman had listened patiently to the secretary's explanation of the reasoning behind the warning, Stimson was aware that the president had not included him in the delegation to the Potsdam conference. He asked Truman if he had not included him because he was concerned for his health. If that were the president's concern, Stimson added, he need not worry; the doctor had given him a clean bill of health. Rather than deflect Stimson's bid to join the delegation, Truman accepted the excuse that the secretary had offered him. The president claimed that he had indeed been worried about imposing on Stimson for health reasons but with that no longer a concern, he would be happy to have him attend the conference.[64]

Truman's receptivity to Stimson's efforts regarding Japan were more apparent than real, but any semblance of agreement with them was about to disappear. On July 3, James Byrnes was sworn in a secretary of state. Byrnes was a former senator from South Carolina, a Supreme Court justice, and most recently, the head of the Office of War Mobilization and Reconversion. The latter post required political finesse and a zeal for horse trading, qualities that he had in abundance. A Senate veteran, Byrnes had befriended Truman when he joined it in 1935. Byrnes had also been considered Roosevelt's most likely running mate in 1944 before Truman got the nod. Years later, Truman wrote in a draft of his memoirs that he appointed Byrnes secretary of state as consolation for having been bumped off the presidential ticket. After Judge Rosenman advised the former president that readers might not think that was sufficient reason to give someone such an important position, Truman revised the draft to say that he had appointed Byrnes because the secretary of state was next in the line of succession, there being no vice president, and he wanted someone with extensive political experience in that post.[65]

Noticeably absent from these explanations was any reference to Byrnes's foreign policy experience. And for good reason. At the time of the appointment, Truman may have thought that Byrnes, who had accompanied Roosevelt to Yalta, had some special insight into FDR's foreign policy. That was not the case. As Truman eventually learned, Byrnes had been an observer, not an active participant at the conference.[66] Byrnes used domestic politics as his point of reference in approaching foreign relations. That put him at odds with Stimson, Grew, and others who thought that in the case of Japan, domestic politics hampered the development of a rational, forward-looking policy. Byrnes's approach also made him more receptive to the complaints raised by those in the State Department like Acheson and MacLeish, who opposed modification of unconditional surrender. Grew had already provoked criticism from MacLeish and Acheson when he told them of his efforts to get Truman to issue a warning to Japan. The two assistant secretaries objected to even the barest suggestion that the United States would commit to allowing the Japanese to keep the monarchy. When the McCloy draft was sent to the State Department, Acheson and MacLeish denounced the idea of allowing the emperor to remain on the throne. They argued strenuously in department meetings that it would take more than a pruning away of Japan's military extremists to transform Japan into a peaceful nation.

In keeping with his brief, MacLeish denounced any attempt to change unconditional surrender without a full public hearing on the issue. On July 6 he took his case directly to the newly appointed secretary of state with a lengthy critique of the McCloy draft warning. MacLeish argued that it was disingenuous to claim that the recently drafted warning was simply an effort to clarify unconditional surrender. The real motivation behind the warning to Japan was to meet Japan's "irreducible terms" regarding preservation of the monarchy. "If we are modifying the announced policy of unconditional surrender to a new policy of surrender on irreducible Japanese terms," he wrote, "the American people have a right to know it." Moreover, if that is what the U.S. intended, it would mean that the Allies planned to treat Japan less severely than it would Germany. He warned that such a discrepancy "will certainly be observed. and resented by a majority of the American people."

MacLeish also questioned the soundness of a policy that left the emperor and the imperial institution in place. He conceded that he was not an authority on Japan, but he believed that the experts had yet to refute the most obvious criticisms made by opponents of the emperor. The Japanese monarchy was an anachronistic, feudal institution "perfectly adapted to the manipulation and use of anachronistic, feudal-minded groups in the country." Should the monarchy remain in place, he asked, what would keep the militarists, large landowners, industrialists, and current office holders from using it to reassert their power once the war was over? MacLeish admitted the possibility that the emperor might assist the Allies in obtaining the surrender of Japanese troops in Asia. He asked, however, if they might be seeking short-term benefit at the cost of long-term trouble with a resurgent Japan. If so, the lives already sacrificed in the war would have been for naught. MacLeish recommended against issuing the warning until it had been fully debated in the secretary's staff committee. If, however, the administration elected to release the warning and thereby change the unconditional surrender policy to surrender based on Japan's irreducible terms, then it should say so "in words that no one in the United States will misunderstand."[67]

It remained to be seen whether MacLeish's memo had hit its mark. Byrnes was leaving with Truman the next day for the Potsdam conference. That night, while attending the president's band concert, Grew told Forrestal that the president was departing for the conference with a copy of the finished warning in hand. Grew feared, however, that it would be "ditched on the way over," because some within the administration viewed it as an attempt "to get the Japanese war over with before Russia has an opportunity to enter."[68]

The next morning, July 7, Grew, once more in the position of acting secretary of state, presided over a meeting of the secretary's staff committee. MacLeish opened the session by discussing the memorandum he had given to Byrnes the day before. Grew replied that he had been charged by the president to prepare the warning with Stimson and Forrestal and that the finished document had been given to the secretary of state to bring with him to Potsdam. Grew added that Stimson, Forrestal, Admiral King, and most likely General Marshall had approved the final wording. A discussion followed in which Grew reprised his arguments for including a statement permitting the Japanese to keep the emperor. When MacLeish repeated his assertion that the emperor was useful to the Japanese military, Acheson reinforced the point. He said that he could not understand why, if the emperor had no importance in Japan's war-making capacity, "the military element in Japan would be so insistent on retaining the emperor." "There must be some reason," he continued, "why the people in control consider the institution to be vital to them."

During this discussion, Assistant Secretary of State James Dunn and legal advisor Green Hackworth intervened to suggest a revision of the offending clause. Why not state simply that the Japanese would be allowed to choose their own form of government? Grew asked Hackworth to draft the statement for the next day's meeting. He also suggested that Dunn bear in mind the committee's discussion when he went to Berlin.[69] At the end of the meeting, Acheson made clear that he hoped that there was nothing in the records of the staff committee to suggest that it had approved the warning. Grew assured him there was not; the committee was not involved in any way in preparing the warning.

That, of course was true, at least up until that day when the committee insisted on revising the crucial clause regarding the emperor. The final version, dated July 9, was drafted by Hackworth and revised again by Dunn. It read, "When the people of Japan have convinced the peace-loving nations of the world that that they are going to follow peaceful lives they shall be given an opportunity to control their destinies along peaceful lines."[70] This fell well short of the language proposed in the McCloy committee and amounted to a major setback for Grew, who misspoke when he told the committee that the president had charged him with preparing a warning. As noted earlier, there is no evidence of Truman telling him to draft a warning and considerable evidence to indicate that neither Grew nor McCloy were told to do so, despite their claims to the contrary.[71] Instead, the evidence indicates that Grew, Stimson, Forrestal, and McCloy felt strongly about the wisdom of issuing a warning and that all were agreed on the necessity of including a pledge to preserve the monarchy despite the fact that Truman had shown no inclination to do so.

Grew and the others could be forgiven if they were unsure of what the president wanted. Truman, following in the footsteps of his predecessor, was evasive and encouraging without being committal. For their part, Acheson and MacLeish were clearly as upset by the process in which policy was being changed as by the policy change itself. For MacLeish, a democratic foreign policy could not exist without an open discussion of the issues. Career professionals like Leahy, Stimson, and Grew viewed public opinion as fickle and uninformed. They believed that their experience had provided them with a sounder basis on which to make policy decisions. The corporate lawyers and brokers who managed the War and Navy Departments also regarded the people as incapable of making sound decisions that protected what they described as "the national interest." Men like Stimson, McCloy, and Forrestal were above the squalid bargaining of electoral politics. Indeed, of the men who filled the highest ranks in the War and Navy Departments, only one, Stimson, had ever run for elected office, and he had lost.

As Grew's lament to Forrestal demonstrated, by the time Truman and Byrnes left for Potsdam, it was becoming difficult to separate the policy of unconditional surrender from American policy toward Russian entry into the war. It was no coincidence that Grew had taken up the idea of modifying unconditional surrender at the same time he was worrying about the extension of Soviet influence in northeast Asia. Hoover had exhibited the same concern in his meeting with Truman and his subsequent memorandum to the president.

However, the battle lines over unconditional surrender were also taking on a partisan hue. Those supporting modification of unconditional surrender were almost all politically conservative by habit and Republican by choice. Opposing them were those who equated unconditional surrender with a democratically oriented policy that was an important feature of Roosevelt's legacy. While Acheson was not a Roosevelt loyalist, he and MacLeish were viewed by their State Department colleagues and outside observers as liberally minded New Dealers. Cordell Hull, an early supporter of Roosevelt and New Deal programs, remained committed to securing the unconditional surrender of the country that had attacked Pearl Harbor when he was secretary of state.[72] Elmer Davis, Roosevelt's appointee as director of the Office of War Information, also opposed modification of unconditional surrender. Davis had survived numerous calls for his head from Republicans during the war. Throughout the summer, he continued to oppose any change in the policy that FDR had announced at Casablanca.

These were the contours of internal dynamics within the Truman administration. Conservative wariness about Russian entry into the war was resisted by those who hoped for continued cooperation between Washington and Moscow. The latter group thought more about subduing Japan than thwarting Soviet ambitions. They believed that America's priority should be to uproot Japan's feudal institutions and encourage the growth of democracy in their place. Opposing them were conservatives who sought an early surrender and postwar stability based on the persistence of the Japanese imperial institution.[73] As is usually the case in Washington, these internal debates did not remain within the confines of government offices. By the summer of 1945, the policy of unconditional surrender had become a subject of vigorous debate throughout the United States.

# 3

# "Popular Opinion Can Offer
# No Useful Contribution"

On the evening of July 6, President Truman, Admiral Leahy, and Secretary
of State James Byrnes departed Washington by train, arriving the following morning in Newport News, Virginia, where they boarded the cruiser
USS *Augusta*. At exactly 7:00 a.m., the *Augusta* got under way. At 8:15, she
joined up with the light cruiser USS *Philadelphia*. *Augusta* took station 1,000
yards astern of *Philadelphia*, and together the two cruisers—designated Task
Force 68—headed for Antwerp, Belgium.[1]

As Truman steamed toward Europe, he left behind mounting worries
about rising prices and the possibility of large-scale unemployment. Critics
pointed to the military's continued dominance of the economy and
complained that the brass hats were stubbornly impeding reconversion
to serve their own interests. Awaiting the president in the Berlin suburb
of Potsdam was an entirely different set of problems, though one no less
daunting. Truman's main objective was to keep the alliance together long
enough to defeat Japan. Following the Army's guidance, the president placed
a premium on securing timely Russian assistance against Japan. But the
conference would also be addressing a host of European problems. The future of Germany headed the list. The fate of the Eastern European countries
"liberated" by the Soviet Union promised to be equally difficult to decide.

After three months in office, Truman had begun to build his own team of
advisors and cabinet secretaries. The exodus of FDR holdovers began in late
June. The first to go was Attorney General Francis Biddle, replaced by Assistant
Attorney General Tom Clark. At the end of June, Lewis B. Schwellenbach,
a former Democratic senator and Roosevelt appointee to the district court
in the State of Washington, replaced the long-serving Frances Perkins as
secretary of labor. Byrnes replaced Stettinius in early July. Secretary of the

Treasury Henry Morgenthau, Jr., like Perkins a long-serving FDR loyalist, was eased out later in July and replaced by Fred Vinson, whom Truman had come to respect for his intelligence and political sagacity. Truman originally planned to have Vinson with him at Potsdam, but then decided to have him stay in Washington to be sworn in so that he could be in the line of presidential succession after Byrnes.[2]

Admiral William Leahy was one of several members from Roosevelt's administration Truman retained. He had served as chief of staff to the commander-in-chief and as the president's representative on the Joint Chiefs. He did not have a formal policymaking role, but he advised the president on military matters and oversaw the White House Map Room, which put him in control of the flow of information. Leahy graduated from the U.S. Naval Academy in 1897 and served in the Spanish-American War the following year. As he climbed the career ladder, he served as captain of the *Dolphin,* a dispatch boat occasionally used for recreation by Assistant Secretary of the Navy Franklin Roosevelt. Leahy's friendship with Roosevelt was an unusual pairing. Like Stimson, Leahy was a reminder of a bygone era. Conservative and uncomfortable with democratic politics, he was out of touch with what he referred to as the "proletariat" of his own country. Nevertheless, the "old snapping turtle," as one columnist referred to him, became one of FDR's trusted aides. Leahy became chief of naval operations in 1937 and held the post for two years before reaching the statutory age for retirement. After that, FDR appointed him governor of Puerto Rico. In 1941, Roosevelt made Leahy ambassador to Vichy France in the hope that he could keep the French fleet out of German hands. While there, Leahy became friends with Admiral Jean Darlan. He returned to the U.S. the following year to become the president's military advisor. When the Allies invaded North Africa, Leahy stoutly defended the compromise with Darlan that provoked widespread criticism from liberals.[3]

Leahy performed numerous valuable functions for Roosevelt, one of the most important being his ability to impartially settle interservice disagreements. When Truman became president, the admiral quickly got the new commander-in-chief up to speed. The two men met every morning to review world developments and frequently went to the Map Room for additional information. Initially, Leahy considered Truman unsuited for the job, a "bush-leaguer," he told his son. He soon changed his mind.[4]

As the USS *Augusta* headed for Potsdam, Truman studied a hefty briefing book that included several documents organized sequentially that dealt with the process of obtaining and implementing Japan's unconditional surrender. The first of these recommended that the United States and its allies use the conference to issue jointly or individually a statement explaining the salient features of the policy. The paper noted that a draft was being prepared for that purpose and then listed the benefits to be expected from such a statement. There followed the familiar justifications: that it would alleviate the Japanese public's fear of the unknown and counter Tokyo's propaganda predicting the extermination of the Japanese people; that it would further divide the militarists from the peace advocates; that it would eliminate concern over the fate of the monarchy and thus remove the most serious obstacle to unconditional surrender; and that it would satisfy the demands at home that the administration try to end the war early by clarifying American war aims.[5]

A second document dealt with the establishment of military government in Japan, with special reference to the role of the emperor. The State Department, with the Joint Chiefs' tentative agreement, recommended that the victors use the emperor to announce Japan's unconditional surrender, as well as to order the surrender of all Japanese forces and compliance with the orders of the designated Allied commander in Japan. Once the surrender was accomplished and the Allies were in control of Japan, they would promptly suspend the emperor's constitutional powers and take him and his family into custody, preferably in a palace outside of Tokyo. The Allied commander would then have to walk a fine line to allow the Japanese people to determine the fate of the institution. The briefing paper cautioned that the Allies should not dethrone Hirohito against the will of the people or attempt to abolish the imperial institution. The first would incite resistance, and the second would be futile since the Japanese would restore the institution once the occupation ended. On the other hand, continued the document, it was possible that the Japanese would eventually decide to do away with the monarchy. Therefore, the designated commander was advised to avoid treating the emperor differently from other Japanese.[6]

In exemplary bureaucratese, the briefing book managed to treat the most politically volatile issue, the fate of the monarchy, as an afterthought, presenting it as a logical and uncontroversial decision. The pledge to leave the emperor in place was sandwiched between the goal of strengthening the peace faction in Tokyo and the need to respond to "a growing body of opinion" in the United States clamoring for clarification of the surrender policy. State Department professionals evidently thought that last point would appeal to the two politicians heading the delegation to Potsdam. When one considered the requirements of occupation, a pledge to preserve the monarchy became even less controversial, though it depended on the emperor's ability to command the surrender of his subjects. After he performed that task, the Allied commander would provide for the continuation of the monarchy, unless the Japanese themselves objected.

The authors of this State Department document did not say why the Japanese might change their minds; they simply said it was a possibility. Here was a problem that required great delicacy on the part of the Allied commander. He would have to maintain the emperor on the throne but be responsive to Japanese opinion if it decided the institution was obsolete. Fortunately, or so it seemed at the time, they had found a way to thread that needle. The key section in the draft warning that Stimson had handed Truman announced that the Allies would withdraw from Japan once they were satisfied that a peacefully inclined responsible government, one that was representative of the Japanese people, had been formed. "This may include a constitutional monarchy under the present dynasty if it be shown to the complete satisfaction of the world that such a government will never again aspire to aggression."[7]

Grew, Stimson, McCloy, and the Japan specialists who prepared the briefing papers for Truman and Byrnes had done their best to make the release of the warning, tentatively titled "Proclamation of the Heads of State," an inevitable outcome of Potsdam. Toward that end, they had expended considerable effort in encouraging the public calls for clarification of unconditional surrender. The advocates of modifying the policy understood that they had to either persuade the public to accept their views on the monarchy or convince the president to disregard popular opinion if it went against modification.

As the internal debate intensified, the proponents of modification employed the traditional tactics of the bureaucratic warrior—the leak of confidential information. On June 7, the International News Service reported an interview with an anonymous government source under the headline "Emperor Valuable to U.S.: Japan Might Give Up, but Must Keep Face." The source, identified as "high official who has spent many years in Japan" and who sounded unmistakably like Joseph Grew, insisted that "the emperor and militarism are two different things, and those who maintain the contrary do not know their history." The "high official" explained how the U.S. could use the emperor to secure the surrender of Japanese troops and

Assistant Secretary of War John J. McCloy, arriving at Gatow Airport in Berlin, Germany, to attend Potsdam. U.S. National Archives and Records Administration.

urged Americans to understand that the U.S. should protect the emperor as a means of shortening the war.[8]

On July 4, *New York Times* columnist Arthur Krock tapped his extensive sources in the administration for an editorial recommending that the decision to maintain the imperial institution be made without reference to public opinion. Krock began by noting the existence of a "wide and emphatic difference of opinion" within the U.S. government on the role of the emperor in Japan. Those on "the highest plane" believed that the Japanese monarchy was not inherently militaristic, and that preservation of the throne would help stabilize postwar Japan. Opponents of modifying unconditional surrender saw the throne as inextricably linked to Japanese militarism, the apex of a broad-based pyramid that had to be lopped off to destroy the entire edifice. Krock's column accurately described the sharp disagreement within the secretary's staff committee. He added a new element, however, when he cited authorities who believed that the occupation was neither "practical" nor "necessary" to pacify Japan and achieve American war aims.

Once the cooperation of the emperor was secured, the U.S. could ensure Japan's demilitarization by patrolling its coastal waters and monitoring its trade. Grew had never gone that far, though Admiral Leahy had. Krock appeared not to choose a side in the debate but nevertheless expressed a preference for the views of those on the "highest plane." The whole issue of the Japanese monarchy "must be answered by high authority on the basis of expert judgment, to which popular opinion can offer no useful contribution."[9] Stimson, Grew, Leahy, and Hoover could not have said it better.

Public opinion nonetheless remained a formidable issue, and a Gallup poll taken in June revealed what advocates of modifying unconditional surrender were up against: 33 percent of respondents wanted to execute the emperor, 11 percent wanted him kept in prison for the rest of his life, 17 percent wanted a court to decide his fate, 9 percent wanted to exile him, 4 percent wanted to leave him alone because he was just a figurehead for the warlords, and 3 percent wanted to use him as a puppet to run Japan. The remainder, 23 percent, had no opinion. In short, 70 percent of participants chose an option that was unacceptable to the advocates of modification. The results were disappointing but not surprising. Grew and the other retentionists thought the poll proved only how uninformed most Americans were. They had a point. The same survey showed that only 54 percent of respondents got the emperor's name correct. Answers included Hara Kari, Yokohama, and Fujiyama.[10]

Americans may not have been able to name the emperor, but they knew enough to hold him accountable for what Japanese soldiers did in his name. Few people could have explained the intricacies of the Japanese constitution and the emperor's role as the head of state and the spiritual, or more accurately, supernatural, embodiment of the nation. They did understand that in service to the emperor, Japanese soldiers were beheading downed American flyers and starving prisoners.

American hatred of the emperor was balanced by a more generalized desire on the part of most Americans to return to peacetime pursuits. Americans were looking past the surrender of Japan and thinking about life after the war. Evidence of this trend could be found in those rising demands to speed up demobilization and bring the boys home, workers leaving demanding war industry jobs in search of more permanent employment, and calls to lift curfews for bars and restaurants and end the ban on horse racing. With Germany defeated, public restiveness with government restraints manifested itself in heated criticisms of the armed forces, especially the Army. The major job in the war had been completed, and Japan's defeat was a forgone conclusion. In this changed atmosphere, more people were willing to ask if there was some way to coax Japan into surrendering without having to endure the losses suffered in bitter victories like Iwo Jima and Okinawa.[11]

In this respect, public attitudes matched the debate over unconditional surrender that was taking place within the government. Press coverage of the issue reflected and shaped the changing public mood. In May, a *Time* magazine cover story featuring Hirohito depicted the emperor's role in unifying Japanese society and asked if removing him from the throne would create chaos and complicate the Allies' goal of demilitarizing the defeated enemy. The author refrained from answering his own question, but his willingness to raise it marked a significant departure from *Time's* previous treatment of Hirohito as the leader of Japan's military and complicit in the militarist's aggression.[12]

The tone of *Time's* story was consistent with publisher Henry Luce's belief that in trying to shape opinion, it was not a good idea to get too far ahead of the readers. Luce, the China-born son of Presbyterian missionaries, founded a publishing empire that included *Time*, the photo journal *Life*, and *Fortune*. The "Republican Party is my other church," he admitted, and he was not above using his publications to promote causes he personally supported. One such cause was the career of Chiang Kai-shek, who frequently appeared on *Time's* cover and was the subject of numerous stories. In May 1945, Luce was beginning to worry that a prolonged war with Japan would facilitate Soviet expansion in northeast Asia to the detriment of Chiang's regime. After he toured the Pacific theater and paid court to General MacArthur, Luce returned to the U.S. determined to change the unconditional surrender policy.[13]

*Time's* lengthy discussion of the emperor was one in a flurry of articles in the press in the weeks between the end of fighting on Okinawa and Potsdam that raised questions about the conduct of the Pacific War. Citing anonymous government sources in the administration or Congress, some debated the best way to defeat Japan, with blockade and bombardment being the preferred method. Others called for clarification of American war aims, while still others candidly questioned the need for an occupation or recommended allowing the Japanese to retain the emperor.[14] Letters poured into the White House and Congress with recommendations and interpretations of "unconditional surrender." These were opinions informed by the press and statements of public officials. Many referred to news stories they had read as well as the president's May 8 statement to Japan and his Memorial Day address.

One did not need an opinion poll to know that most Americans wanted the war to be over. It was more difficult, however, to know what most Americans were willing to do—or put up with—to bring about an end to the fighting. On the one hand, a majority insisted on unconditional surrender and complete victory over Japan. Complicating the picture was a Cantril poll in June 1945 in which 58 percent of respondents reported that they preferred to see the Japanese brought to the brink of starvation by the Navy and American airpower before any invasion. Only 27 percent called for a prompt invasion.[15] As we have seen, however, Marshall and the Joint Staff Planners believed that a policy of siege would prolong the war and increase the likelihood of a negotiated settlement. That, in turn, would make it nearly impossible to achieve the war aims that Americans said they supported: unconditional surrender and punishment of the emperor.

Other polls in June demonstrated growing public concern over casualties, the battle for Okinawa having just ended, but offered little guidance on policy preferences. In a Cantril poll, participants were offered the choice of making peace with Japan after it relinquished control of China and the Pacific islands or continuing to fight at the possible cost of "several hundred thousand American soldiers." The total proportion wanting to fight was 56 percent; those willing to make peace, 37 percent. In a *Fortune* magazine poll that asked a similar question but omitted reference to casualties, the proportion willing to fight rose to 85 percent.[16]

A concurrent survey of soldiers showed support for unconditional surrender but ambivalence about how it should be obtained. Conducted in June, the poll surveyed 2,075 soldiers who had returned to the United States from overseas duty. When asked if they supported "a peace in which both sides would have something to say about the peace terms," 1,332 answered that the United States should keep fighting until Japan was thoroughly beaten, 201 supported negotiations, and 500 were undecided. But when asked how they felt about further service in the war, 1,248 said they should be discharged now and 381 said they should serve a while longer, but not until Japan was defeated.[17] In other words, the majority thought that the job of subduing Japan should be someone else's. That response is understandable given that nearly all the participants in the poll had earned at least one combat star and the vast majority had two or more. The GIs' commitment to unconditional surrender had to be qualified by the knowledge that most of the soldiers participating in the poll believed they would not be sent to the Pacific.[18]

By the end of June, the available evidence, polls and letters, showed a public decidedly uneasy about the human costs of subduing Japan and nervously hopeful that their leaders could formulate some public statement that would induce Japan's surrender. The letters sent to the White House or Congress rarely displayed the desire for vengeance attributed to the public by Hoover, Grew, and Stimson. The common motivating force was the desire to save American soldiers from risking their lives in a war already viewed as won.[19] In that respect, the more Americans learned about conditions in the war, the more insular they became. Missing from letters was any discussion of the geopolitical consequences of victory. Members of Congress, their mailbags bulging with letters calling for the return of GIs from Europe, also appeared more concerned with domestic issues than the fate of Asia once Japan was defeated.

Rather than fret over the territorial implications of Soviet entry into the war, some legislators could not help wondering how Russian assistance would affect American troop deployments. Would Soviet assistance reduce the size of the American force needed to subdue Japan, relieve pressure on the home front, and speed up demobilization? Marshall had anticipated those questions when he spoke to a subcommittee of the House Appropriations Committee in a closed session on May 25. Addressing the House members' concerns, the general explained that the U.S. would probably need fewer troops if Russia entered the war but that remained one of the "imponderables" at present.[20] Although Marshall testified in closed session, members of the House subcommittee promptly divulged much of what was said to reporters. Several congressmen told the press that "there may soon be another sharp reduction in the size of the Army."[21]

Congressional speculation on Russian plans and media coverage of it appeared to violate recently adopted censorship rules recommended by Marshall that advised against press speculation about "future war plans." In keeping with Marshall's wishes, the Office of Censorship instructed the press that speculation about the "intentions of the Soviet Union toward Japan" was a matter of particular concern and should be avoided.[22] Some members of Congress were not willing to defer to Marshall and the Army when their interest collided with those of the military. Domestic politics temporarily pushed thoughts about the future of Asia to the margins of congressional concerns.

Postwar geopolitics remained the domain of Washington insiders. Invariably, considerations of postwar Asia turned back to the question of Russian entry into the war. As noted earlier, when Henry Luce returned to Washington after his tour of the Pacific, he was firmly convinced the war must end before the Russians came in. Luce set to work lobbying senators on the need to modify unconditional surrender, meeting with more than a third of them during an extended visit to the capital. Luce also sought to meet with Truman, but the president departed for Potsdam before it could be arranged. Undeterred, he used his publishing empire to focus public attention on the issue.[23]

John Callan O'Laughlin, the owner and editor of the *Army and Navy Journal*, shared Luce's hopes that Japan could be induced to surrender. O'Laughlin reached a fraction of Luce's audience, but he numbered among his readers and correspondents some of the most influential people in the Republican Party. During the first decades of the century O'Laughlin was a prominent journalist, and, like many Republicans in the 1920s, he had a favorable opinion of Japan and its leaders, some of whom he met when he was secretary to the American Commission to the Tokyo Exposition of 1912.[24] As editor of the *Army and Navy Journal*, a specialized periodical dealing with service news and world affairs, O'Laughlin had access to military officers, administration figures, and members of Congress. He also wrote and circulated a type-written political newsletter to prominent Republicans, including Herbert Hoover, that oscillated between accurately dispensing sensitive military intelligence and peddling spectacularly inaccurate political and diplomatic gossip.

Beginning in April 1945, O'Laughlin's newsletter regularly advanced the thesis that the new prime minister Suzuki was working assiduously to end the war. Each report contained equal parts intelligence reporting and wishful thinking. O'Laughlin recounted the latest information on unauthorized Japanese peace feelers and on Truman's desire to get Russian assistance against Japan.[25]

After several weeks of reporting Truman's efforts to secure Russian assistance, O'Laughlin shifted gears and noted that the occupation of Germany was causing the British and Americans to be concerned about having the Soviets enter the war against Japan. According to O'Laughlin, the British, and to a lesser extent the Americans, were beginning to see the value of

Japan as a counterbalance to Russia. Truman would be willing to come to terms with the Japanese, but they would have to make the first move.[26]

New York Times military analyst Hanson Baldwin voiced the growing concern over the consequences of Russian entry into the war. Baldwin's evaluation of the strength of Soviet and Japanese forces in northeast Asia gave the Russians the edge, but he speculated that geography and limited communications would slow a Red Army advance. Although Russia retained its military advantage, the diplomatic benefit Stalin had gained by bargaining with the Allies over the timing of Soviet entry was waning. Japan was already defeated, Baldwin said, and the United States could, if necessary, compel Tokyo's unconditional surrender. Russia's aid would still be welcomed for its military benefits, he continued, "but it is not strategically essential, and it indubitably would add to the complexity of the political problems this global conflict will leave in its wake."[27]

By May, the growing wariness over Soviet participation that circulated inside the government was common. Officials like Grew and Forrestal shared their opinions with favored journalists who presented them in a positive light. Those not privy to these exchanges of information could nonetheless infer what was taking place from what they read or heard around town. Left-wing critics of the growing anti-Soviet mood that was taking root in some quarters criticized that policy and the process by which it was disseminated to the public. In a June 16 article titled "The Arrest of 'the Six,'" I. F. Stone condemned the arrest of six people connected to the left-wing journal Amerasia, one of whom was the foreign service officer and China specialist John Stewart Service. Stone noted that although the six were arrested under provisions of the 1917 Espionage Act, the charges were "quite vague."

The real crime committed by the six, according to Stone, was not espionage but that they had leaked information critical of the State Department's wholehearted commitment to the Nationalist Government of China. According to Stone, government favorites in the press—such as Ernest Lindley, Arthur Krock, David Lawrence, and syndicated columnist Frank Kent—always received confidential materials. Stone speculated that because the case was so weak, the government's real intention was to intimidate critics of the State Department's China policy, stir up a red scare that would hurt relations with the Soviet Union, and pave the way for a "conditional 'unconditional surrender with Japan.'" Stone perceived Grew and Dooman to be at the center of a campaign supported by the conservative press chains that trumpeted the corralling of the six "spies." He reminded readers that Grew and other "reactionaries" in the department had been sympathetic to Japan's prewar defense that it was trying to save China from communism. "The same crowd in Washington that appeased the Japanese before," he wrote, "are out to save them now from full defeat, and for much the same reason—the old bulwark-against-you-know-what line."[28]

During the last week of June, several Republican senators called for the president to state America's terms of surrender in the hope that Japan could be induced to capitulate. Indiana Republican Senator Homer Capehart announced that the Japanese had contacted U.S. officials with a peace offer that he found agreeable. Without stating the precise terms, he asked, "If the Japanese gave up all their conquered territories, including Manchuria, would this not be all right?" Truman immediately had one of his aides check with the State Department, which promptly refuted Capehart's story. Following an official denial by Grew, Capehart subsequently admitted that the Japanese in question were "influential" businessmen. The rumors briefly subsided, but the episode showed how carefully the Truman White House was monitoring congressional opinion.[29]

On July 2, Republican Senator Wallace White of Maine, the minority leader, called for a statement defining unconditional surrender. White declared that Japan should be told that it faced a choice between annihilation and surrender "with permission to continue peaceful pursuits." Capehart followed White's cautious statement by insisting once again that Washington had received a peace offer from the Japanese.[30] Ten days later, as the Allied delegations began arriving for their summit conference at Potsdam, Capehart made another plea for an Allied statement of war aims. The senator scoffed at the idea of democratizing Japan. In an indirect reference to the emperor question, Capehart said the U.S. should demand Japan's demilitarization and punishment of war criminals but he saw no reason why "we must destroy Japan's form of government and then spend years in occupation and teaching a different form of government."[31] *Time* magazine followed with a call for a statesman-like gesture to try to gain Japan's surrender.[32]

Amid the debate over defining unconditional surrender, O'Laughlin's *Army and Navy Journal* revealed that Truman carried with him to Potsdam a proclamation calling on Japan to surrender and listing American terms. Someone in Washington who was privy to the drafting of the proclamation wanted to make sure that it was released. The editorial, which was published on July 14, accurately described the draft proclamation and highlighted the disagreements over the fate of the emperor. According to the *Journal*, "Liberals and New Dealers" wanted to execute the emperor. Others, according to the editorial, blamed the warlords for Japanese aggression and believed that the emperor did not "involve our security and that the war would only be prolonged if we should fight to destroy Japan's religious and political systems."[33]

Whoever had divulged the proclamation's contents had done so in a way that revealed his political affiliations. The reference to "Liberals and New Dealers" in the journal's article was not intended as a compliment.[34] The ideological contours of the dispute prompted one Japanese commentator to observe that Truman was beginning to feel its effects. The same day it reported the *Army and Navy Journal*'s scoop, the *New York Times* noted that Oya Kusuo of the Japan Broadcasting Service viewed the recent debate over unconditional surrender as an indication of a "conservative yet considerably radical about face on the part of Truman." Oya detected a growing inclination on the part of Americans to reassess FDR's policy of "meddling in the Far East" and predicted that Truman would "liquidate gradually the individual failures of Roosevelt which had all too strongly colored America in domestic administration and foreign policy for more than twelve years."[35]

Public questioning of unconditional surrender became a matter of concern for the Office of War Information (OWI). On June 26, OWI director Elmer Davis had advised the Joint Chiefs of Staff (JCS) and civilian heads of various war agencies that the Japanese were emphasizing the costs of enforcing unconditional surrender with the hope that they could "involve us in a definition" of what it meant.[36] Now he thought it necessary to commence a radio campaign to counter the sentiment "either latent or expressed" that the surrender would be negotiated.[37] Davis was not overreacting. *Time* correspondent Jack McNaughton noted that "round-faced, paunchy" Senator Capehart "put many a nerve in a tizzy recently when he popped off to reporters to the effect that he knew peace advances had been made." McNaughton added that Senator White had spoken for many senators who privately believed that the U.S. needed to tell the Japanese what unconditional surrender meant. He added that White also understood that "how to do it without giving the Japanese the impression that we are war weary is another matter."[38]

★ ★ ★

When senators and journalists referred to peace feelers, they meant Japanese officials or private citizens who were contacting American representatives abroad through intermediaries to begin negotiations to end the war. Historians have described these Japanese officials as "peace entrepreneurs" to capture the independent freewheeling nature of their efforts. But the term could be applied to Americans as well. Scattered through the sprawling wartime American government were officials who believed that Japan could be induced to surrender before the invasion. These American peace entrepreneurs had stepped up their activity after Germany's surrender. By the time Truman arrived in Potsdam in mid-July, their programs were well under way.

The most restrained of these agents was Allen Dulles. Stationed in Switzerland during the war, Dulles ran a wide-ranging intelligence operation for the Office of Strategic Services. Dulles had served in the American embassy in Vienna before the U.S. entered World War I in 1917, and then relocated to Bern, Switzerland, where he was assigned the task of gathering intelligence on German military activities. At war's end, he joined his older brother as a member of the American delegation to the Paris Peace Conference. In the postwar era, Dulles, who like his more famous brother was a partner in the powerful and staunchly WASP law firm of Sullivan and Cromwell, held a number of influential positions in the growing foreign policy establishment, including director and secretary of the Council on Foreign Relations and legal advisor to arms limitations talks at the League of Nations.

After Pearl Harbor, Dulles was recruited to join the OSS by its chief, William "Wild Bill" Donovan, and eventually assigned, once again, to Bern. Dulles was back in his element. Residence in neutral Switzerland, a happy hunting ground for spies, double-dealers, and opportunists, gave him the opportunity to live the life of action and intrigue he had always desired. During the war, his agents collected intelligence on German troop movements, armaments, and plots against Hitler. In March 1945 he entered into lengthy negotiations with German military officers led by the SS General Karl Wolff and eventually secured the surrender of German forces in northern Italy several days before V-E Day. The Soviets had been notified of those talks, but because negotiations involved the surrender of an army in the field, as opposed to a government, the Soviets had been excluded. Stalin accused the Americans of arranging a surrender that would enable the Germans to transfer forces to battle the Red Army. An outraged Roosevelt rejected Stalin's characterization of American efforts, and the two leaders managed to set the affair aside shortly before the president died. Nonetheless, the episode vividly demonstrated the mistrust that lay barely below the surface of the Grand Alliance.

Not long after Germany surrendered, Dulles's organization began receiving information that Japanese representatives in Bern wanted to open talks with the Americans. Dulles doubted that the Japanese had authority from their government to negotiate, but he saw little harm in exploring these opportunities. Contacts were tentative at first. However, by early July both sides were speaking more openly about how the war would end. In one set of talks, Dr. Per Jacobsson, a Swedish banker and formerly an officer of the International Bank of Settlements, represented Dulles, and Kitamura · Kojiro, also an officer of the bank, spoke for Kase Shunichi, Japan's minister to Switzerland. On July 15, Jacobsson told Kitamura that to avoid destruction, Japan needed to accept unconditional surrender, which had recently been defined in a statement by Joseph Grew of the U.S. Department of State. Jacobsson noted that Grew's statement had emphasized the elimination of Japanese militarism but had said nothing about the emperor. He added that Dulles had communicated with Grew and that in Dulles's judgment, Grew's omission of the monarchy from his statement was a clear indication that the United States did not plan destroy the monarchy. According to Jacobsson, Dulles also said that Japan needed to act quickly before Russia entered the war. Once that happened, "it will by no means be so simple to end the war."[39]

Despite Dulles's call for prompt action, the Japanese stalled. Given his early skepticism about the talks, Dulles was not surprised. On July 18, he informed William Donovan that major developments were unlikely. Still, at least the U.S. had established a connection that the Japanese could use "when the situation in Tokyo permits Japan to accept unconditional surrender."[40] That message was forwarded to the president at Potsdam.

As the Jacobsson-Kitamura talks came to a standstill, Dulles responded to another Japanese overture, initiated by Commander Fujimura Yoshiro, a Japanese naval attaché in Switzerland, and communicated through another Dulles associate. According to Fujimura, Dulles, speaking through his associate, told him that Switzerland was a good place to open peace negotiations because the Soviet Union did not have relations with the Swiss and thus there would be "little meddling or surveillance." If the Japanese were in earnest, they should send an admiral to Switzerland "in all haste."[41] That advice was seconded by Captain Nishihara, the Japanese naval counselor at Bern. According to Nishihara, Dulles's secretary, Dr. Gero von Schulze Gaevernitz, a German, told Nishihara's representative that "United States leaders are of the opinion that the Japanese national structure is not to be upset." National structure in this case was a reference to the imperial institution as it currently existed in Japan. Nishihara also said that Gaevernitz had warned the Japanese representative that for the moment the United States found it "advantageous" to work with the Soviet Union. Nishihara added that, according to Gaevernitz, Russian-American cooperation would result in Japan being "torn asunder" just as Germany was.[42]

Fujimura and Nishihara may have been in earnest, but their superiors were not. Japanese officers believed that Dulles was simply trying to exploit divisions within the Japanese military. On July 22 the Navy general staff ordered Fujimura to turn the matter over to Minister Kase and cease all contact with the Americans. The orders ended by affirming Japan's willingness to continue the war and optimistically declared that enemy propaganda and Dulles's efforts "really indicate what difficulties the enemy is facing."[43]

The fruitlessness of Dulles's efforts and of a similar initiative through Sweden provided the Americans little encouragement that the Japanese were ready to surrender. The truculence behind Japan's unresponsiveness was clear. In following Dulles's third-party interactions with the Japanese, the Americans had the benefit of listening in on both sides of the conversation. American cryptanalysts had broken Japan's diplomatic code before the war and learned to decipher and translate messages from the foreign office and Japan's diplomatic posts with remarkable speed. Subsumed under the code-named MAGIC, the collection, decoding, and distribution of these messages remained unknown to the enemy throughout the war. Japanese obliviousness to this monumental breach in security allowed the Americans to eavesdrop on the reprimands Tokyo sent to its representatives in Bern. It also allowed the Americans to see what the Japanese in Switzerland were telling Tokyo, including the statements regarding the emperor and the Soviet entry into the war, both of which were attributed to Dulles. Not surprisingly, OSS summaries depicted Dulles as much more guarded on these points. In Donovan's report to Byrnes, he omitted any mention of the Soviet Union in the conversations and said Dulles had told Jacobsson that "he had no comments to make with regard to dynastic and constitutional questions."[44]

It is possible but unlikely that Jacobsson improvised comments about the emperor and Soviet entry to keep the conversations going. Dulles had interviewed and briefed Jacobsson before sending him to meet the Japanese, and it is difficult to see what Jacobsson would have thought could be gained by misrepresenting the American position. Moreover, it seems unlikely that Dr. Gaevernitz, Dulles's secretary, would make the same statements as Jacobsson regarding the status of the emperor and the threat of Soviet entry into the war without clearing them first with his boss. The Japanese might have embellished what was said to convince their superiors to take the negotiations seriously. In any case, the idea of conducting negotiations away from the prying eyes of the Soviets was certainly consistent with Dulles's conduct of the negotiations with General Wolff. Moreover, his warning about the complications that would arise should the Soviet Union enter the war echoed the views contained in several OSS reports.[45] Finally, there is evidence from this period that Dulles was not above deceiving his own superiors as to what he was doing. When Admiral Leahy asked him if his agents were trying to start talks with the Japanese, Dulles denied knowledge of them and said that he did not believe that any of "his group" was involved. The latter statement was misleading but technically correct in that Jacobsson was not part of Dulles's group. It was blatantly false where Gaevernitz was concerned.[46]

In the end, Dulles's Swiss sojourn was a minor chapter in his long career in espionage. Although the talks fizzled, they were not unproductive. The Americans already knew that the survival of the monarchy was, as Grew put it, one of Japan's irreducible terms. They now had strong evidence that Suzuki's government remained unwilling to talk to the Americans, let alone surrender unconditionally. But those who were not privy to the MAGIC summaries continued to hold out hope that Japan could be coaxed into surrendering, if given the right terms.

One of the leading advocates of this view was Brigadier General Bonner Fellers. Like Dulles, Fellers found his calling during the war, when he served as Douglas MacArthur's military secretary and head of MacArthur's psychological warfare program. Fellers's lifelong interest in Japan began when he met Yuri Watanabe, a Japanese exchange student at Earlham College, a small Quaker liberal arts school in his home state of Indiana. Watanabe introduced the young Fellers to the writings of Lafcadio Hearn, who was famous for his observations of Japanese culture in the Meiji era. Fellers subsequently transferred to the U.S. Military Academy and graduated in 1918. During the interwar period he served three tours in the Philippines and visited Japan on several occasions. On his last stint in the Philippines he served as MacArthur's liaison to Philippine president Manuel Quezon.

In 1934–1935, as Japanese forces consolidated their grip on Manchuria and pressed farther south, Captain Fellers attended the Army's Command and Staff College. There, he combined his professional duties and intellectual curiosity about Japan by writing a paper titled "Psychology of the Japanese Soldier" that predicted Japanese adoption of suicidal weapons. While prescient in some respects, Fellers's treatise also recycled the views on race and ethnicity employed by pseudoscientific scholars like Lothrop Stoddard, the author of the widely read book *The Rising Tide of Color Against White World Supremacy*. Stoddard and other so-called experts on race lectured frequently at Army schools during the interwar period, and their influence could be seen in intelligence reports and lectures produced by officers, including Fellers. In "Psychology of the Japanese Soldier," one reads that "the aborigines of Japan were a dwarfish, stupid race known as Ainus." The Ainus were subjugated or driven out by a "sullen and easily angered" people from Korea who were subsequently conquered by a people of disputed origins whose "tempers were bright." These people, the current rulers of Japan, were, "like all good races," a blend, but their dominant strain was Mongolian.[47] And so on. In 1939, Captain Fellers confidently predicted that the Russians' "strange blend of European and Oriental traits" would prevent them from becoming a major military power.[48]

When war broke out in Europe in 1939, Fellers immediately sided with the noninterventionists. Several aspects of his professional service made that decision a foregone conclusion. First was his adoration of MacArthur, a prerequisite for those wishing to be in the general's inner circle.[49] Second, FDR's apprehensions about MacArthur and the general's loathing of Roosevelt required Fellers, and anyone else wishing to serve MacArthur, to take the general's side and treat Roosevelt as a menace. Fellers gleefully obliged by regularly voicing his suspicions of the president he derided as the "Sailor King." Feller's antipathy toward FDR and his admiration for MacArthur were reinforced by Fellers's relationship with Herbert Hoover. In September 1939, after Germany invaded Poland, a dismayed Fellers told Hoover, "We must not enter the present war no matter who wins!" He added that MacArthur and famed aviator Charles Lindbergh were the best people to lead an anti-interventionist movement. Lindbergh was enormously popular, and FDR feared MacArthur. Moreover, as Fellers noted, "few men, if any, have a more brilliant mind than MacArthur." Hoover replied two days later that he "wholly agreed" with Fellers.[50]

The following June, as France fell to the Germans, Fellers sent Hoover a typed twenty-six-page report on the military situations in Europe and Asia that included analyses of Hitler's rise and the consequences of his likely victory. Among other insights, Fellers's report explained that the American people were being led unthinkingly into war by British and Jewish propagandists. Americans needed to understand that even if Hitler controlled Europe, he could never invade the Western Hemisphere. The most likely outcome was that the world would be divided into three domains. "If we prepare thoroughly to defend our hemisphere; if Japan rids Asia of the White Man, then Hitler's surplus energies are automatically relegated to Africa and the Soviet Union. He should be busy for some time to come."[51]

According to Fellers, strict neutrality was also called for in Asia. The Japanese had been "finagled" out of territorial gains after their victories in 1895, 1904, and 1914, and they would rather be destroyed than let that happen again. Military conditions also made war against Japan a hopeless task. "Should we elect to fight Japan," he wrote, "it is important to know that *we cannot defeat her in Asiatic waters*." Fellers clarified by saying that providing the Japanese Navy secured the nation's lifeline to mainland Asia and did not venture into Southeast Asia, it would hold the advantage against all attackers. Carrier-based fighters did not have the range or power to defeat Japan's navy in its home waters. If an American fleet approached, the Japanese fleet would be safely sheltered in the Sea of Japan and Japanese submarines would dart out to attack approaching ships. Conversely, geography and logistical constraints meant that the Japanese Navy did not pose a threat to the United States. To attack the U.S., the Japanese would have to reduce American and Filipino forces and strike the naval base in Honolulu. Fellers saw no reason why the Japanese would attempt either of those moves, providing the United States remained neutral.

Five years later, in spring 1945, Fellers's strategic predictions had been completely upended. American submarines had severed Japan's lines of communication, ships from the Third Fleet prowled Japan's coastal waters, carrier-based planes struck at enemy airbases in the home islands, American forces slowly liberated the Philippines from Japanese control, and Brigadier General Bonner Fellers had returned to Manila with MacArthur. In addition to serving as MacArthur's military secretary, Fellers oversaw the development of psychological warfare programs to take advantage of the increasingly desperate situation in which the Japanese found themselves. The basis for these programs, which included prisoner interrogations, broadcasts, and leaflets, was Fellers's November 1944 report titled "Answer to Japan." Fellers, like Grew and Stimson, saw Hirohito as a captive of Japan's "gangster militarists." The key, Fellers believed, was to drive a wedge between the military fanatics on one side and the Japanese people and the emperor on the other. Fellers hoped to do that through a massive propaganda campaign emphasizing that the militarists had brought Japan to the brink of ruin and, in doing so, imperiled the existence of the monarchy thereby endangering Japan's spiritual essence.[52]

Fellers saw reason to hope that the rule of the militarists was coming to an end. If Japan's imminent defeat in the Philippines and the heavy bombardment of the home islands were not enough, the prospect of Soviet entry into the war promised to seal the fate of the empire. In March 1945, Fellers told MacArthur that fear of Soviet intentions might lead Japanese "liberals" to depose the militarists and throw themselves on the mercy of the Americans. According to Fellers, the liberals understood that the United States would not expend thousands of lives and risk Japan's destruction just to destroy the monarchy, especially since imperial sanction would help facilitate Japan's surrender on American terms. "When the war in Germany ends," he predicted in a memo, "the likely participation of the U.S.S.R. in Pacific affairs may force the peace group into quick action against the military."[53]

Not long after V-E Day, Fellers's program received an unexpected boost from Washington. "Truman's speech on unconditional surrender for the Japanese," he told radio commentator and MacArthur loyalist Frazier Hunt, "was a brilliant one and a victory for Psychological Warfare Planners." By defining "unconditional surrender" as applying to the military, as opposed to the government, Truman's speech reinforced Fellers's wedge strategy and gave the Japanese a "way out." Fellers still expected that the Americans would have to land on the mainland, but once that happened, he told Hunt, "I believe that there is a fair chance, possibly an even chance, for a surrender on our terms."[54]

By July, shortly before Potsdam, however, Fellers had grown more pessimistic. Japanese soldiers were surrendering in the field, but the militarists remained in control in Tokyo. The Sailor King's policy of unconditional surrender, "which might constitute the most unfortunate phrase of the war," meant one thing to Americans and another to the Japanese. For Fellers, the solution to this problem seemed obvious: the United States needed to do more to clarify its terms. Toward that end, Fellers drafted a seven-point program spelling out the meaning of unconditional surrender. The first six points called for "liquidation" of the militarists and elimination of Japan's empire, army, navy, merchant marine, and military industries. The seventh point called for the creation of "a liberal government, responsible to the people rather than the Emperor."[55]

Fellers believed that the seventh point was the only controversial one in his proposal. "If we were to define our attitude toward Japan's religion, her Emperor and the government which we seek to establish after the war the term 'unconditional surrender' might be clarified to the Japanese." "This might go a long way towards shortening the war," he added. Allowing the Japanese to keep the emperor amounted to non-interference in Japanese religion, Fellers asserted. A hands-off policy on religion would be consistent with the principles stated in the American Constitution and in the Atlantic Charter, which guaranteed people the freedom to choose their own government.[56] Taking a swipe at the late Sailor King, he asked Hunt, "What happened to our four freedoms in which we alleged freedom of worship?"[57]

Like Joseph Grew, Fellers had drawn on his years of experience with Japanese culture to argue that the United States should publicly pledge to preserve the imperial institution.[58] There were other similarities. Fellers decried the emotionalism of those who wanted to eliminate the emperor. And, like Grew, he saw an early surrender by Japan as an antidote to the problem of Soviet entry into the war. By July, however, he was reconciled to the likelihood that it would take an American invasion of the home islands to tip the balance of power in favor of Japanese he referred to interchangeably as "liberals" and "conservatives." Fellers did manage to establish within the upper echelons of MacArthur's command the principle that the emperor could be the spiritual focal point of the reformed postwar Japanese government.[59]

As Truman sailed to Potsdam in early July, the American campaign of strangulation intensified in anticipation of the invasion. Interservice rivalry in the Pacific between MacArthur and the Navy, which had a powerful effect on the war in the Pacific, surged to epic proportions. In the midst of this feuding, Navy psychological warfare specialists mounted a campaign based on themes that MacArthur's men would have found familiar. The Navy's answer to Bonner Fellers was Captain Ellis M. Zacharias.

By early 1945, Zacharias was in the third decade of a career as a specialist on Japanese affairs and intelligence work. His interest in Japanese language and culture began at the U.S. Naval Academy and led to his appointment to Tokyo in 1920 as assistant naval attaché. During his three-year tour in Japan, Zacharias became fluent in Japanese. He subsequently chose an unconventional career path as a specialist in naval intelligence. Zacharias returned to Tokyo as a naval attaché in 1928 but left under a cloud when his superior accused him of trying to usurp his authority. Despite his rough edges and penchant for self-promotion, Zacharias's ability was undeniable. In 1942, he was appointed deputy director of the Office of Naval Intelligence (ONI). Zacharias thought he was destined for the top position in ONI, but his disruptive style and impatience with skeptics earned the ire of Admiral King and J. Edgar Hoover, the director of the Federal Bureau of Investigation.[60]

In 1943, Zacharias was sent to the Pacific, where he commanded the battleship USS *New Mexico*. A year later, he returned to an intelligence post in California. While on duty in the Pacific, he obtained the captured journal of a Japanese officer that revealed the officer's disillusionment with Imperial General Headquarters. Zacharias believed that a well-conceived psychological warfare program could capitalize on that disillusionment and sow doubt and dissension within Japan's ruling elite. His experience in Japan during the great Tokyo earthquake of 1923 had convinced him that the Japanese had to be led out of a crisis. His program would provide that guidance by showing Japan's liberals that they had nothing to fear from unconditional surrender. Zacharias pitched his idea to the OWI and won the approval of Admiral King and Navy Secretary Forrestal. To no one's surprise, Zacharias was put in charge of the program.[61]

Zacharias's made his first broadcast as an official spokesman of the U.S. government on May 8, V-E Day, the same day that Truman gave his brief address to Japan clarifying unconditional surrender. There would be fourteen broadcasts in all. By June, OWI could point to Japanese references to Zacharias's broadcasts as evidence that they were having some positive effect, although their significance was disputed within the government. Those familiar with his career were not surprised by what happened next.

On July 21, while Truman was in Potsdam, Zacharias published an unsigned letter in the *Washington Post* explaining that unconditional surrender applied only to the way the war was terminated. After that, American treatment of Japan would be guided by the Atlantic Charter; the Cairo Declaration; public pronouncements by Allied leaders, including Truman's V-E Day address; and international law. Zacharias ended the letter by assuring Premier Suzuki that if he wanted to know about the future of

Japan's national polity or the emperor, all he had to do was ask. "Contrary to widespread belief, such a question can be answered quickly and satisfactorily to all those who are concerned over the future peace of the Orient and world."[62]

Zacharias reprised the letter's main themes in his broadcast, which was transmitted to Japan on the same day. The broadcast immediately set off a storm of controversy in Washington and surprised the American delegation at the summit conference. In that message, Zacharias told the Japanese that if they surrendered unconditionally, they would be entitled to the rights guaranteed under the Atlantic Charter. He also advised the Japanese to surrender promptly while they had only the U.S. to deal with. The situation would be complicated later, he added.[63] Reporters and officials in Washington pounced. Zacharias's reference to the Atlantic Charter offered a clear suggestion that the Japanese would be able to keep the monarchy. His broadcast seemed to signal a change in the unconditional surrender policy. He appeared to be trying to warn the Japanese that they would have to deal with the Soviets if they did not surrender soon.

Denying that he had overstepped his authority, Zacharias responded to the controversy by saying that his broadcasts were cleared by the State Department. Columnist Arthur Krock, who as we've seen was a proponent of modifying unconditional surrender, went further and cited "persons in authority" who confirmed that the broadcast was approved at Potsdam, meaning by Truman or Secretary of State Byrnes.[64] As Joseph Grew noted privately, Krock was almost certainly wrong. Truman had previously rejected an attempt by Zacharias to include a reference to the emperor in his broadcasts.[65] Less than a week later, the Navy severed its connection to the broadcasts by assigning Zacharias to OWI. Four days after that, he was told to drop "official spokesman" from his broadcasts.[66]

Allen Dulles, Bonner Fellers, and Ellis Zacharias worked independently of each other to find a way to reconcile the Japanese to unconditional surrender. Each believed that the only way to accomplish that task was to tell the Japanese that the United States did not intend to destroy the monarchy. For Zacharias and Fellers, the politically safest way to do that was by citing the Atlantic Charter. Dulles, who worked in secret, did not need to camouflage his intention. All three thought that the prospect of Soviet intervention into the war would provide additional impetus for the Japanese to surrender. Indeed, the movement to clarify and/or modify unconditional surrender was prompted by concern over Soviet ambitions in northeast Asia. Of course, that was not something that American officials would state openly. Although Arthur Krock rarely had difficulty obtaining sources for his columns, he could find no one who would confirm "the widespread surmise" that another purpose of Zacharias's broadcast had been "to end the war before the Soviet Union could enter it.[67] There would be plenty of people willing to do that once the war was over.

Zacharias's broadcast represented the crescendo in a steadily rising chorus of public calls for the United States to clarify what it meant by unconditional surrender. As Truman had sailed to Europe, he was pursued by press speculation about the probability of his issuing a new statement further clarifying policy. We've seen that O'Laughlin's *Army and Navy Journal* had revealed the existence of the document that Stimson presented to Truman and in doing so had accurately depicted the internal dispute over its contents. Krock had followed suit, as did *Time*. In an editorial in its July 16 edition, the magazine presented America's challenge in the Pacific as pitting power against statesmanship. The U.S. had already demonstrated that it had the capability to crush Japanese resistance. What it needed to do now was make "a clear and positive statement of U.S. aims toward Japan of U.S. policy after Japan succumbs to inevitable defeat."[68]

The same week, while Truman traveled to Potsdam, the *Kiplinger Washington Letter* reported that "something less than unconditional surrender for the Japanese is under discussion within our gov't." The newsletter, a business tip sheet founded by economics reporter W. M. Kiplinger, said that the terms being discussed included surrender of the Japanese Army and Navy, the liquidation of Japan's Asian and Pacific empire, and destruction of war industries. "Life of the Emperor to be respected for the sake of religion. (He is a Japanese God.)" According to the newsletter, the Allies, including the Soviet Union, were going to release a list of "terms" for Japan's surrender. They would be "stiff" but "not 'unconditional surrender.'" While the American public may not be able to predict how the Japanese would respond, he added cryptically, "the gov't MAY have some secret clues."[69]

The *Kiplinger Washington Letter* served a business clientele that was primarily interested in war news as it affected economic outlook. *Kiplinger* told its readers that civilian authorities in Washington thought that diplomatic maneuvering made an early end to the war likely. "Evidence of the changed thinking is the rush of new gov't plans to wrestle with internal economic confusion . . . IF Jap war should fold up. . . . You will detect this note of urgency in the news in the next few weeks." "The motive power behind it is the thought that the Japs MIGHT quit."[70]

Kiplinger did not have the renown of publishers like Luce or Hearst, but he had a reputation for reliability among his specialized clientele. He never cited sources so that officials would speak candidly to him.[71] One can discern from his reports that Kiplinger was in close contact with officials in a number of agencies. While his information on Allied "terms" may have come from interviews with personnel in the War, Navy, or State Departments, it is more likely that it came secondhand from his business sources. The Washington depicted in Kiplinger's four-page newsletter was a hive of bureaucracies wielding enormous power over the economy through war contracts. The process of terminating those contracts had begun. The widespread feeling was of a dam about to break. "The earlier the end, the bigger the cut," Kiplinger predicted. "In your own plans, don't ASSUME an early end of the Jap war, but keep alert on it as a contingency, and don't get caught napping," he added unhelpfully.[72]

At the heart of discussion was the so-called Potsdam Proclamation. While Truman and Byrnes were at sea, Grew kept up his campaign to get the president to release the warning to Japan. On July 13, he cabled Byrnes to tell him that he (Grew) had made a statement to the press on July 10 to quell further speculation about Japanese peace feelers. Grew assured Byrnes that the message was unanimously approved by the secretary's staff committee, Navy, and OWI. He then made yet another plea for releasing the warning to Japan. "I hope that early action may be taken on the proposed statement by the President which I gave you before your departure spelling out a little more definitely what unconditional surrender will mean."[73] Grew omitted any mention that the statement had been revised in the Secretary's Staff Committee due to protests from Acheson and McLeish.

Like *Kiplinger* and *Time*, most news outlets correctly identified the contents of the draft warning that Truman carried with him to Potsdam. Grew and others had made certain of that. They had also done their best to raise expectations that the warning would be issued in conjunction with the Big Three meeting. In that respect, I. F. Stone was correct: government officials arbitrarily decided when and with whom they could share supposedly secret information. But by the summer of 1945, it appears that American officials had become so confident in American power that they were also becoming careless in choosing what to share.[74] Kiplinger's reference to American officials having "secret clues" as to Japanese thinking probably meant little to most American readers. Foreign intelligence specialists may have seen it as evidence that American code-breaking efforts were paying off.

By the time Truman arrived in Potsdam on the evening of July 15, what had begun as press speculation that he would issue a clarification of unconditional surrender had assumed a tone of certainty. We do not know how the campaign behind it affected the president's thinking about the issue. Truman had of course asked Grew to put the subject of a warning to Japan on the conference agenda. However, once Truman, Stalin, and Churchill arrived at Potsdam and began meeting, they decided to work without a formal program. Each participant was free to introduce subjects of interest to them.[75] Truman never put unconditional surrender on the agenda, and it is simply not known whether he ever had any intention of introducing the subject or if that was something he decided once he arrived in Berlin. We do know that on July 16, his first full day in Berlin, Truman learned that the strategic outlook in the war had changed dramatically. That evening, Stimson received word that an atomic device had been successfully detonated in the desert in New Mexico. The secretary promptly brought the report to Truman and Byrnes. Both men were, according to Stimson, "greatly interested, although the information was still in very general terms."[76]

The following day, July 17, Stalin visited Truman at his residence in the suburb of Babelsberg and confirmed his previous commitment to have the Soviet Union enter the war against Japan.[77] The atomic bomb and Soviet entry into the war now had to be factored into the president's calculations on ending the war. As Truman processed this new information, he also had to deal with the daily schedule of the conference and still conduct White House business concerning domestic affairs.

The schedule was demanding. The foreign ministers met in the morning. That allowed Truman to conduct government business. Daily plenary sessions usually started after lunch to accommodate the nocturnal habits of Churchill and Stalin and ended with formal banquets that often ran past midnight.[78] The Joint Chiefs enjoyed a lighter work schedule. They did not attend the plenary sessions but met instead with their British counterparts to finalize command responsibilities in the Pacific and reorganize theater boundaries. The Combined Chiefs of Staff (British and American) met twice with the Russian military delegation to confirm Soviet entry into the war against Japan and establish operational boundaries.

The Joint Chiefs held their first meeting on July 17. Their first item of business was consideration of the warning to Japan. The draft they saw, the Stimson-McCloy draft, contained an explicit pledge to permit the Japanese to establish a "constitutional monarchy under the present dynasty if it be shown to the complete satisfaction of the world that such a government will never again aspire to aggression."[79] Admiral Leahy opened the meeting by informing the Chiefs that the Joint Strategic Survey Committee (JSSC) had recommended that the JCS support the document under consideration but they had also suggested a change to the next to last paragraph, the one referring to the emperor.

The JSSC was an interservice group of senior officers empowered to think broadly about the future of American security.[80] In early July, Forrestal had given a copy of the draft warning to the Joint Chiefs for their comment. Admiral King had in turn passed that version on to the JSSC, which balked at the provision allowing the Japanese to preserve the monarchy "under the present dynasty." Unlike the Secretary's Staff Committee, the uniformed elder statesmen of the JSSC were not worried about appearing to appease the Japanese. Instead, they criticized the clause's ambiguity. One problem with the phrase "under the present dynasty" was that the Japanese might infer that the Allies planned to depose the current emperor and replace him with someone else. Conversely, they worried that Japanese radicals, primarily communists and socialists, might object to having the monarchy preserved in any form. To avoid misinterpretation, the JSSC recommended that the provision be rewritten to read that "subject to suitable guarantees against further acts of aggression, the Japanese people will be free to choose their own form of government."[81] That was the same idea recommended by Green Hackworth and James Dunn from the State Department, more economically stated.

That revision had provoked a sharp protest from the warning's original authors in the Army's Strategy and Policy Group (S&P). "Page Mr. Stimson!" someone jotted in the margins. The colonels in the S&P objected that the radical element in Japan was too small to be a factor in the government's decision to surrender. They were willing, however, to revise their draft to make it unmistakably clear that they did not intend to dethrone Hirohito. Most of all, they insisted that "we should not beat around the bush but should state unequivocally what we intend to do with the Emperor." In their revised draft, which was dispatched to Potsdam, the crucial clause now read,

"The Japanese people will be free to choose whether they shall retain their Emperor as a constitutional monarch."[82]

That is where things stood when the Joint Chiefs took up the subject in Potsdam on July 17. Having introduced the JSSC's recommendations, Admiral Leahy redirected the discussion by explaining that "the matter had been considered on a political level and consideration had been given to the removal of the sentence in question." Leahy added, however, that he thought the Joint Chiefs could consider the JSSC's draft from the military point of view. According to the secretary for the meeting, "the Chiefs spent considerable time discussing the application of the unconditional surrender formula to Japan." Unfortunately, the minutes provide a terse record of this critical discussion. We know only that Marshall took the lead in warning against doing anything that would imply that the Allies planned to remove Hirohito from the throne "since his continuation in office might influence the cessation of hostilities in areas outside of Japan proper." In addition, Marshall recommended that the Chiefs convey that idea to the president in a paper accepting the JSSC's revised wording on the emperor. According to the minutes, the Joint Chiefs agreed with Marshall and directed the committee secretary to draft a memorandum with those provisions for the president.[83]

The absence of a more detailed record leaves one only able to speculate why Marshall accepted the views of the Joint Strategic Survey Committee over those of his own staff officers in S&P. The same could be said for Admiral King and the other Navy representatives present. In light of their reluctant support for the invasion of Japan, it would have made sense to support the McCloy committee's recommended modification of unconditional surrender. Perhaps Leahy's introductory remark—stating that the subject of the emperor, and the sentence involving his fate, had been considered at the "political level"—was a way of telling the Joint Chiefs that the question had been decided by Truman. The Chiefs may also have concluded from their reading of the intercepted Japanese messages over the previous several weeks that no proclamation, regardless of what it said about the emperor, would induce Japan to surrender.

The following day, July 18, the Joint Chiefs approved a memorandum for the president that substituted the Joint Strategic Survey Committee's wording for that of the McCloy committee. Gone was the reference to a constitutional monarchy under the "present dynasty." The crucial twelfth point in the warning now read, "Subject to suitable guarantees against further acts of aggression, the Japanese people will be free to choose their own form of government."[84] Leahy's comment that it had been decided on the "political level" to delete the offending passage implied that Truman and Byrnes intended to issue an edited version of the warning at some point. The most that can be said is that they were not in a hurry to do so.

Their inclination to move slowly was reinforced when Byrnes had solicited his predecessor Cordell Hull's views on the text as well as the timing of the McCloy committee's warning. This was the second time Hull was asked to comment on a proposed statement to the Japanese. When Hull replied on July 16, he zeroed in on paragraph 12, the section regarding the preservation of the monarchy. Hull questioned if anyone could predict how the Japanese would respond to the warning, but he thought it likely that the militarists would try to interfere. If the warning failed to induce Japan's surrender, the Japanese would be encouraged and there would be "terrible political repercussions" in the U.S. Would it not be best to wait for Soviet entry into the war and the climax of the American bombing campaign? Byrnes replied immediately in writing, which Grew read to him over the phone on July 17. "I agree that issuance of statement should be delayed, and when made, should not contain the commitment to which you refer." Hull was uncertain what commitment Byrnes meant. Grew answered "I would not have interpreted it as a commitment, but I thought what he had in mind was paragraph 12 of the proposed statement," meaning keeping the monarchy, about which Hull had taken no definitive stand. The two men discussed the passage briefly, and Grew said that he agreed the warning should be delayed.[85]

This was disingenuous on Grew's part. He of course thought that it shouldn't be delayed. His efforts and those of the other retentionists to apply pressure on the president to issue a warning were, however, not enough to overcome Hull's objections. Several days later, on July 19, Grew wrote to Byrnes in Potsdam, asking how he should handle queries from the press regarding the imminence of an Allied statement on unconditional surrender. Grew suggested a lengthy "elucidation" that said in part that Truman had taken papers on the subject with him to Potsdam but that "no plan altering the policy already announced has been formulated." He went on at some length to state that implementation of the policy of unconditional surrender would depend on when Japan surrendered. The longer the war lasted, the harsher the treatment Japan would receive. Byrnes's reply, two sentences in

all, simply instructed Grew that he should refer the press to Truman's previous statements on V-E Day and Memorial Day.[86]

As of July 21, Byrnes and Truman were aware that Hull had counseled
delaying release of the warning and removal of paragraph 12. They also
knew that the Joint Chiefs recommended revising paragraph 12 to delete
reference to the monarchy. They may have known that the Secretary's Staff
Committee had recommended revising paragraph 12 to eliminate mention
of the emperor. Byrnes also knew that MacLeish strongly objected to the
draft warning, particularly the passage regarding the emperor. The future
release of a warning to Japan clarifying unconditional surrender seemed
probable but not definite.

The only thing that seemed certain at this point was that when it was
released, the warning would not contain the original passage from the
McCloy committee, permitting the Japanese to have a constitutional monarchy under the present dynasty.

American intelligence reports detailing Japanese military activities and
eavesdropping on diplomatic communications seemed to have reinforced
Truman's unwillingness to compromise on the emperor. The president continued to receive his daily briefings on the information collected through
MAGIC decrypts of Japanese diplomatic messages and analysis of Japanese
troop dispositions, which were processed through a military intelligence
program code-named ULTRA.[87] Those two sources showed that the
Japanese refused to accept anything resembling unconditional surrender.
Instead, Tokyo was employing diplomacy to avoid the full consequences of
defeat while simultaneously preparing for a bloody showdown on Kyushu.

The prospect of diverging views among the Allies gave the Japanese
reason to hope for a more favorable outcome than unconditional surrender.
Japanese diplomats in Sweden and Switzerland thought that England's
greater interest in European conditions would lead the British to pressure
the Americans to soften their terms. They also thought Japan could count
on "ever greater war weariness" developing in the U.S.[88]

Soviet mediation might be another way to mitigate Japan's defeat. As
we've seen, that was the route chosen by the emperor in mid-June. By early
July, however, efforts to engage the Russians through their ambassador in
Tokyo had failed to elicit a favorable response. After more dawdling, Foreign
Minister Togo persuaded the emperor to dispatch former prime minister
Prince Konoe Fumimaro to Moscow as his personal emissary. On July 12,
Togo instructed Ambassador Sato Naotake to inform the Soviet foreign

minister that the emperor wanted to send Konoe to Moscow with goal of ending the war, although the message made no mention of mediation.[89] That such a move was an exercise in self-delusion was almost immediately noted by Sato. Japan could offer the Soviet Union nothing it could not take when it chose to, he pointed out. Nevertheless, Sato persisted in trying to interest the Soviets in Tokyo's proposal to send Prince Konoe to Moscow on a high-level but unspecified mission as the emperor's representative.[90]

On July 15, after several failed attempts to get Soviet approval for the mission, an exasperated Sato told Foreign Minister Shigenori Togo that his government would have to face the facts. If it wanted to terminate the war, it would have to accept unconditional surrender or "terms closely approximating thereto." In a subsequent message Sato confessed that he remained uncertain about the government's views on ending the war. On July 17, Togo replied that the "directing powers" remained convinced that Japan's armed forces could still "deliver considerable blows" against the enemy, but they confessed doubt that they could withstand the repeated

Satō Naotake. 22nin no Scijika courtesy National Diet Library.

attacks that were likely to follow. Nevertheless, Japan would not accept anything like unconditional surrender. Lest Sato's doubts continue, Togo reiterated "The Emperor himself has deigned to express his determination and we therefore made this request of the Russians."[91]

For American intelligence officers, these and other similar cables provided compelling evidence that the Japanese militarists still controlled the government, and that the emperor was supportive of their efforts to force the United States to abandon unconditional surrender. An Army intelligence (G-2) analysis of the first several messages in the Sato–Togo exchange sent to General Marshall in a memorandum on July 13 considered several interpretations of Tokyo's actions and concluded that the Japanese government "clique" was engaging in diplomatic maneuvers to stave off defeat and avoid surrendering. The proposed mission to Moscow, according to G-2, was motivated by the belief that "Russian intervention can be bought by the proper price." As for Tokyo's willingness to fight rather than accept unconditional surrender, G-2 surmised that Japanese rulers were hoping that "an attractive Japanese peace offer will appeal to war weariness in the United States."[92]

The invocations of Japan's fighting spirit and the predictions of American war weariness contained in Japanese diplomatic messages revealed the premises on which Japan's strategy rested. Decrypted Japanese Army and Navy communications showed how the generals and admirals in control of the government sought to implement that strategy. Beginning in June, ULTRA decryptions had discovered a steady buildup of Japanese forces on Kyushu, one that exceeded anything the Americans thought possible. Imperial Headquarters identified Kyushu as the next likely target because the experience of the previous two years showed that the Americans would choose to direct their next assault at an objective within range of land-based aircraft. Topography dictated the landing sites on the three broad beaches in the southern and southwestern part of the island. The weather set the schedule: first an attack on Kyushu sometime after September, and the next assault, most likely on Honshu, early in 1946.[93]

During the June 18 meeting at the White House in which the president approved OLYMPIC, the code name for the invasion of the home islands, Marshall advised the president that Japanese reinforcement of Kyushu was "possible but that it was becoming increasingly difficult and painful" because of American air and naval forces, and that all communication between Kyushu and the other main islands would be destroyed.[94] By July, the Japanese had managed to reinforce Kyushu anyway. ULTRA intercepts kept locating newly formed divisions on Kyushu. Others originated in Manchuria or Honshu and had been sent south. On July 22, while in Potsdam, Marshall learned that G-2 had identified three new infantry divisions on Kyushu, raising the total to nine.[95] Two days later, he informed British and Russian military leaders that there were an estimated five hundred thousand troops on Kyushu. "At the present time," Marshall added, "the most noticeable movements of Japanese troops have been toward Kyushu."[96] The Americans could also follow the Imperial Headquarters' efforts to convert Kyushu into a base for suicide weapons, including kamikaze planes, midget submarines, and piloted torpedoes. Taken aback by the size of the escalation, American officials were also disturbed to learn that the Japanese had correctly identified the beaches where OLYMPIC forces would be coming ashore.[97]

ULTRA revealed the size of the Japanese reinforcement but not the quality of the troops or their equipment. Other information collected through diplomatic messages indicated that the Japanese were stretched thin in terms of food and vital supplies, especially fuel. On the other hand, ULTRA revealed Imperial Headquarters' determination to inflict intolerably high casualties on the invaders through the use of suicide weapons and large-scale counteroffensives near the beaches.[98]

Staff officers in Imperial Army Headquarters found other reasons for hope. Reporting on the political situation in the U.S., they concluded that partial demobilization might backfire by sending mixed signals to the public. On the one hand, demobilization and the initial moves toward reconversion suggested the war would soon be over. On the other, according to their report, "predictions of increased casualties along with the indefinite war objectives may become factors contributing to decreased fighting morale among the people and the military." American press reports enabled the Japanese to identify many of the conditions that were troubling the Pentagon. "Rejection of the National Conscription Law, increases in labor strife, criticism of strategy, et cetera are obstacles to the success of the government's war measures," they observed. Despite these signs of restiveness in the American public, Japanese planners predicted that it would take at least one more battle, on a scale larger than Okinawa, to force the Americans into a negotiated settlement.[99] A statement or warning clarifying unconditional surrender—even one containing a pledge to preserve the monarchy, assuming the proper wording could be agreed upon—would almost certainly confirm the views of Japanese officials who detected a weakening of American resolve.

American officials had a chance to see how the Japanese would respond to just such a warning when Captain Zacharias made his controversial July 21 broadcast, assuring the Japanese that they would be entitled to the rights contained in the Atlantic Charter if they surrendered. The first response, however, came from the American press. Some journalists emphasized the warning aspects of the message and disregarded the reference to the Atlantic Charter. Columnist Anne O'Hare McCormick reported from Potsdam that the broadcast had been orchestrated by the administration and that its warning to end the war before the Russians entered was proof that Stalin and Truman were coordinating their policies on Japan.[100] The editors of the *New York Times* focused on Zacharias's reference to the Atlantic Charter and asked if the administration was softening its policy of unconditional surrender. If that was the case, they added, the announcement should come directly from Truman and only after consultation with America's allies. The editors noted that Japanese spokesmen had recently crowed about Truman ending American "meddling" in Asia; Zacharias's broadcast would only further encourage them to think they were winning the propaganda war.[101] Unbeknown to the editors, the Japanese naval counselor in Bern had forwarded to Tokyo the views of a Japanese journalist who cited Zacharias's previous broadcast as evidence that the Americans were seeking peace before the Russians entered the war.[102] The *Washington Post's* editorial page took the opposite view from the *Times*. The *Post*, whose editorial page editor favored clarification of unconditional surrender, said that Zacharias's broadcast did not represent a change in American policy and noted that it had not been disavowed by the government.[103]

Given the confusion created by Zacharias's broadcast, it seemed almost obligatory for Truman to say something to clarify the situation. Grew thought so. The day after the broadcast, he sent a telegram to Byrnes noting the heavy coverage that the broadcast had received. Grew told Byrnes that the press was giving special attention to Zacharias's introduction as an official spokesman and the implications for the Japanese monarchy contained in his mention of the Atlantic Charter. He added that the Associated Press was reporting that Truman and Churchill and possibly Stalin would be issuing a statement clarifying the meaning of unconditional surrender in the next few days.[104] There was no reply from Byrnes and no statement from Truman.

In the meantime, Tokyo radio elaborated on themes addressed in Zacharias's broadcast. One commentator said that if the United States would abide by the Atlantic Charter, excluding the section that called for disarmament of countries that threatened the peace, Japan would willingly stop the conflict.[105] No mention was made of a surrender. Another broadcast by Domei News Agency, the official news agency of Imperial Japan, explained that the Americans were rushing to end the war because they feared that the Soviet Union, "already freed from the demands of the war against Germany," might gain ascendency over the U.S.[106]

Somewhat oddly, the Tokyo broadcaster employed an Aesop's fable to suggest to America the benefits of taking a lenient approach to ending the war. The fable recounted the contest between the sun and wind over who was more powerful. The wind sought to demonstrate its power by forcing a man to give up his coat. The wind blew violently, but that only made the man grip his coat more tightly. The sun went next, and by warming the man got him to willingly shed his coat.[107]

The lesson wasn't lost on some on the American home front. On July 23, Nebraska Republican Senator Kenneth Wherry, who a month earlier had tried to cripple the OPA and who disliked the phrase "democratic processes," because it "sounded too close to socialism," announced that a high military official had given him a copy of a letter addressed to the president that called on Truman to end the slaughter in the Pacific.[108] The "letter" Wherry described sounded very much like the documents that Stimson had handed Truman when he delivered the draft warning. According to Wherry, the letter described Japanese attempts to negotiate an end to the war and recommended that Truman tell the Japanese people that the emperor would remain on the throne. Wherry also endorsed the letter's recommendation for a postwar Allied control council for Japan as opposed to a full military occupation.[109]

In the days that followed Wherry's revelation, other prominent Republican senators spoke in favor of a negotiated settlement, one that would allow the emperor to remain on the throne. These were answered by four Democratic senators, including the majority leader Alben Barkley. Three opposed any change in the terms, the one exception being Elbert Thomas of Utah who had been a missionary in Japan before the war.[110]

All this talk of peace and modification of unconditional surrender coincided with the rising tempo of American attacks on Japan's home islands. Admiral William Halsey's Third Fleet conducted what he termed a "big parade" up and down the coast of Japan's main islands, part of a "softening up" strategy leading up to OLYMPIC. Battleships fired shells at Japan's coastal cities while carrier-based aircraft strafed and bombed Japanese airfields. The

Americans estimated that in eleven days of the campaign they destroyed or damaged more than 800 Japanese planes, 125 locomotives, and 374 ships totaling 159,000 tons. During the same period, B-29 Superfortresses flying from the Marianas firebombed cities and medium bombers attacked from newly constructed bases on Okinawa.

The home islands lay practically helpless before the onslaught. Japan's navy had been sunk in the Philippine Sea, and its air force was unable or unwilling to challenge the attackers. Japanese morale already appeared to be cracking under the strain. Japanese newspapers called the government's predictions of fracturing Allied unity "political superstition," while police tried to bring a growing number of peace agitators and slackers into line.[111]

It was by almost any measure a lopsided affair. But it was not enough to dispel the prospect of an invasion, one that terrified most Americans, given what had happened on Tarawa, Saipan, Iwo Jima, and of course Okinawa. Army and Navy officers scanning the intelligence estimates for the buildup on Kyushu, as well as backlogged shipping schedules and the chaotic results of the simultaneous discharge and redeployment of GIs, had even more reason for worry. An American victory was inevitable, but what form it would take and when it would occur was anyone's guess. Major George Fielding Elliot, a writer for the *New York Herald Tribune* and widely considered the dean of military analysts at the time, summed up the situation for his readers. Imaging what had become the typical conversation on the war, Elliot noted that no one was willing to predict when the war would end. "But what's your guess, now, off the record?" was the usual question. "No use guessing. There are too many unknown factors," was the reply.[112]

For Elliot, at least, the biggest unknown was Japanese psychology. The Japanese faced a choice between surrender and certain destruction. That was known. Which they would choose was not. In his articles, Elliot noted that Americans had been in contact with Japan for only eighty years. Distance and unfamiliarity with language and culture made mutual understanding difficult. Those obstacles were compounded by the unpredictable ways people behaved in wartime. Americans were far more familiar with Germans and yet repeatedly surprised by them during the war. Under the circumstances, there was nothing to do about the war against the Japanese except "keep plugging away until they surrender or are utterly destroyed."[113]

Elliot's columns offered cold comfort to the families of GIs slated for the invasion. And, as popular as they were, they were competing against a growing number of commentators, officials, and legislators who argued that the United States could do more to end the slaughter. Elliot thought Truman had said enough when he told the Japanese they need not fear extermination or enslavement. But advocates of modifying unconditional surrender insisted the United States could do more to induce Japan to give up. By Potsdam, there were plenty of experts who believed that the time was fast approaching when the nation's vast power would need to be tempered by statesmanship. And that meant a negotiated surrender.

# 4

# "They Will Yield"

Writing in his journal on July 25, the midpoint of the Potsdam Conference, Truman reported that he had had a "most important session" with Lord Louis Mountbatten, the British commander of the Southeast Asia Command (SEAC), and General George Marshall. "We have discovered the most terrible bomb in the history of the world. It may be the fire destruction prophesied in the Euphrates Valley Era, after Noah and his fabulous Ark." Truman proceeded to adopt a more clinical tone in describing the power of the new weapon. Referring to the several reports he received, he noted, among other details, the small amount of explosive material, a mere 14 pounds; the dimension of the blast's crater, 1,200 feet in diameter; and the reach of its impact, a steel tower toppled a half mile away, men knocked off their feet 10,000 yards from the blast.[1]

The details Truman cited were contained in a report by Major General Leslie Groves, the head of the Manhattan Project, that Stimson delivered to the president's residence on July 21. According to Groves, the atomic bomb test had been "successful beyond the optimistic expectations of anyone." Groves conservatively estimated that the power from the blast exceeded 20,000 tons of TNT. Among the unauthorized observers of the test was "a blind woman who saw the light."[2] Stimson noted that the president was "tremendously pepped up" by Groves's report, and several participants at the conference, including Churchill, detected a firmer attitude on the part of the president at that day's plenary session.

It took several days, however, for Truman to consider the profound implications of America's entry into the atomic age. His biblical musings on July 25 capped off a period of ten days, both before and at Potsdam, during which he received almost daily warnings about Russian intentions. Those alarms were accompanied by reports of Japanese preparations for the American invasion and, even more unexpectedly, predictions of economic disaster at home. As Truman sifted through this information he also had to decide if he would issue a warning to Japan. By the twenty-fifth, he felt he had some clarity on all these issues, including the question of Japan's unconditional surrender.

Problems with the Russians had started almost immediately. Before the Potsdam Conference began, T. V. Soong, the Chinese foreign minister, had flown to Moscow to negotiate a treaty between China and the Soviet Union that would implement the terms of the Far Eastern agreement made at Yalta without Chiang Kai-shek's knowledge. As talks got underway, Ambassador Harriman warned Truman that Stalin was demanding rights that would give him complete control of the key ports and railroads in Manchuria as a prelude to sealing the area off from foreign access.[3]

As noted, on July 17, the first day of the conference, Truman and Secretary of State Byrnes met with Stalin at the "Little White House," the president's residence at the conference. Stalin told Truman that the Soviet Union would be ready to join the war by mid-August but that the Red Army still needed to complete negotiations with the Chinese confirming the rights granted to the Soviets at the Yalta Conference. Stalin added that the Russians had agreed to recognize Chiang's government as the sole authority in China and promised to refrain from interfering in China's internal affairs. When Byrnes asked about the remaining disagreements, Stalin complained that the Chinese were trying to undermine the Russians' preeminent interests in the two main Manchurian railroads and the ports of Dairen and Port Arthur, as called for in the Yalta agreements. However, he expected Soong to return to Moscow at the end of July to complete the negotiations.[4]

Later that day, Truman and Byrnes told Admiral Leahy that Stalin had confirmed Soviet readiness to join the war against Japan, pending the outcome of negotiations with China. According to Leahy, they also said that they believed that an agreement could be reached only through "radical concessions by China." They concluded that the Russians would enter the war even without an agreement.[5] That evening, however, Truman wrote in his journal that he had discussed the Chinese situation with Stalin and "Most of the big points are settled." "He'll be in the Japan War on August 15. Fini Japs when that comes about." After a brief description of the day's luncheon, Truman ended the entry, "I can deal with Stalin. He is honest—but smart as hell."[6]

On July 18, the second day of the conference, Stimson brought Truman a second report on the atomic bomb test. This one contained more details

Seated in the garden of Cecilienhof Palace in Potsdam, Germany, L to R, seated: British Prime Minister Clement Attlee, President Harry S. Truman, and Soviet Prime Minister Josef Stalin. L to R, standing: Adm. William Leahy, British foreign minister Ernest Bevin, Secretary of State James Byrnes, and Soviet foreign minister Vyacheslav Molotov. Presidential Collection of Harry S. Truman.

than the first, though it was not a full report on the bomb's potential. During their conversation, Truman said that he had clinched the "Open Door in Manchuria," which was a reference to America's historic defense of the principle of nondiscrimination in trade in China. Stimson remained skeptical and urged the president to get a specific promise regarding the so-called Open Door in writing.[7] Truman was unfazed by Stimson's wariness about Soviet intentions. That evening he wrote his wife, Bess, "I've gotten what I came for—Stalin goes to war on August 15 with no strings on it. He wanted a Chinese settlement and it is practically made—in better form than I expected."[8]

The same night, Truman confided to his journal that Stalin had told him and Churchill about the Japanese request to send an envoy to Moscow. Truman deemed Stalin's evasive reply to the Japanese acceptable. "Believe the Japs will fold up before Russia comes in. I am sure they will when Manhattan appears over their homeland." Truman went on say that he had invited Stalin to America, where Stalin had never been. Both men agreed that they were misunderstood in the other's country and pledged to rectify that situation.[9]

Some historians have cited Truman's comment about Japan surrendering before the Russians entered the war as evidence that he no longer sought their assistance and remained hopeful of keeping them out of Manchuria. His additional journal entries were therefore written with future readers in mind. Having narrowly averted a break with the Russians after he became president, Truman was making it clear to posterity that he wanted cooperation with Stalin. The question is therefore, If that were the case, why even put in writing his hopes that Japan would surrender early? The uncertainty about Truman's thinking in this critical period is compounded when one compares what he allegedly told Leahy with what he is supposed to have said to Stimson. Leahy recorded that Truman and Byrnes believed the Chinese would be forced to make radical concessions. Stimson said the president was exceedingly pleased that he had clinched the Open Door. Then, of course, there is the upbeat letter to Bess and his journal, in which he noted confidently, "Most of the big points are settled."

What are we to make of these seemingly conflicting reports and what they suggest about Truman's thinking about the Soviets and the Japanese surrender? Leahy's record of his conversation with Truman is the outlier. Perhaps the ever-skeptical Leahy applied his own more sinister interpretation to Truman's and Byrnes's comments on the Stalin-Soong negotiations. Unfortunately, there is no way to know that. At this early point in the conference, we simply can't be sure whether Truman was worried about Soviet designs on Manchuria and therefore contemplated ending the war before the Soviets entered. In any case, Truman's optimism about the Stalin-Soong talks, whatever its source, would not last much longer.

On July 19, the day after he wrote Bess, Truman received a telegram from Chiang, asking for the president's help in fending off Stalin's demands. Over the next several days, Byrnes reported on expanding Soviet demands in the foreign ministers' meetings, including claims to Italian colonies and a base in the Black Sea straits. Truman witnessed the same from Stalin in the plenary sessions. There was little give and take on European issues. Truman held firm. He opposed the Soviet assignment of part of eastern Prussia to Poland and refused to recognize the Soviet-backed governments in Romania and Bulgaria. During one session, Churchill said that British representatives in Bucharest were practically confined by the Russians, it was if an iron fence had fallen around them. "All fairy tales," Stalin replied.[10]

Truman's interactions with Stalin during the early days of Potsdam were hardly encouraging, but, again, apart from holding his ground in the plenary sessions, the president left little record of how Russian conduct affected his thinking about ending the Pacific War. Stimson, however, left a clear account of his stiffening attitude toward the Soviets. As noted, the secretary urged Truman to get a pledge in writing from Stalin that he would abide by the Open Door in Manchuria. This was an issue of special significance to Stimson, dating back to 1931 when, as secretary of state, he watched helplessly as Japan seized Manchuria and transformed it into the puppet state of Manchukuo. Truman was less invested in the sanctity of the Open Door as an expression of actual American interests, though he understood the political significance of the principle. Byrnes, who had promoted Roosevelt's accomplishments at Yalta, had even more at stake in making sure that Chiang was not forced to abandon the Open Door. Neither Truman nor Byrnes wanted a cardinal principle of American foreign policy to be sacrificed to Soviet aggrandizement. Stalin's behavior at the conference during its early days—as well as Chiang's plea for help— indicated that the Americans needed to do something to prevent that from happening.[11]

A strategy of delay initially seemed an option. Stalin had told Truman that the Russians would not enter the war until they had negotiated an agreement with the Chinese. Perhaps the Chinese, with American backing, could stall the Russians. On the other hand, Truman knew that the Army was counting on Soviet assistance in subduing the Japanese in northeast Asia. On July 21, the same day that Truman received Groves's full report, the State Department sent Byrnes a news summary showing that press opinion strongly favored Soviet entry into the war as a way of shortening the conflict and saving American lives.[12] Uncertain of how to move next, Truman asked Stimson to find out if General Marshall still considered Soviet aid essential in defeating Japan. When Stimson did, Marshall replied that by massing their troops on the Manchurian border, the Soviets were already tying up Japanese forces so they would not be available to reinforce the home islands. He added, however, that even if the U.S. went ahead without the Russians and forced Japan's surrender, the Red Army could still invade Manchuria and seize what it desired. Marshall suggested that one way to gauge Soviet intentions was to have Truman tell Stalin that since the British military delegation was leaving Potsdam soon, the Joint Chiefs planned to do the same.

Like Marshall, Truman appears to have surmised that there was no way to keep the Russians out of Manchuria. The president found himself facing the same dilemma FDR had confronted. Was it better to grant the Russians the rights formerly held by Imperial Russia, and thereby hope to limit Soviet aggrandizement, or to risk the possibility of Russian dominance of northeast China unrestricted by any international agreement, however shaky? Truman decided an agreement was preferable. On July 23, the same day he asked Stimson for Marshall's views, Truman sent Chiang a telegram, reminding him, and anyone who would later question his role in this exchange, "I asked you to carry out the Yalta agreement, but I have not asked you to make any concessions in excess of that agreement." Truman ended by requesting that Chiang send Soong back to Moscow to complete the negotiations.[13]

The next day, July 24, Stimson told Truman what Marshall had said about the Soviets already occupying Japanese forces. However, he left out the general's conclusion that even if Japan surrendered to the Americans before the Soviets came into the war, the Russians would take what they wanted. Stimson no doubt knew that crucial piece of information would have convinced Truman to urge Soong back to the negotiating table. Stimson did pass along Marshall's suggestion that he ask Stalin if there was any reason for the Joint Chiefs to stay at the conference. Truman said he would put the question to Stalin at the end of the afternoon's meeting, though he noted that Admiral Leahy had called for a meeting of all three military staffs either that afternoon or the following morning. So much for Marshall's stratagem for divining Soviet intentions, if that is what it was. The general would be able to ask the Russians himself when they met.[14]

Much of what was taking place within the American delegation at Potsdam was being improvised in response to new information and inflected through the personal views of different officials. Coordination was slipshod or nonexistent. Perhaps most telling, no meeting between Truman, Churchill, and their military staffs had been organized to jointly assess the potential impact of the atomic bomb on their planned operations. A swarm of policymakers and would-be policymakers huddled on the sidelines seeking news and trying to influence decisions. Secretary of the Navy James Forrestal had not been invited to the conference but happened to be in the neighborhood and stopped in. Ambassador Harriman flew in from Moscow to offer his insights to the president should he request them, though he wound up spending most of his time meeting with Stimson and Assistant Secretary of War McCloy. Truman sat at the center, relying on the small contingent of advisors: Byrnes, Byrnes's right-hand man Benjamin Cohen, Charles Bohlen, and Admiral Leahy.

Fred Vinson was perhaps the one person Truman would have wanted at the conference and had been unable to bring with him. Nevertheless, Vinson made his views known to the president by way of three cables, all of them warning of impending economic disaster unless the administration took immediate steps to speed up reconversion. In the first cable, which Truman got on July 19, Vinson laid the blame for the impending crisis squarely on the military. The Army was refusing to furlough coal miners, paving the way for a fuel shortage by winter. The same was true of railroad men. Clogged traffic on the West Coast trunk lines was causing spoilage of foodstuffs headed east. More workers were needed to unsnarl traffic. Vinson warned that unless the Army relented, "this will become worse and not better and may even threaten the army's ability to complete redeployment in the desired length of time." Overall, Vinson complained, the Army was keeping more men in uniform than it could possibly need in a one-front war against Japan. "I urge your most serious consideration of this problem on your return," he added. "We need manpower for the war effort and for reconversion. With some help now reconversion can proceed faster, and a small impetus now will save much trouble for the economy when the shock of V-J Day comes."[15]

Vinson followed up with a shorter, more powerful, message. Vinson asked the president to request from the JCS an immediate "reappraisal of all military requirements and of the strategic considerations on which these requirements are based." He also wanted OWMR involved in the study. Vinson acknowledged that Japan's hopeless military situation did not mean the war would end soon and the U.S. had to prepare for the worst. "On the other hand," he added "the demonstration of our naval and air superiority requires the continued re-examination of our needs for winning the war."[16]

On July 21, Vinson followed that message with his third and final cable reiterating his bewilderment at the Army's insatiable need for men. The Army currently claimed it needed "7,242,000 personnel plus 1,150,000 civilians to maintain 3,000,000 troops against Japan, as compared with 8,300,000 when there were 5,000,000 in active theaters last spring." Vinson urged the president to act or there would be "real trouble during the coming winter."[17]

It is worth noting that although Vinson implicitly supported a strategy of siege to defeat Japan, he stopped short of recommending modification of unconditional surrender. As outgoing director of OWMR and the soon-to-be secretary of the treasury, he was acting well within his jurisdiction when he pointed out the effects of current military policies on reconversion. Whatever temptation Vinson might have had to weigh in on the unconditional surrender debate would have been checked by his familiarity with Truman's views on the subject. It will be recalled that Truman had first handed Hoover's memorandum recommending modification of unconditional surrender to Vinson. He knew that Truman had declined to take Hoover's advice. Vinson also knew that despite repeated calls in Congress and the press, Truman had not altered his stand on the issue. Vinson had already given Truman plenty to think about. There was no point in exceeding his authority by weighing in on national policy.

The president responded to Vinson's ominous cables by telling him that he "very much appreciated" his memoranda. "They have been a great help to me," he added.[18] In typical fashion, Truman did not specify how they were helpful, nor did he comment on Vinson's request that he call for the JCS to make an immediate reappraisal of strategic assumptions. In fact, Truman made no mention of what action, if any, that he planned to take. That did not mean that he did not take Vinson's warnings seriously. At that moment, however, there was little that the president could do. He was in Potsdam. The Joint Chiefs were coordinating plans with the British and Russians, the centerpiece of which was the American invasion of Japan's home islands.

Adopting a strategy of protracted warfare, a siege, as Vinson and others supported, in order to spare the American economy was not practical. Nor was it an appealing alternative once Truman believed that he now had the means of ending the war earlier than expected—and with an unconditional surrender. That possibility began to come into view once the president received the Groves report on July 21, the same day that he received the last of Vinson's cables. Knowing that the bomb test was successful was of immense importance to Truman, but it would be several days before he learned when the bombs would be ready. On July 24, Stimson told the president that a uranium bomb would be available shortly after August 1. A plutonium bomb would be ready around August 6. A second plutonium bomb would be ready by August 26. After that, three would be available in September.[19]

Things now seemed clearer. According to Stimson, Truman replied that he now had the cue for his warning to Japan, a copy of which had just been sent to Chiang Kai-shek for his approval.[20] Stimson knew from Byrnes that the warning did not mention the monarchy, and he acknowledged that there was no chance of reinstating the critical passage now that the warning had been sent to Chiang. Nevertheless, he tried to salvage the situation. Stimson confided to Truman that he "hoped that the President would watch carefully so that the Japanese might be reassured verbally through diplomatic channels if it was found that they were hanging fire on that one point." It was a shrewd suggestion entirely in keeping with Stimson's approach to policymaking. Stimson was telling the president that he could still reverse his position on the emperor and that he did not have to announce that change in a public proclamation. It could be done quietly, behind the scenes, diplomatically. As he had done so often when confronted with a request to make a commitment to preserve the monarchy, Truman deflected it with a vague assurance. According to Stimson, Truman replied that "he had that in mind, and that he would take care of it."[21]

The president was more emphatic in supporting another of Stimson's proposals. Before ending their meeting, Stimson told Truman that he opposed any attempt to include the ancient capital of Kyoto on the target list for the atomic bombs. Stimson believed that the destruction of Japan's cultural center would be a "wanton act" that would deeply embitter the Japanese people. Targeting Kyoto, Stimson insisted, ran counter to American interests. It would preclude "what our policy demanded, namely a sympathetic Japan to the United States in case there should be any aggression by Russia in Manchuria."[22]

In short, by July 24, after the confusion of the early days of Potsdam, the pieces were falling into place. After learning about the Japanese buildup on Kyushu and confirming Japanese diplomatic intransigence, Truman had been told that the Army's plan for an invasion would, in addition to costing thousands of American lives, throw the domestic economy into chaos. Even Soviet assistance, which Truman had eagerly sought, was being presented by his advisors as a potential danger. As evidenced by his query to Stimson, Truman was losing interest in obtaining the Soviet Union's timely entry into the war. Nevertheless, the president believed that he could not use the new weapon against Japan without providing the Russians some advance notice. Following the July 24 plenary session, Truman informed Stalin, almost casually, that the United States had a powerful new weapon that would soon be ready for use against Japan. Stalin appeared to take the news in stride and replied that he hoped it would help end the war quickly. Truman, Churchill, and other observers thought that Stalin did not understand that the president was referring to the atomic bomb. No one sought to correct the Soviet leader's misapprehension. Satisfied that he had fulfilled his obligation, the president said no more on the subject.[23]

The following morning was when Truman met with Lord Mountbatten and General Marshall, separately, before attending the day's plenary session. Apart from describing the meetings as "most important," Truman's notes contain this comment: "At 10:15 I had General Marshall come in and discuss the tactical and political situation. He is a level headed man—so is Mountbatten." Fortunately, we have Mountbatten's and Marshall's accounts to flesh out Truman's record. "The president told me, as a great secret," Mountbatten wrote, "the story of the atomic bomb." This was in fact the third time in less than a day that someone had told Mountbatten about the bomb. The previous afternoon, Marshall told him about the bomb and swore him to secrecy. He was, Mountbatten wrote in his diary, "not to tell a soul—not even the Prime Minister, with whom General Marshall knew I was dining that night."[24] Following his dinner with Mountbatten, Churchill took Mountbatten into his study and closed the doors. "I have a great secret to tell you." After he shared the secret with Mountbatten, Churchill advised the Allied commander to instruct his staff to begin planning for the possibility of Japanese surrender in the next few weeks.[25] Apart from the comical aspects of this melodrama—Mountbatten does not say if he tried to look surprised when Churchill and Truman shared their "secret"—the lack of coordination between the Allies on incorporating the bomb into their plans is striking. Mountbatten diplomatically called attention to the makeshift nature of this approach when he recommended that Truman inform General MacArthur. He added that it would be best if the timing of the bombs could be arranged so that the field commanders were ready to occupy Japanese-held areas as soon as Japan surrendered. Truman demurred on this point, explaining that he did not want the war to continue a day longer than necessary. In his diary entry, Mountbatten acknowledged the soundness of the president's thinking, but he added that an early surrender of Japan "is clearly going to present the wretched commanders with extremely difficult problems."[26]

Truman's meeting with Marshall centered on the likely impact of the bomb on military planning. But it also addressed the impact of an early surrender on the domestic economy. It is possible, even likely, as some historians have suggested, that Marshall briefed the president on the most recent evidence of the Japanese fortification of Kyushu.[27] The best evidence of what occurred at this meeting can be found in the briefing papers that Marshall prepared for the president, as well as a digest of those papers Marshall sent to Stimson after both men had returned to Washington. The report, titled "Status of Demobilization Plans to Meet an Early Defeat of Japan," began with Marshall explaining, "This is the substance of the report I made to the President at TERMINAL (Potsdam), he being concerned over the possible adverse morale effect over jobs, etc."[28] Here was evidence that Vinson's warnings about the state of the American economy had gotten the president's attention.

Overall, Marshall's report offered a surprisingly optimistic account of how the Army would be able to make the transition to peace without adversely affecting the American economy. It also touched on the Army's ability to secure postwar objectives in Asia if Japan suddenly surrendered. MacArthur's and Admiral Nimitz's staffs, it noted, were working on contingency plans for operations in case Japanese resistance collapsed. U.S. forces would be employed in the occupation of Japan and Formosa, but the Army also anticipated opening several ports on the China coast to supply Chinese troops and facilitate their liberation of areas held by the Japanese below the Great Wall. The Army might also occupy parts of Korea, though it would need political guidance on that objective before adding it to its list of responsibilities. The report cautioned that because American forces were dispersed throughout the Pacific and still being organized for the invasion of Kyushu, it might take up to three months for them to occupy all the strategic areas in Japan and Korea.

This meant that the U.S. would be dependent on Japanese cooperation to occupy the home islands and disarm the millions of Japanese troops still in the field. Given the expected delays in moving troops into Japan, the Army endorsed a plan in which MacArthur would, at first, garrison key strategic points in Japan and "administer the country through the existent Japanese ministries and administrative machinery." The Army also recommended using "Japanese Imperial headquarters, or a portion thereof," to secure the surrender of Japanese troops throughout the empire. Although the briefing paper scrupulously refrained from mentioning the emperor, the reference to ministries and Imperial Headquarters tacitly reinforced the Joint Chiefs' previous recommendation that nothing be done to prevent the U.S. forces from using the emperor to facilitate the surrender and occupation.[29]

Following his meeting with Truman, Marshall instructed MacArthur to add the occupation of key points in Korea to his list of objectives in the event of a Japanese collapse. That evening, when Truman wrote about the apocalyptic implications of the bomb—the "fire destruction prophesied in the Euphrates Valley Era"—the president wrote that he and Stimson were agreed that the bomb would be used on purely military targets and that the Allies would issue a warning to Japan asking its leaders to surrender and save lives. "I'm sure they will not do that," he wrote, "but we will have given them the chance. It is certainly a good thing for the world that Hitler's crowd or Stalin's did not discover the atomic bomb. It seems the most terrible thing ever discovered, but it can made the most useful."[30] The remainder of this lengthy July 25 entry referred briefly to his meetings with Mountbatten and Marshall before shifting to a summary of the day's plenary session in which Russia's attempt to change Poland's western border at Germany's expense, the "Bolsheviki land grab," was the main subject.

The next day, Truman released the Allied warning to Japan. Secretary Byrnes showed the warning, titled the "Proclamation by the Heads of Governments, the United States, China, and Great Britain," to Soviet foreign minister Molotov as a courtesy. The Russians requested time to study the document, but it had already gone to the press by the time they received it. Byrnes unconvincingly explained that he did not ask for Soviet input because they were not in the war yet and he "did not wish to embarrass them."[31]

Issued on July 26, the Potsdam Declaration, as the warning became known, closely resembled the draft produced by McCloy's subcommittee and delivered to Truman by Stimson. The opening paragraphs warned that Japan's armed forces would be annihilated and its homeland devastated. They also referred to the "terms" the Japanese must accept, which suggested that there were limits to what the Allies demanded. There were also limits to the Allies' patience. "There are no alternatives," it continued. "We shall brook no delay." The proclamation stated that Japan would be demilitarized and those who "deceived and misled the Japanese people" into following the path of aggression would be removed from authority. Japan would be deprived of the areas it took by force and subjected to a military occupation. The declaration promised the Japanese people a more hopeful future by stating that the "Japanese Government shall remove all obstacles to the revival and strengthening of democratic tendencies among the Japanese people. Freedom of speech, of religion, and of thought, as well as respect for the fundamental human rights shall be established." Japanese military forces would be permitted to return to their homes, the Japanese would not be enslaved, and the nation would not be destroyed. Japan would have "access to, as distinguished from control of, raw materials" and, in keeping with Truman's earlier pronouncements, called for the unconditional surrender of "all of Japanese armed forces." The declaration concluded by warning, "The alternative for Japan is prompt and utter destruction."[32]

The main difference between the Stimson draft and the final version was the deletion of the clause in the draft permitting the Japanese to retain a constitutional monarchy under the current dynasty. In its place was the wording suggested by the Joint Chiefs, pledging that the Allies would withdraw from Japan once their objectives had been obtained and "there has been established in accordance with the freely expressed will of the Japanese people a peacefully inclined and responsible government."[33]

Without question, possession of the atomic bomb reinforced Truman's decision against modifying unconditional surrender. It did not, however, determine it. Truman had resisted modifying unconditional surrender because he believed that it was politically unpopular. But he also saw no indication that Japan's decision whether to surrender was hanging on the fate of the emperor. Japanese diplomatic messages showed that they were seeking an alternative to surrender. Those messages and military preparations revealed that the Japanese believed that a weakening of American resolve would lead to negotiations either before or immediately after the climactic battle on Kyushu. Under such circumstances, an American pledge to preserve the Japanese monarchy would encourage the Japanese to think that additional concessions were possible. As troubling as Truman found it, the bomb provided the president a way out of his dilemma. He could avoid the political risks of making a promise about allowing the emperor to remain on the throne and still end the war well before OLYMPIC started. Truman and Byrnes expected the power of the atomic bomb to make Japan see the reasonableness of the Allies' terms.

During the previous three months, Truman had rejected the advice of those who proposed modifying unconditional surrender as a means of ending the war before the Russians entered. He did not change his mind about unconditional surrender at Potsdam even though his experience with Stalin made him more wary of Soviet intentions. That wariness led Truman to be less forthcoming with the Russians, but it did not translate into concessions toward Japan. The president made only the barest of gestures in telling Stalin about the atomic bomb and excluded the Russians completely from consultation on the Potsdam Declaration. At the same time, the president deleted from the warning the concession on the monarchy.

Nevertheless, according to Admiral Leahy, "some indulge the hope that this statement will bring about an unconditional surrender by the Japanese Government before the Soviet Government joins the war."[34] As the tone of his comment indicates, Leahy disdained such thinking. And, as already noted, Truman doubted that the proclamation would induce Japan's surrender. That meant that as long as preparations for the invasion of Japan consumed American military resources, there was little the United States could do to balance Soviet power in northeast Asia.

The atomic bomb had the potential to change that equation. Walter Brown, one of Byrnes's advisors, recorded that the secretary was hoping for time, "believing that after [the] atomic bomb Japan will surrender and Russia will not get in so much on the kill, thereby being in a position to press for claims against China."[35] According to James Forrestal, Byrnes told him that "he was most anxious to get the Japanese affair over with before the Russians got in, with particular reference to Dairen and Port Arthur. Once in there, he felt, it would not be easy to get them out."[36] Not everyone in the American delegation invested such hopes in the bomb. Leahy, for one, continued to insist that the new weapon would not work.[37]

Truman, on the other hand, did view the bomb as the winning weapon, although we do not know if he thought the U.S. could capitalize on a sudden surrender to thwart Soviet ambitions in northeast Asia. It is tempting to see Truman's inclusion of Korea in MacArthur's occupation responsibilities as evidence of the president's desire to beat the Russians onto the peninsula. There is circumstantial evidence to support that thesis. Despite the urgings of their diplomatic and military advisors, Truman and Byrnes left Potsdam without establishing a trusteeship formula for Korea or discussing long-term occupation responsibilities with the Russians. During his presentation to Truman on July 25, Marshall had said that if Japan suddenly surrendered, troops might land in Korea but would need political guidance first. The general made it clear, however, that logistical constraints worked against a speedy occupation of the peninsula. American forces were spread throughout the Pacific, there was a backlog in shipping, and the continued demobilization of low-point men meant that it might take as long as three months to occupy key points in Japan and Korea. That timetable notwithstanding, Truman instructed that MacArthur add Korea to his responsibilities.

Such thinking owed more to impulse than to coherent strategy. There was no serious operational planning, no coordination at the Joint Chiefs level, let alone with the British, and significantly, no mention of what was to happen in Manchuria when Japan surrendered. American might was cresting in the Pacific, yet the United States was ill-prepared to project that power onto the mainland of Asia. The biggest irony in this scenario was, as Marshall intimated, that if the Japanese suddenly surrendered unconditionally, the Allies would find themselves dependent on the cooperation of the Imperial Japanese Army.

The Allies did not have to wait long for Japan's response to the Potsdam Declaration. Before the proclamation was announced, *Domei* reported that officials in Tokyo were calmly waiting for the Allies to issue a proposal. Expectations were running high that the conference would release some statement on the war. The Japanese began to receive the anticipated statement by way of shortwave radio broadcast early on the morning of July 27.[38] Within the foreign ministry, some officials concluded that Japan would have to acquiesce to the Allied demand for surrender. They noted that having finally defined "unconditional surrender," the Allies would not be open to negotiations. Others interpreted the omission of any mention of the emperor positively. The ultimatum promised the Japanese they could choose their own government, they noted. That meant that they could maintain the monarchy if the Japanese people desired it, which they almost certainly would. Most important, the Cairo Declaration had called for Japan's unconditional surrender. The Potsdam Declaration called for the unconditional surrender of Japan's armed forces. Foreign Minister Togo, unwilling to speculate, thought Tokyo should say nothing for the moment while it sought Moscow's help in clarifying several points in the declaration.

After these discussions, Togo headed off to a meeting with Hirohito. He explained to the emperor that the Allied declaration was a general statement containing broad principles in need of further definition. He planned to seek Russia's aid in obtaining more specific information about the Allies' intentions. Hirohito, having already read the declaration, agreed.[39]

On the afternoon of July 27, the Big Six met to discuss what was now being termed an ultimatum. Togo recommended no response while the Japanese determined the status of their opening to Moscow. In this respect, the omission of the Soviet Union from the declaration's signatories was encouraging. The military rejected that approach and insisted on a strong denunciation of the declaration. Togo fended off that demand and advised that it might be possible to obtain further clarification on some of the terms stated in the declaration. Premier Suzuki sided with Togo, explaining that the best course of action would be for the government to *mokusatsu* the proclamation, which meant to kill it with silence. In common use, the term could also mean to treat something with silent contempt or even just to ignore it. The military leaders were satisfied, and Togo had prevailed, momentarily. The same day, the cabinet ratified that decision. Shortly afterward, a carefully edited version of the declaration was given to the press with instructions that it be treated as a straight news story.[40]

The newspapers printed the censored text, but they also stated that the government's policy was *mokusatsu*. Quoting a government source, the *Asahi Shimbun*, a major daily, informed readers that "since the Joint declaration of America, Britain, and Chungking is a thing of no great value, it will only serve to re-enhance the government's resolve to carry the war forward unfalteringly to a successful conclusion!" Exactly how Suzuki's use of the potentially inflammatory *mokusatsu* found its way into the press remains a mystery. With the press having gone beyond simply printing the declaration, the military demanded an official government statement rejecting the ultimatum to steady the troops in the field. Only Navy Minister Admiral Yonai objected. That afternoon, Suzuki provided the desired denunciation at a press conference. Reading from a prepared text, the premier stated that he regarded the Allied declaration a rehash of the Cairo Declaration. "The government does not regard it as a thing of any great value; the government will just ignore it [*mokusatsu*]. We will press forward resolutely to carry the war to a successful conclusion."[41]

Two days later, on July 30, the United Press reported Suzuki's description of the Potsdam Declaration as merely a repetition of the Cairo Declaration. Suzuki was quoted as saying that the "Japanese government ignores this proposal of unconditional surrender for the simple reason that it does not attach any importance to this declaration." The Associated Press reported Suzuki as saying that the imperial government would take no notice of it. The *New York Times* reported more categorically that Suzuki had put the government's official seal on its rejection of the surrender ultimatum. The *Times* quoted Suzuki as saying that there was "no change whatsoever in the fundamental policy of our Government in regard to the prosecution of the war."[42]

What all this revealed is that the Japanese government could not stick to a policy approved at the cabinet meeting for even twenty-four hours. Suzuki had sought to ban official comment on the declaration while the

government sought answers from Russia. Instead, he found himself having
to publicly state that the government was ignoring the ultimatum. The
reports from the AP and UP, which were widely circulated throughout
the U.S., did not employ the most inflammatory definition of *mokusatsu*—
killing by silence. The AP paraphrased the premier as saying Japan would
take no notice of the declaration. UP quoted him as saying the government would ignore it. The *New York Times* went further in calling Suzuki's
response a rejection, but the main emphasis of its reporting was that Japan
would continue to prosecute the war. Equally important, as the AP and
*Times* noted, Suzuki's comments followed a statement by the head of the
Political Association of Great Japan and other "spokesmen" describing the
Allied declaration as a further indication of "war weariness" in their own
countries. In short, the American press betrayed no confusion about the essence of Suzuki's statement: defiance.

It was Japanese officials who seemed uncertain of what they were
doing. American observers could hardly be faulted for not knowing that
Suzuki had backtracked on the cabinet's decision to withhold comment
on the declaration. The premier's decision to reverse course confirmed
what American intelligence officers had surmised: that the Japanese government remained unwilling to accept unconditional surrender. The
outcome would have been the same even had the Japanese press not reported the government's views in its morning editions or had Suzuki not
responded to the planted question from the press. The senior leadership,
at least, was agreed that Japan should fight on while it sought clarification
of the Potsdam Declaration from the Soviet Union. That decision led the
increasingly frustrated Ambassador Sato to wonder if anyone in Tokyo
knew what they were doing.[43]

Japan's military leaders remained committed to fighting the climactic
battle on their homeland. Anything else was inconceivable to them. Suzuki,
Togo, and Admiral Yonai Mitsumasa, the least belligerent of the military
members of the Supreme Council, did not invest as much confidence in the
outcome of *Ketsu-Go*, but they also did not take seriously the Allies' ultimatum. Togo believed there was still time to confer with the Russians. Yonai
counseled patience. "Churchill has fallen," he told a confidant "America is
beginning to be isolated. The government therefore will ignore [the decla-
ration]. There is no need to rush." When Suzuki learned that some of Japan's
leading businessmen had advised acceptance of the Potsdam Declaration, he
scoffed at the idea. The premier insisted that the Allied declaration proved

that "they will yield before we do."[44] All of the supposed moderates were agreed that the situation called for steely determination and nerve.

And where was his majesty at this critical moment in the empire's life? Neither the emperor nor the military leaders were willing to entrust the fate of the national polity to the mercy of the Allies. The Potsdam ultimatum was deemed unacceptable because it did not guarantee the preservation of the *kokutai*, of which the emperor system was the central component. Hirohito decided to put his trust in the Russians instead. If he had any questions as to why Suzuki reversed himself and issued an official verdict on the ultimatum, he never voiced them. As the American aerial assault on Japan intensified, Hirohito was preoccupied with preserving the symbols of his divine right to rule. On July 25 and again on July 31 he instructed Marquis Kido to ensure the safety of three ancient relics kept at shrines on the southeastern coast of Honshu, the main island of Japan. The three sacred items were a mirror, a curved jewel, and a sword that had been handed down through the ages as emblems of the true monarch. The "imperial regalia," as the relics are called, were stored in special containers, and no one, not even the emperor, could see them.[45] Losing them would call into question the emperor's fitness and might weaken his claim to rule.

The American public, which was the other intended audience for the Potsdam Declaration, responded more favorably to the Allied warning. Senators Wherry, Capehart, and White, the three Republicans who led the call for modification of unconditional surrender—while professing to want only clarification of the doctrine—all pronounced themselves pleased with the document. (Wherry hedged slightly, calling it a "step in the right direction," but otherwise supported the ultimatum.[46]) The Republicans' favorable response stemmed from their confidence that the omission of the emperor from the declaration indicated that the U.S. did not intend to remove him from power.

That is how two prominent journalists who supported retention interpreted the document. Constantine Brown reported that American military and diplomatic authorities were predicting that Japan would fold soon, possibly before the Russians entered the war. Summarizing information received from "reliable quarters," Brown explained that the fate of the Imperial House was the main issue preventing the Japanese from accepting the terms of the Potsdam Declaration. According to Brown, the warmongers had been able to use their support among the Japanese people to force the emperor to go to war in Asia. As the tide turned, however, the militarists lost support and the masses looked to the emperor to save them. The peace faction, which according to Brown included business leaders, civilian political leaders, representatives of the nobility, and the middle class, was growing stronger, but its success hinged on the fate of the emperor. The doves needed a specific pledge that the Allies would "leave the present monarchic form of government untouched, as was the case when Italy surrendered unconditionally." Japanese peace "brokers" strengthened their case by noting that the abolition of the monarchy would produce chaos and make Japan ungovernable. If the Allies left the imperial institution alone, Brown concluded, "a surrender of the Japanese could be arranged without dely."[47]

The *Washington Post's* Ernest K. Lindley cited reports from "informed quarters" and government "Japan experts" to conclude that the emperor held his fate in his own hands. The Allies reserved the right to try Hirohito as a war criminal if evidence warranted it, but the emperor could contribute to his own preservation if he cooperated with the Allies in ending the war. Lindley noted that the ultimatum, which was similar in most respects to the draft Truman took to Potsdam, promised the Japanese that they could choose their own form of government. That could mean "the imperial institution as an appurtenance of a constitutional monarchy," but it would have to be stripped of all ties to the military. Lindley also predicted that the military occupation would be limited to certain points in Japan—if the government acted in good faith. In short, the ultimatum offered strong incentives for the Japanese to end the war without delay.[48]

The columns by Brown and Lindley promoted an interpretation of the Potsdam Declaration that meshed with what both commentators perceived as the nation's main objectives in Asia: an end to Japanese militarism and an early end of the war, ideally before the Soviet Union joined in. They thought these goals could be achieved through a limited occupation and the cooperation of Japanese civilian politicians and business leaders. Preservation of the monarchy was essential to this program because it was the biggest obstacle to peace and because abolition of the imperial system would provoke revolution. No one would benefit from that, except perhaps the Russians.

Brown and Lindley, it will be recalled, were among the journalists whom I. F. Stone identified as receiving favored access to government officials. Thus, as far as liberal proponents of a stricter definition of unconditional surrender were concerned, those arguments were predictable. What made them worrisome, however, was that they reflected the views of unspecified officials in Washington. Liberals had no way of knowing how much support those officials had for their ideas. Even more worrisome was the possibility that those officials, Joseph Grew and Eugene Dooman being among the likely suspects, appeared to be signaling to the Japanese that they could expect leniency if they promptly surrendered.

Liberals viewed a soft peace and exclusion of the Russians as two sides of the same coin. Advocates of modifying unconditional surrender could say their main objective was to save American lives, but liberals believed that their limited postwar objectives in Japan made it clear that the real aim of the "emperor worshipers" and "soft peace boys" was to maintain Japan as a bulwark against Russia and revolution. Liberals did not mince words in describing their opponents. While Truman was at Potsdam, delegates representing 115 farm, labor, civic, fraternal, and women's groups sent the White House a petition that unanimously approved of resolutions calling for the removal of "reactionary" officials in the State Department who were seeking to "extend American domination over the world's markets" and "working feverishly now to prevent the complete defeat of Japanese imperialism" so as to leave "reaction strong in the Far East."[49] The ideological battle even affected otherwise nonpolitical social occasions. On July 24, Mrs. Henry Wallace, wife of the former vice president and progressive stalwart, was stunned when Grew's wife told her that if Russia attacked Manchuria, "we must now think about strengthening Japan." Wallace noted that his wife was "horrified at Mrs. Grew's indiscreet frankness." "Of course," he continued, "a statement of this sort merely confirms one's belief that a high percentage of the State Department is composed of 'the people,' who want to make sure 'the people' come out on top everywhere in the world. Therefore, they have a great deal in common with the Nazis and fascists wherever they may be."[50]

A cartoonist for the *Washington Post* graphically illustrated how widespread Wallace's views were, at least among liberals. The cartoon, titled "Birds of a Feather," showed two characters walking in opposite directions on the same sidewalk. Closest to the viewer was a caricature of paunchy, cigar-clutching, countrified, long-haired congressman of the old school with "Our Russophobes" written across his ample middle. He was carrying a placard that read "Russia Can't Be Trusted, We'll Have to Fight Them Sooner or Later, Write Your Congressman." Across from him was a bespectacled and buck-toothed uniformed Japanese labeled "Jap Propagandist." He was holding a sign that read "Impossible for Allies and Russia to Stick Together.

"Birds of a Feather." *Washington Post*, July 29, 1945.

Eventual Bustup Make Opportunities for Illustrious Sons of Heaven to Negotiate 'Soft Peace.'" The Japanese was saying to the Russophobe "Remarkable Coincidence. We Both Work Same Side of Street."[51]

The two main liberal periodicals, the *New Republic* and the *Nation*, the latter which boasted being "America's Leading Liberal Weekly," also feared that while Truman was at Potsdam, he would issue a statement weakening unconditional surrender. The *Nation* detected a strange contrast between America's "massive and relentless military offensive against the Japanese and the note of hesitancy, almost appeasement, which has crept into our political warfare." In particular, the editors worried that Zacharias's broadcast would show the Japanese that the U.S. was as anxious about the Russians as they were. That would almost certainly lead the enemy to think there was a way out of the war by playing the Allies off against each other.[52] The *New Republic* warned that the Japanese would hold out if they thought there was a possibility of a rift between the Allies. The editors had no objection to a joint declaration demonstrating Allied unity, providing it did not lead to negotiations or soften the meaning of unconditional surrender. Nor did they oppose the overthrow of the emperor, providing it was done by the Japanese. The most effective way to accomplish that would be for the Americans to use the military occupation of Japan to strengthen democracy throughout the country.[53]

The release of the Potsdam Declaration and its apparent rejection confirmed for the editors of the *New Republic* the belief that Japan's leaders were playing for time. Only a clear, decisive military victory would bring about Japan's surrender on American terms. The Allies could not soften their demands. "To gain surrender now at the cost of losing the peace would have been to sacrifice all the effort so far made." The editors of the *Nation* went further. They claimed that American officials were contributing to Japanese recalcitrance. According to the *Nation*, the only way to eradicate Japan's malignant old guard was to attack it at the source. "If the Imperial Palace were brought squarely into our propaganda—as well as our aerial and naval—bombsights, the Japanese people might understand that when we spoke of democracy we meant democracy." Only then would the Japanese people see that surrender meant "a chance to win a free life" that the emperor, militarists, and industrialists had denied them.[54]

The liberals received unexpected support from Hanson Baldwin, the *New York Times* military affairs reporter. Baldwin worried that the Allies' silence on the fate of Hirohito perpetuated the State Department's mistaken efforts to treat the militarists as separate from the emperor. He considered that approach to be misguided; the emperor was so closely linked to the militarists through "kinship, custom tradition" that it was difficult to see how one could be eliminated without the other. Baldwin also insisted that only a full occupation of Japan could uproot Japan's military culture. He warned that anything less could leave Japan as capable of starting another war as Germany was after World War I.[55]

While commentators and administration officials aired their views, the broader public was responding in ways that were likely to disappoint both sides in the debate over unconditional surrender. According to a *Foreign Affairs* survey, a week after the Potsdam Declaration had been issued, 54 percent of those polled either had not heard of it or read it. Of those who knew about the ultimatum, 1 percent thought it was too hard on Japan, 15 percent thought it was not hard enough, 24 percent thought it just right, and the remaining 6 percent had no opinion. On the other hand, in a Gallup poll conducted during the period July 27 – August 1, that asked whether the Japanese should be allowed to choose their own government, which was a provision of the declaration, 60 percent said no, 34 percent said yes, and 6 percent had no opinion. A different *Foreign Affairs* survey found that 26 percent of respondents believed the Japanese should be allowed to decide if they wanted to keep the emperor system of government; 66 percent wanted to do away with it. But according to a Gallup poll, only 48 percent of respondents thought that Japan should not be able to have an emperor; 37 percent believed Japan should not be barred from having an emperor.[56]

In other words, unsurprisingly, the polling data skewed toward relatively stern treatment of Japan, although it did not rise to the level of vindictiveness that conservative opponents of unconditional surrender attributed to the public. The Gallup poll showing that only a plurality wanted to do away with the emperor was surprising in light of the frequently cited poll in June that found a vast majority wanting to punish the emperor. Perhaps the answers depended on how the questions were asked. Or perhaps some Americans did not object to the idea of a monarchy as much as they objected to the monarch. There is not enough supporting information to draw a conclusion. What stands out is that 54 percent of Americans did not even know about the ultimatum. The poll appeared to confirm General Marshall's fear that Americans were already looking past the war.

As the war of words escalated in Washington, the actual war against Japan continued unabated. At the end of July, the Army Air Force announced that it would soon be hitting Japan with more than eight thousand planes, the most to date. These did not include naval aircraft launched from carriers operating in Japanese waters. The striking capacity of long-range B-29 bombers was also about to increase given the capture of bases in Okinawa. The attackers would also benefit from the protection of long-range Thunderbolt fighters. The shorter trips would require less fuel and permit the planes to carry heavier payloads.[57] Also at the end of July, Admiral William "Bull" Halsey's Third Fleet planes were in the nineteenth day of a prolonged attack against Japanese naval and air bases. Meanwhile, General Curtis LeMay issued a list of eleven Japanese cities that were targeted for complete destruction by B-29s.[58] Two days later, a destroyer task force from Halsey's Third Feet steamed straight into the Suruga Gulf to shell the city of Shimizu, a key link in Japan's railway net.[59]

Reports of the relentless air and naval attacks against Japan's home islands might easily have led some military leaders to think Japan was on the verge of surrendering. But Japanese Imperial General Headquarters refused to capitulate while its main force remained intact in the home islands. And so the air raids and shelling continued while the Americans prepared for the invasion of Kyushu. OLYMPIC, scheduled for November 1, would send fourteen divisions and two regiments against three separate beaches at the southern tip of Kyushu. There would also be supporting operations against several smaller islands off the southern coast of Kyushu. Once the invading force had gained control of the southern third of Kyushu, the buildup for the second stage of the invasion would begin. In stage two, code-named CORONET, twenty-five divisions would eventually land in the vicinity of Tokyo and drive into the heartland region of the Kanto Plain. The assault on Honshu, which depended on the transfer of divisions from the European theater, was not expected to take place before March 1, 1946.

OLYMPIC and CORONET were aimed at the heart of the Japanese empire. Other Allied operations would subdue the widely dispersed and undefeated Japanese forces that controlled much of China and Southeast Asia. During their meetings at Potsdam, the Combined Chiefs of Staff, first meeting separately and then with their Soviet counterparts, had agreed on geographical responsibilities and operational boundaries that would enable each of the Allies to gradually retake territory conquered by the Japanese since 1931. The loosely coordinated operations served a dual purpose: to crush all elements of Japanese resistance and to secure territory deemed vital to the postwar interests of each of the belligerents.

Nationalist China, having been at war the longest, had the most at stake in reestablishing sovereignty over the vast areas controlled by the Japanese. Seven years after having been pushed out of the prosperous coastal areas and consigned to the less-developed western interior, the Nationalists were taking the offensive. By the summer of 1945, Nationalist troops had cleared northern Burma and reopened land communications between southwestern China and India along the newly built Stilwell Road. The next step was a move against the south China coast. Operation RASHNESS, as the offensive was called, would open a port along the coast to facilitate the creation of thirty-nine divisions along American lines. Another offensive, tentatively dubbed CARBONADO, would bring Nationalist troops into the vicinity of Hong Kong, Britain's colonial bastion. Chiang had made no secret of his intention to reclaim Hong Kong for China "at the proper moment." By early summer, Chinese troops, trained, armed, and advised by Americans, began preparing for operations in the Hong Kong area. Thus, it seemed possible that China's first major offensive of the war might embroil the United States in a showdown over Britain's most important colony in East Asia.

Chinese and British success in Burma set the stage for future British operations to the south. Southern Burma, Thailand, Malaya, Sumatra, and Singapore formed the area of operations for the Southeast Asian theater, commanded by Lord Mountbatten. Southeast Asia Command (SEAC) was created in 1943 to clarify command responsibilities among the Americans, Chinese, and British operating in Asia. The political implications of the re-organization were obvious. American critics drew attention to these by sarcastically insisting that the theater acronym really stood for "Save England's Asian Colonies."

As operations in Burma neared completion, Mountbatten planned for Operation ZIPPER, an assault on the Port Swettenham–Port Dickson area on the west coast of the Malay Peninsula in the fall. ZIPPER would be followed by an attack on Singapore in December and the recapture of Hong Kong a few months after that. After a four-year hiatus in European rule, Mountbatten hoped to retake Southeast Asia gradually in stages, so that the British could restore order and undo the damage done to European prestige by Japan's stunning victories in 1941–1942.

To further pare down American responsibilities in Asia, the Americans and British agreed to expand the boundaries of the Southeast Asian Command to include Indochina below the sixteenth parallel, all of Thailand, Java, the Celebes islands, and Borneo. This agreement added half a million square miles to Mountbatten's command. The British area of interest now consisted of one and a half million square miles, much of it occupied by undefeated Japanese armies. It was with this situation in mind that Mountbatten later remarked that the decision to enlarge SEAC "was not as flattering as it may sound."[60]

In contrast to SEAC, Soviet preparations for the invasion of Manchuria were nearly completed. In the three months after Germany's surrender, the Red Army redeployed more than thirty divisions from the European theater to the area bordering Manchuria. More than one thousand trains rolled across Siberia carrying seven hundred thousand battle-tested troops and the supplies they would need for the invasion. In all, one and a half million men, five and a half thousand tanks, and an equally impressive number of artillery pieces and self-propelled guns were being massed for the offensive. To conduct the campaign, Stalin created a special high command for the Far East, headed by former chief of the general staff marshal Aleksandr Vasilevskii. The high command stealthily assembled troops well behind their designated jumping-off points and moved most often at night. In his instructions to the general staff, Stalin emphasized the need for a swift, decisive campaign. Speed became even more imperative once Stalin learned that the United States had added the atomic bomb to its arsenal. The final timetable for AUGUST STORM aimed for victory in thirty days.[61]

Compared with the Russian preparations, American arrangements for OLYMPIC were lagging. The movement of men and supplies to the Pacific was hampered by numerous obstacles. Manila harbor was clogged with ships deliberately sunk by the Japanese. The construction battalions needed to erect facilities for the influx of troops were slow in arriving. The status of troops designated for OLYMPIC was also a problem. Some of the divisions had only recently withdrawn from combat in the Philippines. They would have less than two months to rest, re-equip, and absorb replacements for the men lost to combat and disease. In addition, they would also need to replace veteran high-point men with inexperienced GIs from the European Theater or the U.S. As General Marshall later observed, the Army was losing its first team on the eve of its biggest campaign in the Pacific.

Planners thought that OLYMPIC could be conducted with units already in the Pacific, once they received replacements for high-point men and casualties. The second phase of the invasion, the attack on the Tokyo–Kanto Plain region, depended on troops redeployed from Europe. Redeployment was just getting underway and already facing a backlog in shipping. There were several causes for that problem. One was distance. It took a ship three times as long to make a round trip to the western Pacific as it did to Europe. Demobilization added to the scarcity of shipping. The second was political. Although redeployment was supposed to be the top priority, Army staff officers conceded that they had reversed priorities in response to demands from Congress and the public to hasten the return and discharge of high-point men. That included GIs in the Pacific, which, in turn, required more ships to bring those men home and ship their replacements out from the U.S. The third source of the problem was MacArthur. As Admiral King seemed all too happy to explain to Marshall, MacArthur had held on to most of the freighters sent into his theater, using them as floating storehouses for ongoing "mopping up" operations in the Philippines. Repeated pleas to the general to release some of those ships were having little effect.[62]

Japanese Imperial Headquarters meanwhile prepared for the climactic stage of the war by repositioning its forces and husbanding supplies and resources, including special attack (suicide) weapons, and by issuing orders emphasizing the importance of the Japanese soldier's spiritual strength and devotion to the emperor.[63] In practical terms, this resulted in the Japanese Army consolidating its forces in China by gradually withdrawing north and along the coast, in anticipation of American landings. Field Marshal Terauchi Hisaichi, the commander of Imperial Japanese Army's Southern Area, could do little to coordinate defense of Southeast Asia. Japanese garrisons were isolated and poorly provisioned. Widespread food shortages and abuse of the inhabitants had squandered whatever goodwill had been created when the Japanese drove out the Europeans four years earlier. In the summer of 1945 Tokyo belatedly began implementing plans for Indonesian independence, starting with Java. Terauchi issued the standard orders, commanding soldiers and officers to fight to the death, but he also planned for the wholesale slaughter of the thousands of prisoners under Japanese control if defeat became inevitable.[64]

In Manchuria, the renegade Kwantung Army, which had initiated Japan's invasion of China in 1931, dug into defensive positions and waited for the Russian attack. Over the course of the war, Imperial Headquarters had siphoned off nineteen infantry and two armored divisions for combat in the Pacific. Inexperienced and ill-equipped recruits filled out the order of battle, creating a formidable force on paper only.[65] Japanese commanders planned to defend only a small portion of southeastern Manchuria. This decision was poorly communicated to the Kwantung Army's field commanders, and not at all to the million and a half Japanese civilians living in Manchuria. Implementation of this new defense plan did not begin until June 1945. Even then preparations proceeded slowly.

Through much of the summer, Japanese observers watched nervously as the Soviet Union transferred forces to the Siberian frontier. Preparations for the Red Army's campaign in Manchuria were nearing completion when Colonel Shiraki Suenari told his superiors on the Imperial Japanese Army's general staff that the Red Army was not equipped with winter clothing. That could mean only one thing—that the Russians were planning to attack in August. Shiraki's warning made little impression on his colleagues.[66]

Planning continued on the assumption that the Red Army would not attack until autumn or the following spring.

To prepare for the decisive battle for the home islands, Imperial General
Headquarters continued to pour troops into Kyushu. The Americans' preference for land-based air coverage of operations convinced Japanese Imperial
Headquarters that Kyushu would be the first battleground. The geography
of Kyushu enabled Japanese strategists to predict the most likely sites for
the invasion. Seasonal weather patterns—in this case, the approaching typhoon season—suggested an invasion date sometime in fall. The Japanese
would have nearly 900,000 men in fourteen divisions to repel the invaders.
If OLYMPIC came off as expected, the Americans would be committing
650,000 troops to the invasion.[67]

The guiding assumption of Allied planning at Potsdam was that the war
would continue for at least several months, possibly a year. That thinking
changed dramatically with the success of the atomic bomb test in mid-July.
As noted, on July 25—the day Stimson told Truman when the first atomic
bombs would be ready, and the day after the Combined Chiefs of Staff had
agreed to the final arrangements for Southeast Asia and met for the first
time with the Russians—Truman instructed General Marshall to request
MacArthur's plans for the rapid occupation of Japan *and* Korea. Similarly,
Churchill instructed Mountbatten to notify his staff to be prepared for an
early Japanese surrender. The prime minister prohibited Mountbatten from
explaining the reason for the sudden change of plan. As the admiral recalled,
"My SEAC staff had to rush forward all our plans for landing in Malaya and
Singapore, and just take my word for it that there would be no opposition."[68]

As Mountbatten's statement indicates, existing operational plans would
have to serve as the template for the surrender operations. Nevertheless,
the logistical demands imposed by accelerated timetables promised to be
a source of ongoing difficulty. American commanders in the Pacific were
a small step ahead of SEAC in planning. Before the Potsdam Conference
began, the JCS had asked MacArthur and his Navy counterpart, Admiral
Chester Nimitz, to work up plans for the occupation in the event that
Japanese resistance collapsed before OLYMPIC. MacArthur's preliminary
plan was code-named BLACKLIST; Nimitz's was CAMPUS. It did not
take long for the two commanders to revert to the interservice squabbling
that had been a standard feature of the American war in the Pacific. The
stakes were raised when the commanders learned about the atomic bomb.
A Japanese surrender was a real possibility.

Desiring speed above all else, the Joint Chiefs tentatively decided that Nimitz's plan, which envisioned a naval show of force in Tokyo Bay and Marine landings at key points along the shore, offered the quickest means of enforcing the surrender. MacArthur protested that naval forces were not suited for such responsibilities. He added that command and control of all surrender operations should follow the structure established for OLYMPIC, which would put him in charge. MacArthur eventually got to the heart of the matter. "It would be psychologically offensive to ground and air forces of the Pacific Theater," he told the Chiefs, "to be relegated from their proper missions at the hour of victory."[69] Marshall thought a compromise was possible. What was needed, he explained, was some variation on MacArthur's BLACKLIST that would also provide for the rapid movement of naval forces into key areas during the period between capitulation and the arrival of MacArthur's main force. "We are trying to end the war with Japan," he reminded MacArthur.[70]

The urgency with which the Allies approached planning for a sudden end to the war was in marked contrast to the desultory fashion in which the Japanese sought an alternative to unconditional surrender. Of course, the Allies, including the Russians, knew about the atomic bomb and the Japanese did not. One can see how the Japanese would regard the threatening passages in the ultimatum as promising a continuation of the siege they were already enduring. Japanese intelligence did not forecast any dramatic escalation in the war until November at the earliest. That gave Togo and his foreign ministry aides time to study the Potsdam Declaration, parse key phrases, and ponder their subtleties and nuances. In doing so, they gave almost no attention to what under other circumstances would have stood out as the clearest message contained in the ultimatum: that delay would bring "prompt and utter destruction."

# 5

# "A Great Victory Has Been Won"

The thirteenth and final meeting of the Big Three at Potsdam ended with the approval of the joint communiqué at 12:30 a.m. on August 2. At 7:15 a.m., Truman departed the Little White House for Gatow Airfield and the C-54 plane that would deliver him to an airfield in Southwest England. Secretary of State Byrnes, who was next in the line of succession (given there was no vice president), flew in a separate C-54. Their destination was the USS *Augusta*, anchored in Plymouth Roads. The 800 mile flight took them over the Isle of Wight to Harrowbeer Airbase, 10 miles outside Plymouth. After a short trip by car, the president's party arrived at Mill Dock and boarded Admiral Sir John "Ralph" Leatham's barge, which took them to the *Augusta*. At 11:20 a.m., the president boarded the cruiser after an absence of seventeen days.

The day's main events consisted of meetings with King George VI, who was aboard the battle cruiser HMS *Renown*, also anchored in Plymouth Roads. The president, Byrnes, and Admiral Leahy had lunch with the monarch on the *Renown*. This was ostensibly a social call, but the participants did discuss the situation in the Pacific. During that conversation, Leahy confirmed his skepticism about the atomic bomb by making a bet with the king that the new weapon would not work. Later that afternoon, Truman repaid George VI's courtesy by playing host to His Majesty on the *Augusta*. The formalities completed, *Augusta* got underway a little before 8:00 p.m. Truman was headed home.[1]

As the president steamed west, in Manila, General MacArthur's intelligence chief, Major General Charles A. Willoughby, was updating estimates of Japanese strength on Kyushu. On August 2, ULTRA showed that there were 545,000 Japanese servicemen on the island. Five days later, the number had risen to 560,000. American cryptanalysts also recorded a steadily increasing number of aircraft moving into range of the Kyushu invasion beaches. Most of these were trainers being converted into suicide planes, similar to those that had attacked the U.S. fleet off Okinawa to such devastating effect. The Japanese were also amassing a flotilla of suicide watercraft, including small surface vessels, midget submarines, and human-piloted torpedoes.[2]

The evidence of the Japanese buildup on Kyushu prompted the planning officers on the Joint Chiefs of Staff to explore alternatives to OLYMPIC, and with a sense of urgency not usually found in routine contingency planning. On August 4, the Joint War Plans Committee (JWPC) forwarded a report to the Joint Staff Planners (JSP) recommending that in light of "the possible effect upon OLYMPIC operations of this buildup and concentration," the JSP should instruct MacArthur and Admiral Nimitz to "review their estimates of the situation, reexamine objectives in Japan as possible alternatives to OLYMPIC, and prepare plans for operations against such alternate objectives."[3] Attached to the report was a draft memorandum for MacArthur and Nimitz explaining that conditions on Kyushu did not require an immediate change in their directive, but did warrant serious consideration of OLYMPIC's prospects and an evaluation of possible alternatives.

As the Americans considered options to OLYMPIC, in Moscow, Japanese Ambassador Sato grew increasingly frustrated with his government's inability to act. Tokyo needed to abandon any expectation that the Soviet Union would help Japan find a way out of the war. Stalin had no incentive to act on Japan's behalf. Everything that Japan could offer, the Soviet Union could take anyway. Sato made his case to the government as directly as diplomacy would permit. "Your way of looking at things," he wrote, "and the actual situation in the Eastern Area may be seen to be absolutely contradictory."[4] Sato's assessment had no impact on his government's position. In reply, Togo urged the ambassador to press for a meeting with the Russian foreign ministry. He also confided, "It is difficult to decide on concrete peace conditions here at home all at once. . . . . [W]e are exerting ourselves to collect the views of all quarters." To reassure Sato, the foreign minister added that there was a "disposition" to make the Potsdam Declaration "the basis of our study concerning terms."[5]

That one sent Sato over the edge. Nearly two months had passed since the emperor had agreed to seek Russia's good offices, and the government had yet to agree on the terms it would accept to make peace. It was time to end the dithering. Sato replied by admitting that he had telegraphed his "humble opinions in outspoken terms," but he sincerely doubted that the Russians would receive him unless he could offer concrete terms on which Japan would make peace. Sato knew that a negotiated armistice was no longer possible and that only surrender would end the fighting. Sato was prepared to go to extraordinary lengths to make his government confront that reality. He reminded Togo that only two months ago, the minister of war had told the Diet that an invading army would be destroyed first at sea and then at the water's edge. "This was evidently a miscalculation," he noted, since the events of the past month had shown "that there are no longer any grounds for statements of this kind." The enemy was coming, and there was nothing Japan could do to stop him. The military may want to continue the war, but the outcome would not be in doubt. The inevitable sacrifices would not stave off defeat. "If things come to such a pass, it will become absolutely necessary," he wrote, "to avoid any situation in which the ill will of the people would focus itself upon the Government and the Military and even extend its evil influence to the Imperial House." The only way out of this nightmarish situation was for the government to accept unconditional surrender, providing the monarchy was preserved. The ambassador concluded by asking Togo to show his report to the emperor and read it to the Supreme Council for the Direction of the War.[6]

Events moved too quickly for Japanese leaders in Tokyo to respond to Sato's message. The Big Six would soon be meeting but under circumstances no one, not even Sato, anticipated. Perhaps there is no clearer indication of how far the two governments were from ending the war than the fact that the Japanese official most willing to challenge his government's stand on unconditional surrender continued to insist on a condition that American officials found unacceptable. Sato's recommendation that Japan accept unconditional surrender on one condition, preservation of the monarchy, was unacceptable to Tokyo and to Washington. The Japanese government was still trying to avoid surrendering. Truman had been unwilling to make a concession on the emperor when it appeared that only an invasion would compel Japan's unconditional surrender. There was little chance he would modify the doctrine now that the U.S. had the atomic bomb.

Sato had framed his recommendation in terms that he thought officials in Tokyo would find unassailable. They needed to surrender now to preserve the emperor from the wrath of the people. Former prime minister Konoe was animated by the same concern about impending revolution.

Wartime Japan was a place of surveillance and compulsion. The military police (*Kempeitai*) brutally enforced regulations and squelched dissent. Police
informants watched their neighbors for evidence of halfhearted enthusiasm
for the war. And yet, signs of dissent and weakening morale were everywhere by the summer of 1945. Perceptive observers knew that the fall of
Saipan in the summer of 1944 spelled disaster for Japan. Mention of that defeat could earn one a trip to the police station for a punishing interrogation.
Widespread malnutrition and disease were taking a deadly toll on Japanese
civilians. B-29s and carrier-launched planes appeared unchallenged overhead. Even the dullest observer knew defeat was inevitable. Government
pronouncements suggesting otherwise were simply unbelievable.

Four years of propaganda, censorship, and constant intimidation had
failed to stamp out criticism of the government and small but meaningful
acts of subversion. Underground groups distributed antiwar pamphlets;
owners of small businesses traded on the black market and undermined
the authority of the petty tyrants the government sent to compel their
obedience. Japanese families in Tokyo went about their business on July
30, the anniversary of the Meiji Emperor's death, without hoisting flags
in his honor. Teenage boys silently prayed for the war to end before they
reached draft age. Others sought medical deferments. Coercion was omni-
present. Sacrifice came grudgingly. Even the revered kamikaze, the flower
of the nation's youth who gave their lives for the emperor, were in most
cases terrified young men subjected to intense social pressure and afraid of
dishonoring their families. They had to be plied with alcohol before they
jammed themselves into the cockpits of their missiles for the one-way flight
to glory.[7]

Were Sato and Konoe right? Was Japan on the verge of revolution?
Japan's modern era had its share of popular rebellions. Perhaps something
similar would have occurred had the war continued. But in the summer
of 1945, survival—of families, coreligionists, and local communities—took
precedence over political organization and mass protest. Such inward-
looking motivation might not have inspired rebellion, though it nevertheless smacked of subversion by placing individual preservation ahead of the
Yamato peoples' devotion to the emperor and Japan's unique national polity.

While Sato warned of incipient rebellion unless Japan surrendered,
George Marshall was dealing with a bureaucratic uprising within the Joint
Chiefs. On August 6, his deputy chief of staff notified him that at its next
meeting the JCS would be assessing the prospects for operation OLYMPIC.

Over the next few days, the possibility that the invasion of Kyushu might be scrubbed in favor of another part of Japan or, more likely, replaced altogether by a continuation of blockade and bombardment, led Marshall to seek MacArthur's input on the continuation of OLYMPIC. MacArthur, not surprisingly, emphatically insisted that nothing be done to change the invasion he was designated to command. Admirals Nimitz and King, however, were prepared to reopen the question, which had only appeared to have been settled at the June 18 White House meeting. That confrontation would have occurred concurrently with an economic reassessment of the Army's invasion plans. As the USS *Augusta* approached Norfolk, Virginia, John Snyder, Truman's close friend and newly appointed head of the Office of War Mobilization and Reconversion, was planning on being dockside when the president disembarked. Snyder's plan was to brief Truman on OWMR's recommendations for cutting military expenditures to speed reconversion on the train back to Washington. Marshall's strategy for compelling unconditional surrender through an invasion was in jeopardy.

As opposition to the Army's invasion plan developed over the first days of August, the entire outlook for the Pacific War changed dramatically. On August 6 (Washington time), the first atomic bomb was exploded 1,900 feet above the city of Hiroshima. Hiroshima was one of few Japanese cities that had not been the target of conventional bombing raids. Rumors had circulated among the inhabitants that the Americans were so taken with the city's beauty that they were sparing it to use as their headquarters. People had started their daily routines early that morning when a lone B-29 flew over the city. Air raid sirens warned of the plan's approach, but when the weather plane passed out of sight the all-clear was given.

Sirens did not sound when, an hour later, three more planes flew into view. One, the *Enola Gay*, dropped the 10-foot-long bomb that floated down at the end of a parachute until it reached the desired altitude and detonated. Nearly everyone within 1.3 miles of the epicenter was either instantly killed or badly injured. The view from the *Enola Gay* was almost instantly obscured by an enormous mushroom cloud of dust and debris. Underneath the cloud, a radioactive black rain fell on the devastated city.[8]

In Washington, the government released a prepared statement, explaining that the new weapon was an atomic bomb and threatening Japan with further destruction if it did not surrender.[9] Although the Japanese government soon had authoritative reports that most of Hiroshima had been destroyed by a single bomb, the military members of the Big Six refused to surrender.

Instead, they downplayed the importance of the "new type of highly destructive bomb," telling citizens they could protect themselves by wearing white clothes. Newspapers practically ignored the atomic bomb in favor of upbeat stories, including reports of a promising rice harvest. After failing to convince the cabinet to act, Togo went to the palace on August 8 to brief the emperor on the atomic bomb. The emperor agreed with Togo that Japan had to surrender, although he allowed that it might be possible to obtain concessions from the Allies. Hirohito instructed Togo to convey the imperial will to Prime Minister Suzuki. Although Suzuki had recently taken to espousing a hard line against surrender, he and Togo agreed to call a meeting of the Supreme Council for the Direction of the War for the following day, August 9.[10]

While the Japanese government outwardly acted unconcerned, in Washington Colonel Charles Bonesteel, in the Army's Strategy and Policy Group (S&P), tried to predict Japan's next move. After the war, Bonesteel would tell historians that he and other Army officers had doubted the wisdom of unconditional surrender. Writing in the immediate aftermath of the destruction of Hiroshima, he gave no hint of that skepticism. Bonesteel predicted that the Japanese would most likely seek "elucidation," really concessions, on some points in the Potsdam Declaration. He expected that some officials in Washington would favor agreeing to those concessions, but advised the head of S&P, Brigadier General George A. "Abe" Lincoln, against making concessions to either group. Bonesteel assumed that the biggest question Japanese officials had was "how many atomic bombs we have and where are we going to drop the next one!" The fate of the imperial institution was most likely their next major concern. The Allied ultimatum was equivocal in dealing with the emperor. Bonesteel added that if the Japanese government was as concerned about the monarchy as "some of the 'Japanese experts' pretend" then "a further elucidation might have beneficial results." He emphasized, however, that the main point was that the declaration allowed the U.S., presumably with Allied consent, to take any action it wished regarding the emperor.

The occupation of Japan was most likely next in order of importance to the Japanese. Bonesteel concluded that an occupation was necessary to impress the Japanese with the reality of their defeat and to guide the "Japanese into the form of government best fitted to achieve our aims." He conceded that some authorities said the Americans would make an "unholy mess" of governing Japan; nevertheless, he thought it better for the Americans to make the attempt than for them to let the Russians do it. Bonesteel concluded his analysis by dismissing the concerns of those who worried that if the United States did not adequately address Japanese concerns, the Japanese government would strike a deal with the Soviet Union. Sounding very much like Ambassador Sato, Bonesteel asserted that Russia could take what it wanted from Japan without unnecessarily risking a breach with the United States that would, he believed, amount to "an open declaration of war on us by the U.S.S.R."[11] Confirmation of Bonesteel's analysis regarding Russian intentions was not long in coming.

Bonesteel's use of quotation marks around the words "Japanese experts" suggested his skepticism regarding those who insisted that the emperor and the imperial system should be treated as sacrosanct in Japanese culture. The success of the atomic bomb may have permitted greater skepticism toward these "experts." It probably also made him and other officers less willing to appease the Japanese now than when an invasion seemed the only way to compel Japan's unconditional surrender.

Not so Ellis Zacharias. The captain planned a broadcast for August 11, his fifteenth, that would solicit directly the emperor's aid in bringing an end to the war. Archibald MacLeish found the tone of that broadcast so objectionable that he fired off an outraged protest to Joseph Grew, calling for its immediate cancellation. Surely there were limits, even in psychological warfare, to how far the U.S. was willing to go to persuade the Japanese to surrender? "The obsequious almost lick-spittle attitude" in which Captain Zacharias approached the Japanese throne would, MacLeish complained, "make Thomas Jefferson and a considerable number of other Americans whirl in their graves." He attacked the broadcast on practical grounds as well. He noted that the Soviet foreign minister had recently appealed to the Japanese people to surrender. An American appeal to the emperor could not fail to invite unfavorable comparisons. "We have let the Russians take our coat before this," he wrote. "I don't see why we should let them take our pants as well."[12] Zacharias's fifteenth broadcast never reached the airwaves. The day it was scheduled to air, it was rendered superfluous by other developments.[13]

On August 8, Ambassador Sato finally was summoned to the foreign ministry by Foreign Minister Molotov. When Sato saw Molotov, he greeted him in Russian, only to be cut short by the foreign minister. The ambassador then stood silently as Molotov read to him the Soviet Union's declaration of war against Japan, effective August 9. It was 5:00 p.m. Moscow

time. Less than an hour later, just past midnight local time, the Red Army
struck at Japanese forces in Manchuria. The weakened Kwantung Army was
caught completely off guard. Various intelligence estimates had predicted
a Soviet offensive in August, but the prevailing view in Imperial General
Headquarters and in the headquarters of the Kwantung Army was that no
attack was possible before September, and that it was more likely that the
Russians would wait until the next spring. Assuming that war was unlikely
in the immediate future, the Kwantung Army was implementing a major
reorganization of its forces. The Russians attacked before those plans were
completed and while numerous Japanese field officers were away from their
posts engaged in routine business. Soviet forces capitalized on this intelligence failure with devastating effect. Moving troops at night and maintaining
signals security, the Russians were able to traverse the Gobi Desert and build
up a force in Outer Mongolia in numbers that far exceeded Japanese expectations. The offensive against Manchuria involved attacks along three axes.
These consisted of an assault from the east, based in the Maritime Provinces,
another from the northeast, and the third from the west in Outer Mongolia
along what the Russians termed the Trans-Baikal Front. A fourth vector of
attack aimed at southern Sakhalin and the Kurile islands, with Hokkaido,
the northernmost home island, as the ultimate objective.

The assault from the east began at night in a driving rainstorm without
any preparatory bombardment. The Russians swiftly outflanked the nu-
merically inferior Japanese and avoided fortified positions while driving
deep behind enemy lines. On the Trans-Baikal Front, the Russians advanced under the cover of darkness and dense fog. By the morning of
August 11, elements of the Russian army had crossed the supposedly im-
passible Khingan Mountains and burst into open territory. The Americans
had predicted that it would take the Red Army thirty days before it could
advance in Manchuria. In less than thirty hours, the Russians had driven
deeply behind Japanese lines. Here and there, isolated Japanese units fought
back with admirable bravery, but the Soviet onslaught moved more swiftly
than either the Japanese—or Americans—imagined possible.[14]

On August 9, General Yamada Otozō, commander-in-chief of the
Kwantung Army, called on Pu Yi, the last emperor of China and the nom-
inal head of Japan's puppet state of Machukuo, at his palace in Hsinking
(Changchun) to notify him of Russia's declaration of war. As Yamada nervously assured His Excellency of a Japanese victory, air raid sirens sent them
into the cellar for shelter. The men emerged unharmed a short while later,

but there was no more talk of victory. When Yamada returned to the palace the following day, he informed Pu Yi that the Japanese were withdrawing to prepared positions in the mountainous region in the south along the Korean border. Pu Yi requested two days to move his family and belongings. He relented and left the next day, August 11, after his Japanese attaché warned him that if he tarried, he would be the "first one murdered by Soviet troops."[15]

Although the Japanese had realized that Soviet belligerence was likely at some point, the sudden Russian declaration of war and the startling success of the Red Army's offensive in Manchuria left them stunned and demoralized. Nevertheless, the Big Six remained deadlocked on the question of unconditional surrender. On August 9, the Supreme Council for Direction of the War met at 11:00 a.m. in the basement of the Imperial Palace to determine Japan's response to the twin calamities of the atomic bomb and Russia's declaration of war. A half hour into the meeting, the members learned that a second atomic bomb had exploded over Nagasaki. The intended target was Kokura, on northern Kyushu, but cloud cover forced the crew of *Bock's Car* to select Nagasaki, a port on northwest Kyushu, which was an alternate on the target list. The plutonium bomb missed its target area and thus inflicted fewer casualties than might otherwise have occurred. The hills on which the city was built also limited the destruction caused by fire. Nevertheless, an estimated thirty-eight thousand people died from the blast and its immediate aftereffects. Apart from devastating another major city, the attack clearly demonstrated that the Americans had more than one bomb.

The impact on the deliberations of the council was negligible. Although the four military members of the council showed some willingness to consider surrender, they agreed to do so only if the Allies would accept several key conditions. The first was that the imperial institution would remain intact and there would be no harm done to the emperor. The military chiefs also insisted on limiting the Allied occupation to a few remote points on Japanese territory and on disarming their own troops. Japanese soldiers and sailors were prohibited from surrendering, they noted; therefore they could hand over their arms only to their own officers. Finally, they insisted that the Japanese alone would conduct the war crimes trials.

For his part, Togo sought to reduce the four conditions to one: preservation of the imperial household. That was a construction that could potentially reduce the emperor to the figurehead that Grew and Stimson already believed he was. Suzuki and Admiral Yonai, both of whom supported Togo, were silent. Togo argued strenuously on behalf of narrowing the conditions to one. He failed to persuade the military, however, and the meeting ended in deadlock.[16]

Two cabinet meetings held in the afternoon and early evening similarly failed to achieve unanimity and thus by default endorsed the outcome of the Supreme Council. In the meantime, peace advocates worked behind the scenes to follow Togo's lead and narrow the conditions to one—the preservation of the monarchy in some, as yet undetermined, form. Leading this effort was the former prime minister, Prince Konoe, the man who been chosen as the emperor's envoy to Moscow. When Konoe met with Marquis Kido, he was dismayed to learn that Kido supported the four conditions. If Kido supported that position, so did Hirohito. Konoe countered by enlisting the support of Prince Takamatsu, the emperor's younger brother, who could not change Kido's mind. Konoe then turned to Shigemitsu Mamoru, a former foreign minister and long-time friend of Kido's. Shigemitsu succeeded where the others had failed. Following his meeting with Shigemitsu, Kido conferred with Hirohito and then reported that the emperor would attend a meeting of the Big Six that evening.

The fateful meeting convened at 11:30 p.m. on August 9 in the basement of the palace. The Big Six were joined by several other officials, including Baron Hiranuma Kiichiro and, of course, the emperor. Each member was given the text of a proposed statement that accepted the terms delineated in the Potsdam ultimatum providing that "said declaration does not comprise any demand which prejudices the Emperor's status under national laws." This was a broader construction of imperial prerogatives than Togo's original language referring to the preservation of the imperial household, but it was not broad enough to satisfy some of those present. Suzuki opened the meeting by stating the four conditions. Togo followed by making a case for only one condition, which was contained in the draft statement. Navy Minister Admiral Yonai broke his silence by agreeing and then fell silent again. That brought an immediate rejoinder from General Anami Korechika, the war minister. Anami vigorously defended all four conditions and insisted that it would be better for all one hundred million Japanese to die than to surrender under the terms of the Allied ultimatum. It is not clear if Anami believed that or if he felt compelled to utter such insanity to placate his more fanatical junior officers. Anami concluded by warning of civil war at home if the government tried to surrender. Chief of Staff Umezu seconded his views.

Baron Hiranuma then weighed in. An accomplished prosecutor, Hiranuma had served in the Ministry of Justice and as chief of Japan's Supreme Court. There was no doubting his credentials as a patriot. He had been an ultra-nationalist supporter of Japan's expansion into Manchuria and an equally ardent supporter of the emperor's divine status. He now employed his prosecutorial skills to the sole purpose of defending the sacred status of the emperor. Hiranuma began by demolishing the military's defense of the four conditions. Under his questioning it became painfully clear that neither the Army nor Navy had a credible plan for Japan's defense. More important, the domestic situation was bad and getting worse by the day, a point affirmed by Suzuki. The real danger, Hiranuma warned, was that civil disturbance would come from continuing the war, not ending it. That did not mean, however, that he favored the statement placed before the council members. Hiranuma faulted the statement for implying the emperor derived his authority from the national laws. That was not the case, he declared. The emperor's authority was of divine origin. Therefore, the preservation of the *kokutai* required a change in the statement to read "said declaration does not comprise any demand which prejudices the Emperor's prerogatives as a sovereign ruler."[17]

When all had said their peace, Suzuki, as prearranged, declared that they must turn to the emperor and ask for his guidance. Hirohito began by saying that continuing the war would destroy the nation and prolong the bloodshed and cruelty in the world. Ending the war would restore world peace and spare the nation. He proceeded to outline the deteriorating military situation. The military wanted to wage a final battle for the homeland, but time and again the military's plans had not been matched by performance. It pained His Excellency to see his troops disarmed and their leaders turned over to their enemies for trial. Nevertheless, it was time to bear the unbearable. The emperor decreed that he wished his government to accept the Potsdam Declaration on the basis proposed by Foreign Minister Togo. With that, Hirohito left the room. As he departed, Suzuki rose and declared, "His Majesty's decision should be made the decision of this conference as well." It was 2:30 a.m. on August 10.

By law the emperor could provide guidance to the government, but the cabinet nonetheless had to vote its approval before that guidance became policy. Sometime before 4:00 a.m. the cabinet dutifully assembled and gave the desired consent. Though he had lost, Anami was not ready to surrender. As the cabinet meeting broke up, he asked if Suzuki would support a continuation of the war, should the Allies reject the one condition. Suzuki said he would. By 7:00 a.m., the Japanese response to the Potsdam Declaration was dispatched to the U.S. by way of Sweden and Switzerland. The key passage in the Japanese reply stated that the Japanese government would accept the terms in the Potsdam Declaration providing they did not "comprise any demand which prejudices the Emperor's prerogatives as a sovereign ruler."

The Japanese radio broadcast of the message was received in Washington on August 10 at about 7:30 a.m. That morning, Truman met with Stimson, Leahy, Forrestal, and Byrnes to discuss the Japanese peace offer, which had not yet arrived through official channels. Records of what occurred during the meeting conflict. Byrnes complained to his assistant immediately after the meeting that by the time he had arrived, Leahy had already persuaded Truman to accept the Japanese offer. Byrnes maintained that he had opposed acceptance of the Japanese offer, but there is reason to doubt other aspects of his account, especially his contention that Leahy had convinced the president to accept Japan's offer.[18] According to the diary of White House assistant Eben Ayers, Byrnes arrived *before* Leahy, making it unlikely the admiral had swayed Truman before Byrnes arrived.[19] Leahy's official diary notes only that he attended the meeting and that a reply to the Japanese was being prepared. There is no mention of a discussion or even who was preparing the reply. Truman's personal record for the day is also of little help. The president's notes combine his meetings of August 9 and August 10 under a single entry for the latter date.[20] Moreover, these notes do not even mention the meeting, which, according to his appointments book, was held at 9:00 a.m.[21]

The various accounts do agree on some essential facts. Leahy and Stimson favored accepting Japan's offer. Byrnes was opposed. Stimson recorded the fullest account. His entry for that day begins by noting that the Japanese had broadcast the text of their reply in plain language over the radio. The secretary had been ready to go on vacation, noting later that such news "busted our holiday." He then referred to the question of the emperor contained in the Japanese reply. Stimson recalled that he had told Truman that deletion of the clause regarding the emperor from the Potsdam Declaration might cause problems. Stimson fumed that the anti-emperor agitation in the U.S. had been fomented by people "who know no more about Japan than has been given them in Gilbert and Sullivan's 'Mikado.'" To his dismay, he had just learned that Acheson and MacLeish, in addition to the normally sound Harry Hopkins, were united against the emperor. They were, he lamented, "three very extraordinary men to take such a position."

When Stimson arrived at the White House, he found Byrnes "troubled and anxious" about making any concessions on the emperor. Admiral Leahy, however, "took the good plain horse-sense position that the question of the Emperor was a minor matter compared with delaying a victory in the war which was now in our hands." When Truman asked for his views, Stimson said that "even if the question hadn't been raised by the Japanese we would have to continue the Emperor under our command and supervision" in order to ensure the surrender of Japanese forces scattered through the empire. The alternative, he added, would be "a score of bloody Iwo Jimas and Okinawas all over China and the New Netherlands." Stimson also suggested a bombing halt as a humane step while the situation was sorted out, but Truman rejected the idea on the "correct but narrow reason" that the Japanese offer had not been officially received in Washington. His recollection of the meeting ended with the bland observation, "After considerable discussion we adjourned to await the arrival of the final notice."[22]

We do not know with certainty what was discussed, but according to Forrestal's diary, Byrnes questioned whether the Japanese reply, given its condition, met the definition of unconditional surrender. Leahy said it did. Byrnes thought the administration would be exposed to criticism if it made a concession to the Japanese. Forrestal noted in his diary that Byrnes's concerns could be "met by an affirmative statement on our part in which we could see to it that the language of surrender accorded fully with our intent and view."[23] The wording of the proposed statement was left to Byrnes, who suggested that Stimson also draft a reply. Byrnes returned to his office and set to work with Ben Cohen, his main advisor. They were joined by Grew, Dooman, and Japan expert Joseph Ballantine. Within a few minutes, Cohen had drafted a statement that included the following crucial sentence: "From the moment of the surrender the authority of the Emperor to rule the state shall be subject to the authority of the Supreme Commander of the Allied Powers, who will take such steps as he deems proper to effectuate the surrender terms."[24] The remainder of the reply required the emperor and high command to sign the surrender documents, ordered the Japanese to move Allied prisoners of war to locations where they could be easily retrieved, reiterated the ultimatum's declaration that the eventual form of Japan's government would be determined by the freely expressed will of its people, and closed by saying that the Allies would occupy Japan until the terms contained in the Potsdam Declaration were met.

Across the Potomac, at the Pentagon, Stimson was discussing the matter with McCloy and several advisors. The secretary was surprised that McCloy "was intrigued with the idea that this was the opportunity to force upon Japan through the Emperor a program of free speech, etc. and all the elements of American free government." Stimson rejected that idea as unrealistic. The most important thing was to secure Japan's surrender before the Russians got too deep into Manchuria and before they could claim a share of control of postwar Japan. Stimson called Byrnes, who read to him the statement Cohen drafted. Stimson noted in his diary, "While a compromise, it was much nearer my position than McCloy's."[25]

Byrnes presented the final draft to the cabinet that afternoon. According to Commerce Secretary Wallace, Byrnes laid special emphasis on "the top dog commander over Hirohito being an American." Truman said that the British had already approved the response and then, according to Wallace, "interjected most fiercely" that he did not expect to hear from the Russians. Stimson followed by voicing his concern that the Russians would delay the surrender until they could push farther into Manchuria, to which Truman replied that it was in American interests that they not push too far.[26]

Although the participants in the deliberations over Japan's surrender offer disagreed as to how the American reply was drafted, it is clear that if they accepted the offer without revision, as Leahy and, apparently, Stimson wanted, it would have seriously compromised the supreme commander's authority and most likely limited the scope of the occupation. That is without question what the Japanese intended when they transmitted their offer. Asked if maintaining the emperor's prerogatives meant "no changes in the states' governing system or no change in the position of his Imperial Majesty," a Japanese representative in Sweden replied that although he had no official instructions on that point, he felt that "the words include both interpretations."[27]

None of the accounts of the August 10 meeting at the White House provide a reliable account of Truman's thoughts regarding the Japanese offer. We do know that he ultimately rejected Leahy's and Stimson's advice. Apart from that, however, we do not know what, if anything, he contributed to the weighing of options. It is easy to imagine how anxious Truman would have been about making the right decision. He had steadfastly refused to make concessions on the emperor all summer. Now, if he yielded, the war would be over. Truman may have recalled that at Potsdam, Stimson had predicted that "the reassurance of the Japanese on the condition of their dynasty" might "make or mar" their acceptance of the Potsdam Declaration.[28]

Military considerations appeared to tip the balance of the argument toward conceding the point to Japan. As Stimson explained, the Allies would need the cooperation of the emperor to ensure an orderly surrender of imperial forces throughout Asia. The emperor could also ease the way for occupation forces entering the home islands. Yet the president still refused to grant the explicit assurances about their emperor that the Japanese desired and that Leahy and Stimson, and before them Herbert Hoover and Joseph Grew (as well as various Republican senators), had recommended giving.

What was Truman thinking? There is no question that he worried about the public's reaction if he appeased the Japanese at the eleventh hour. He also had to consider how the Allies would react to a unilateral revision of the Potsdam Declaration. But those concerns were joined by another. Simply put, Truman did not trust the Japanese. He remained wary of making any decision regarding the emperor that might cost the United States the opportunity to achieve its postwar aims for Japan. Not long after he instructed Byrnes to draft a reply to the Japanese, Truman voiced his concerns about the impending surrender to Democratic congressman Mike Mansfield. Truman's notes say only that Mansfield, who had visited China at FDR's request in 1944, "came in to ask for a trip to China. He was once a resident there and seems to know a great deal about the country. I postponed decision on it."[29] Mansfield, however, told *Time* correspondent Frank McNaughton that he and Truman had covered considerably more ground than the president's notes indicate. Using notes he made immediately after speaking to Truman, Mansfield reported that Truman said that any Japanese surrender would have to "embrace unequivocally all Japanese forces in the field." Truman was especially worried about the potential for mayhem posed by the Kwantung Army in Manchuria. Mansfield added,

> The suggestion of special guarantees to Hirohito, that his status be retained, was deeply distasteful to Truman. He favored no assurances—i.e. that to give the emperor any assurance would constitute something less than unconditional surrender, even if it is a face-saver for the Japs and a life-saving device offered us. It retains for Japan the nuclear rallying point for future nationalism. Truman was not friendly to this part of the Tokyo suggestion, but obviously had to consult with Moscow, Chungking, and London. His idea was to make

it a complete surrender without any concessions to Hirohito, come hell or high water.

According to McNaughton's notes, Mansfield said Truman told him that the U.S. would keep the Pacific islands it needed for its security, "police the hell out of Japan for many years, destroy its war potential, and insure the peace of the Pacific."[30]

Truman's notes for August 10 also show that later that day he met with Senator Warren Magnuson (D-Washington) to talk about "a road to Alaska through British Columbia and his bill on scientific research." But Magnuson told McNaughton that he and Truman discussed the surrender. Magnuson found Truman "ill disposed to make special guarantees to the emperor." He told McNaughton that the president thought Hirohito was "a war criminal just as much as Hitler or Mussolini, in many respects, and now was trying to weasel his nation out of war, preserving meanwhile its essentially totalitarian structure." Truman realized, however, that the U.S. might need to retain the emperor in place "without special concessions" to facilitate the surrender of imperial troops. Magnuson inferred from Truman's comments that the U.S. would make a counteroffer that would enable the emperor to remain "but that the government would be made over to be essentially democratic, using the emperor (in polite language) as a glorified figurehead."[31]

How accurately Mansfield and Magnuson reported Truman's comments, as opposed to projecting their own views onto the president, is impossible to know. McNaughton's report does appear to be flawed in some respects. He records Mansfield as meeting with Truman for nearly an hour, an almost unimaginable span of the president's time, especially since the congressman was scheduled for only fifteen minutes in the appointments book. On the other hand, Mansfield's and Magnuson's accounts, as relayed by McNaughton, present a consistent picture of Truman's attitudes toward the emperor and the surrender. The most important point to emerge from those meetings was that Truman did not accept the views of his conservative advisors that Hirohito was a mere figurehead manipulated by Japan's military clique. The president judged him guilty of abetting Japan's aggression and feared that the imperial institution could serve as the focal point of Japanese nationalism in the future.

Those concerns were what led Truman to reject Stimson's and Leahy's advice to accept Tokyo's offer on August 10. It stands to reason that Truman did not arrive at those views for the first time on August 10, and that they had influenced his decision to reject earlier suggestions from Hoover and other conservatives to make concessions on the emperor. McNaughton's account also indicates that Truman thought in terms of a thorough occupation that would, as McNaughton says he put it, "police the hell out of Japan" as it democratized Japanese society, a position that also differed from the limited occupation desired by Leahy, Stimson, Hoover, and various Republican senators. "They wanted to make a condition precedent to the surrender," Truman wrote in his diary. "Our terms are 'unconditional.' They wanted to keep the Emperor. We told 'em we'd tell 'em how to keep him, but we'd make the terms."[32]

The British and Chinese quickly approved Byrnes's draft reply to Japan. The British, however, suggested deleting the requirement that the emperor sign the surrender documents. The Australians strenuously protested against any attempt to spare the emperor from public humiliation, but their objections were ignored when Truman sent his response to the Japanese.[33] The Russians proved a little more difficult. After sparring with Ambassador Harriman over the issue of the supreme commander—they wanted a veto over his appointment or a joint command—the Russians fell into line and approved the reply without qualification. Harriman's message conveying Moscow's approval reached the president on the morning of August 11. Truman promptly sent the reply to the Japanese through the Swiss embassy and released it over the radio so that it would reach the Japanese more quickly.[34]

Once it appeared possible that the war was about to end, the members of the State War-Navy Coordinating Committee (SWNCC, pronounced "Swink")—comprising assistant secretaries from each department and the Joint Staff Planners, which consisted of uniformed representatives from each of the services—set to work addressing the politico-military issues that would arise from Japan's surrender. On the night of August 10–11 the two committees met in adjoining rooms in the Pentagon to draft the documents that would spell out the steps Japan must take in order to complete the surrender. Perhaps the most significant one was General Order Number One, a directive to be issued by the Imperial General Headquarters to Japanese field commanders, informing them to whom they should surrender their arms. The surrenders would be a moment of military high drama because of the Japanese Army's previous insistence on disarming itself. They would also be political acts of major consequence for the future of postwar Asia.

As the committees began their work, they were informed that Secretary of State Byrnes wanted the United States to accept the surrender of Japanese troops in Korea as far north as possible. Aided only by a *National Geographic* wall map of Asia, Colonel Bonesteel and Colonel Dean Rusk decided on the thirty-eighth parallel, north latitude as the surrender boundary on the peninsula. The area below that line, which would become the American zone, contained Seoul, the capital; two ports, Inchon and Pusan; and at least one prisoner-of-war camp known to be holding Americans. When Bonesteel and Rusk submitted their handiwork to the larger committee, discussion ensued regarding the desirability of moving the line to the thirty-ninth parallel. The Navy's representative favored this adjustment because the line, if continued onto the mainland, would place the ports of Dairen and Port Arthur in the American zone. The Army, with the support of the State Department, fearing that the Russians would reject the entire General Order and put American chances of entering Korea at risk, vetoed this change.[35]

By the morning of August 11, the committees completed their work on the territorial provisions of the General Order. According to the draft, all Japanese troops in China (excluding Manchuria), Formosa, and Indochina north of the sixteenth parallel were to surrender to the representatives of Chiang Kai-shek. The Russians would take the surrender of Japanese forces in Manchuria, Korea north of the thirty-eighth parallel, and Karafuto (southern Sakhalin). Mountbatten was designated to take the surrender in Southeast Asia, including Burma, Thailand, Malaya, Borneo, the Netherlands Indies, and French Indochina south of the sixteenth parallel. Nimitz and MacArthur would divide the remainder of Japan's empire between their two commands. Nimitz would take the surrender in the bypassed areas of the central and western Pacific, as well as unspecified "other Pacific Islands." MacArthur would take control of "the main islands of Japan, minor islands adjacent thereto, Korea south of 38th° north latitude and the Philippine Islands."

The boundaries established in the General Order offered technical guidance to the Allied and Japanese commanders. The staff officers who drafted its provisions were able to complete their task in a short time because they used the operational boundaries agreed upon at Potsdam as their guide. The one exception was Korea, for which they received specific instructions from the State Department. The problem was that only the Russians had conducted the operations envisioned at Potsdam. Most of China and

Southeast Asia, and all of Japan's home islands, remained under the control of Japanese troops. The General Order commanded the Japanese troops in those areas to surrender to Allied commanders, who might take weeks to reach them. In the meantime, the Japanese were expected to retain control of the areas they occupied.

The General Order depended on the emperor's cooperation to effect the unconditional surrender of Japanese armed forces as demanded in the Potsdam Declaration. The precariousness of the situation was obvious to all. Japanese forces, even in defeat, maintained enormous residual power to disrupt the reassertion of Allied control over much of Asia. They could achieve that through overt resistance, a refusal to surrender, or through less direct means, such as by aiding insurgent groups in China and Southeast Asia.

After completing the draft of General Order Number One, the Joint Staff Planners also wrote a draft directive outlining General MacArthur's responsibilities in order of importance. The occupation of Japan held the highest priority. Seoul was second. Landings on the China coast came last and were subject to the progress of the other two missions. Sometime during August 11, the president revised the directive to include the occupation of Dairen and a port in Korea immediately after Japan surrendered. The Dairen operation, which Army officers vetoed the previous night, was revived, although it was not included in the General Order. The Russians had to approve the General Order, but they would not be privy to MacArthur's orders. If the general succeeded in getting troops into Dairen, they would be arriving unannounced into the area that the Soviets viewed as theirs by virtue of the Yalta agreement. That same day, the Joint Chiefs received word from the British that they wanted to release elements of the Royal Navy from American control so that they could occupy Hong Kong. Byrnes said only that the United States should not be asked to participate in or approve the operation without Chinese acquiescence. He recommended that the British take the matter up with the Chinese.

Meanwhile, MacArthur and Nimitz were instructed to further expand their operations beyond those contemplated in their contingency plans. On August 12, McCloy gained approval for landings at Tientsin on the north China coast just below the Great Wall. Later that day, Byrnes agreed to have Admiral Nimitz take the surrender of Japanese forces in the Kuriles below the operational line agreed on at Potsdam. This would place Paramushir and all the islands to the south in the American zone. All concerned knew that the Yalta agreements stipulated that the islands would be turned over to the Soviets. Nevertheless, McCloy and some of the Army's planners desired American landing rights on at least one of the islands to facilitate the occupation of Japan. The Army's planners had advised the president and secretary of state to discuss the matter with the Soviets at Potsdam, but the conference had ended without any mention of the Kuriles. The Kuriles were now on the American itinerary, although, like Dairen, they were not included in the General Order.

For the most part, support for the enlargement of American responsibilities came from the president's civilian advisors. Ambassador Harriman, McCloy, and Navy Secretary Forrestal took the lead in calling for landings in Korea, Dairen, north China, and the Kuriles. These officials had sought to prevent Soviet aggrandizement in northeast Asia. That is one reason they supported modification of unconditional surrender. An early surrender would prevent Russia from claiming Allied support for its attack on Japan and possibly limit Soviet gains there. Truman's refusal to compromise on the emperor and the Japanese government's obduracy dashed those hopes. They were revived by the sudden and unexpected imminence of Japan's surrender. Freed from preparations for the invasion, American forces could project their power into the area previously conceded to the Russians. Or so they hoped.

The Army and Navy staff officers charged with drafting directives to MacArthur saw the surrender planning from a different perspective. These officers were aware of the political implications of the surrender, but they were most concerned with the logistical challenges entailed in coordinating the movements of America's far-flung naval and land forces. The staff officers were especially concerned with making the surrender as orderly as possible. There were nearly three million Japanese troops outside of the home islands. As the Army's top planner Brigadier General George A. Lincoln later explained, staff officers had to draft a General Order that the Allies would accept, or there would be chaos throughout Asia. Unannounced occupations in Dairen and the Kuriles increased the risk of undesirable confrontations. A breakdown in Allied cooperation risked more than could be gained by beating the Russians to Dairen or the Kuriles.

The official American reply to Japan's qualified acceptance of the Potsdam Declaration reached the foreign ministry early in the morning of August 12. Foreign Minister Togo hesitated to accept the Allied terms because he knew they would be rejected by the military. He was correct on that score. The junior staff officers in the Military Affairs Bureau, who had long terrorized their superiors with their zealous devotion to the mystical *kokutai*, demanded immediate rejection of Byrnes's note. Their superiors were less adamant, but they fell into line. Army Chief of Staff Umezu and Navy Chief Toyoda petitioned the emperor to reject Byrnes's note on the grounds that it would make Japan a slave nation. Hirohito rejected that advice and told them to wait for receipt of the official note.

The handwriting was on the wall. Hirohito was prepared to sacrifice the military to preserve the throne. Later that day, Hirohito called a meeting at the palace of his extended family. The thirteen princes in attendance pledged to support the emperor's decision to accept the American offer.[36] At the same time, the cabinet rejected the American reply. Only Togo favored acceptance. Togo had of course expected military opposition, but he was dismayed to find Suzuki siding with the uniformed officers. The prime minister not only insisted on preserving the emperor's prerogatives, he added a second condition by opposing Allied disarmament of Japanese troops.

Unaware of the emperor's wishes or perhaps unconcerned, Japanese field commanders also denounced the American response to Japan's peace offer as soon as it was translated. Count Terauchi Hisaichi, commander of Japanese forces in Southeast Asia, was particularly defiant. "Under no circumstances," he warned, "can the Southern Army accept the enemy's reply." The commander in China, General Okamura Yasuji, blandly stated that Soviet entry into the war did not change things. "I am firmly convinced," he said, "that it is time to exert all our efforts to fight to the end with the determination for all the army to die an honorable death without being distracted by the enemy's peace offensive and the domestic passive policy."[37]

Army staff officers in Tokyo agreed with those sentiments. On August 12, they drafted a paper rejecting the Allied reply and vowing to fight on even if it meant the destruction of the empire. At the same time, the zealots on the general staff plotted to seize the palace to "protect" the emperor. One of the officers' main concerns was that the Americans would destroy the imperial line of succession by exiling Hirohito to China, as the scholar and government advisor Owen Lattimore had recommended, holding Crown Prince Akihito in the United States, and executing the remaining members of the imperial family. To guard against that possibility, the officers prepared to stow a prince from a collateral family in Niigata prefecture until the Americans left Japan.[38]

The Supreme Council for the Direction of the War and the cabinet convened on the morning of August 13 but were interrupted when Umezu and Toyoda were summoned to the palace. There, the emperor told them to cease all offensive operations while negotiations with the Allies proceeded. The chiefs promised to obey His Majesty's wishes unless they were attacked. The council meeting resumed when the chiefs returned but ended in stalemate. Togo reported the results to Hirohito, who told him to convey his acceptance of the Allied reply directly to the backsliding Suzuki. When the cabinet met later that afternoon, the tide had shifted noticeably in favor of acceptance of the Allies' reply. Suzuki finally took control and, reversing his position, argued in favor of acceptance. Although twelve out of fifteen ministers approved acceptance of the reply, that was not enough to make the decision stick. Suzuki ended the meeting by announcing that he would call on the emperor and tell him the position of each of the cabinet members and ask for the emperor's sacred decision.

The following day, August 14, American planes dropped leaflets on Japanese cities informing the inhabitants of the state of negotiations. Fearing that the leaflets would stir popular resentment against the throne, or even prompt the military to revolt, Marquis Kido hastened to the palace and advised Hirohito to summon the cabinet and Supreme Council for the Direction of the War. The unprecedented meeting of both groups was scheduled for 10:00 a.m. Caught by surprise, some of the officials hustled to the palace in their street clothes, there being no time to don the required formal attire. The emperor entered almost an hour later. Dressed in his military uniform, Hirohito sat in silence as Umezu, Toyoda, and Anami argued against acceptance of the Allied reply. When they finished, the emperor reaffirmed his decision to surrender. He added that he would announce the news over the radio so his subjects, especially those in uniform, would understand that the decision to surrender represented the imperial will.[39]

The imperial conference had ended. The drama, however, continued throughout the day into the next morning. At 1:00 p.m., following the imperial conference, nineteen haggard and despondent cabinet members met at Suzuki's official residence to approve the emperor's decision. The meeting lasted well into the evening with several intermissions. The final text of the rescript was not ready for the emperor's approval until 8:00 p.m. All agreed that the emperor should record his message to his subjects rather than read it live. Considerable time was spent debating the text of the imperial rescript. Anami recommended revisions to soften the blow to army commanders in the field. The most misleading of these read "having been able to preserve the *kokutai* . . ."

Written in formal Japanese, the tortuously worded rescript was evasive and insincere. It began with Hirohito reciting his previous justification for the war. Japan had fought, he said, to ensure the country's "self-preservation and the stabilization of Asia." After four years of war filled with gallantry and sacrifice, the war had "developed not necessarily to Japan's advantage." The enemy's use of atomic weapons changed everything. Japan faced obliteration if it continued to fight. Civilization itself hung in the balance. It was to spare the millions of his subjects and all civilization that His Majesty accepted the Potsdam Declaration. In doing so, Hirohito apologized to Japan's supporters in Asia. Those of his subjects who had died in the war were eternally in his thoughts. The way forward would be difficult. He asked his subjects to endure the unendurable as one family, avoid fraternal strife, and strive to enhance "the innate glory of the Imperial State and keep pace with the progress of the world."[40]

The emperor's scribes had labored under extraordinarily difficult circumstances. They had to transform Japan's naked aggression in Asia into a war of liberation and transform the commander-in-chief into a man of peace. It was a tall order. Reading the rescript, one could almost see Hirohito shedding his uniform in favor of civilian dress. Over the next few months, Hirohito and his retainers would cultivate the image of the emperor as a peacefully inclined helpless onlooker to Japan's fifteen-year war.[41]

At 11:00 p.m., three hours after the cabinet meeting ended, the foreign ministry telegraphed Switzerland and Sweden with the request that representatives of those governments transmit to the Allies the news that the Japanese government had agreed to surrender in keeping with terms of the Potsdam Declaration and the Allied stipulation concerning the status of the emperor. The message stated further that the emperor would issue the necessary orders to all imperial forces to surrender and dispose of their arms as directed by the Supreme Commander for the Allied Powers. While Japan's agreement to surrender was being sent to the two neutrals, Hirohito was in his office in the Imperial Household Ministry recording his momentous address to his subjects. The windows were closed and shuttered, and the room was distressingly hot and stuffy. The emperor's pronunciation of several words in the first recording were indistinct, so a second pressing was made. That, too, was imperfect. Although the emperor was willing to try again, it was decided to spare His Majesty further embarrassment and make do with the second effort. Hirohito departed, and the recordings were placed in a safe in a vault beneath the palace.[42]

In the anxious interval between the Allied reply on August 11 and the emperor's decision to surrender on August 14, American military officials hoped for the best but prepared for the worst. On August 12, the assistant chief of staff for Army intelligence warned that the Japanese government might drag out negotiations to weaken American resolve and predicted that any attempt by the government to surrender would be resisted by dissident elements in the Japanese military.[43] The next day, General Marshall had a deputy check with an officer attached to the Manhattan Project about the feasibility of using atomic weapons for tactical purposes. The ensuing conversation between Marshall's representative, General John E. Hull, and a spokesperson for General Groves, Colonel L. E. Seeman, revealed that although everyone understood the immense power of the atomic bomb, the only framework they had for comprehending it was the more familiar one of conventional weapons. Hull wanted to know whether the bombs, as many as nine of which might be ready by November, could be used against Japanese forces and communications centers located close to the invasion beaches. "Suppose you did get a dud or an incomplete explosion," Hull asked, "what safety factor should you consider, one, two, three days?" The two men discussed the matter of timing, and then Seeman offered, "Another thing you may be likely to consider is that while you are landing you might not want to use it as it could be dud." "It is not something that you want to fool around with," he added.[44]

Fortunately for all involved, the use of nuclear weapons in conjunction with OLYMPIC never advanced beyond this cursory investigation of their viability as tactical weapons. The inhabitants of Japanese cities, however, were not spared from one last round of devastating conventional attacks. On August 14, after a pause of three days, American B-29s resumed missions over Japan. Planes from the Far Eastern Air Force based on Okinawa and carrier-based aircraft from Halsey's Third Fleet also blasted targets in Japan. In one raid, more than six hundred planes attacked Kyushu.[45] The *New York Times'* Hanson Baldwin acknowledged how agonizing it was to send Americans into battle when victory was assured. Nevertheless, the U.S. needed to maintain pressure on Japan until the government surrendered. Baldwin speculated that the Allied reply subjecting Hirohito to the Allies' supreme commander was holding up acceptance in Tokyo. "Yet such a stipulation," he wrote, "was absolutely essential to the purposes for which we fought, if the Emperor were to be permitted to remain at all." Baldwin suggested that at the very least the Allies would have to remove Hirohito, and that abolition of the monarchy itself might be necessary. He noted that custom and blood ties linked the imperial family to the military and industrial classes in Japan. That made it "problematical whether the military class can be eliminated without removing the Emperor."[46]

The Allies would soon have an opportunity to test Baldwin's hypothesis. Later on the fourteenth, U.S. officials received word through Swiss diplomats that the Japanese government agreed to surrender. At a hastily called press conference that evening, a relieved and elated Truman announced, "I deem this reply a full acceptance of the Potsdam Declaration which specifies the unconditional surrender of Japan. In the reply there is no qualification."[47] After reading the Japanese message and stating that General MacArthur would serve as the supreme commander to receive the surrender, he concluded the conference with an abrupt "That is all." With that, the reporters broke for the doors to file their scoop.

As Army intelligence had predicted, dissidents in the Imperial Army tried to prevent the emperor from issuing the surrender decree. Officers stationed in Tokyo had been plotting a coup for several days, with the support of several senior leaders in the army. Anami refused to scotch the plot and remained a passive onlooker as it unfolded. On August 14, when they learned of the emperor's decision, the mutineers decided to seize the imperial palace and destroy the emperor's recorded message announcing the surrender. A brief clash ensued in which one of the plotters killed the commander of the First Imperial Guards Division. Rebellious soldiers ransacked the palace looking for the emperor's recording. Without the full support of the military, however, the mutiny was doomed. By daybreak on August 15, the plot had been thwarted. Anami committed ritual suicide, although he lingered for several hours before breathing his last. That morning the leaders of the mutiny, realizing they had failed, committed suicide in front of the palace. Hundreds of soldiers and sailors would follow their example over the next few days.[48]

At noon on August 15, the emperor's recording was delivered to Tokyo Radio. A national broadcast shortly before dawn had alerted the Japanese to expect a message from His Majesty later that day. Across Japan, people waited in uncertainty to hear for the first time "the jeweled voice." Most expected that the emperor would urge them on to fight to the end. What they heard was a high-pitched voice speaking in archaic Japanese that many

Reporters scrambling around (and, in one case, sprawling across) a table at the
White House, evidently picking up press releases announcing the Japanese
surrender. U.S. National Archives and Records Administration.

could not comprehend. The deliberate obfuscation of the text, its omission
of the words "defeat" and "surrender," contributed to the confusion. It was
only after a commentator explained that the emperor had agreed to surrender that they knew for certain that the war was over.[49]

The Japanese received the news with a mixture of shock, relief, and trep-
idation. They had survived, but what was to become of them now?[50] In
the United States, cities everywhere erupted in celebrations. Having nervously waited for Japan's response for days, Americans cut loose. In some
cities, notably San Francisco, the point of debarkation for soldiers and
sailors heading to the Pacific, the partying was marred by looting, brawling,
and vandalism. Numerous people were injured, and some even killed, by
stray gunfire, surging crowds, and flying debris. In the aftermath of these
outbursts, Truman declared Sunday, August 19, a day of thanksgiving. "The
nation could do with some prayer," he commented.[51]

The war was over, but victory would not be secured until the Allies ensured the surrender of Japanese armed forces. Three million of the emperor's warriors occupied territory across China, Southeast Asia, and the bypassed islands of the Pacific. Another two and a half million remained on the home islands, undefeated in battle, and, until August 14, ready to repel enemy invaders. As Marshall and Stimson had warned, the emperor's orders would be instrumental in obtaining their compliance with the terms of the Potsdam Declaration. In his message of acceptance on August 14, Hirohito had agreed to order the surrender of all military forces to the Allied commanders as designated by the Supreme Commander of the Allied Powers. First, however, the emperor would have to wait for the Allies to agree on the boundaries contained in General Order Number One.

Bonesteel's draft of the order had been completed on August 11, though various officials had sought to revise sections of it. One key addition, made by McCloy, specified that the Allied commanders listed in the order were "the only representatives empowered to accept the surrender, and all surrenders of Japanese forces shall be made only to them or their designated representatives." McCloy inserted that final provision with China in mind. The revised order would command the Japanese to surrender only to Chiang Kai-shek's representatives. It also held them responsible for resisting the efforts of Chinese Communist troops to disarm them. The separation of American and Russian boundaries posed a different problem. The Joint Staff Planners had assumed that surrenders in the Kuriles and on the Liaotung Peninsula would be handled by the Russians since both were treated as areas of Soviet influence or outright control in the Yalta Far Eastern Agreement. McCloy, however, wanted the U.S. to take the surrenders of Japanese forces in the southern Kuriles so that the U.S. would be in a better position to obtain landing rights there during the occupation of Japan. Concerns about Stalin's commitment to the Open Door in Manchuria inspired plans for a similar operation aimed at the Liaotung Peninsula even though it fell within the Soviet zone.[52]

The Joint Staff Planners showed little enthusiasm for surprising the Russians by sending ships unannounced into an area of obvious significance to them. Revising the General Order to include the peninsula was, however, out of the question. Stalin would certainly reject that. The JSP sought a way out of their dilemma by drafting a message for the president to send to Stalin, informing him that American ships were operating in the Yellow Sea to prevent the Japanese from destroying port facilities and to discourage a continuation of hostilities. The peninsula would remain in the Soviet zone, and Soviet commanders would be informed of the arrival of American ships. Success of the operation would depend on Stalin's consent and, equally important, the arrival of American forces ahead of the Russians. The JSP also prepared a similar message to inform the Soviets about impending operations in the southern Kuriles.

The ad hoc and risky operations in the Kuriles and the Liaotung Peninsula were all that remained of the proposal to check Soviet influence in northeast Asia first proposed by Joseph Grew in May. At that time, the Army opposed such an effort because Soviet aid was needed in the war against Japan. As an alternative, as we've seen, Grew proposed modifying unconditional surrender in the hope that the Japanese might capitulate before the Russians entered the war. The JCS unanimously rejected that gambit while the campaign on Okinawa was dragging on. When the administration finally decided to issue a clarification of its surrender demands, Truman, with the Joint Chiefs' concurrence, deleted what Grew and Stimson had considered the key passage in the Potsdam Declaration. Throughout the final months of the war, Truman's primary objective was to obtain Japan's unconditional surrender. The Joint Chiefs designed their strategy accordingly. Those priorities remained once Japan was on the verge of surrendering. The occupation of Japan would have the first charge on MacArthur's resources. Then came Korea below the thirty-eighth parallel. China finished a distant third.

Those priorities were evident in the tepid response of Army and Navy officers to the eleventh-hour proposals to occupy Dairen and the southern Kuriles. Brigadier General Lincoln, the head of S&P, and his Navy counterpart, Admiral Matthias Gardner, both expressed doubt about the proposed operations on the Liaotung Peninsula. Gardner thought that Dairen would have to have the same priority as Japan for the Americans to reach the port ahead of the Russians. "We may not get there anyhow. It may be all washed out anyhow," he added. Lincoln agreed that the Americans did not have much of a chance regardless of what they did. A short while later, their immediate superiors reached a similar conclusion.

What little suspense that remained about the outcome of the operations evaporated as soon as the draft General Order was sent to the Allies. Reviewing the order, Stalin reminded Truman that all the Kuriles were to come into Soviet possession as promised in the Yalta agreements. He also wished to specify that the Liaotung Peninsula was part of Manchuria and thus in the zone where the Japanese would surrender to Soviet commanders. Stalin raised no objection to the division of Korea, but he wanted Hokkaido, Japan's northernmost main island, included in the Soviet zone. American-Soviet sparring over surrender boundaries dragged on for several days. Truman rejected Stalin's bid to occupy Hokkaido. The operation to occupy Dairen was quietly canceled, though the president made a clumsy and ultimately unsuccessful attempt to obtain the desired landing rights in the Kuriles. Neither Truman nor Stalin were happy about the outcome of these exchanges, but it is doubtful that they were surprised. The Americans would control Japan's home islands, and the Russians, with Red Army troops descending on the Kuriles and Liaotung Peninsula, would secure the areas most important to them.[53]

While Stalin and Truman determined the boundaries separating their forces during the surrender operations, the emperor ensured that his subjects would obey the instructions in the General Order when it was finally issued. On August 17, he issued a rescript to the military. Like his radio broadcast, this message was couched in vague language and omitted mention of defeat or surrender. His Majesty thanked his subjects for their undying loyalty and sacrifice but noted that Soviet entry into the war had so altered the situation as to put the nation's existence at risk. Therefore, he was "about to make peace" with the Allies. After conveying his grief over the death of so many of his loyal subjects, Hirohito expressed his trust "that you officers and men of the Imperial forces will comply with our intention and will maintain a solid unity and strict discipline in your movements," and in doing so, "leave an everlasting foundation for the nation."[54]

The continuing bellicosity of field commanders outside Japan and the rebelliousness of junior officers in Tokyo convinced Hirohito and Imperial General Headquarters that extraordinary measures would be needed to bring the armed forces to heel. On August 17, three princes were dispatched to the headquarters in Southeast Asia, China, and Manchuria to communicate directly the imperial will. On August 20, Prince Higashikuni, the emperor's uncle and the newly appointed prime minister, found it necessary to make a cryptic radio broadcast to warn mutinous officers to obey the surrender rescript. Those who could be identified were shipped out of the city, while small groups of insurgents, seeing their plans foiled, committed suicide. In the meantime, Prince Takamatsu made a special trip to Atsugi Airfield outside Yokohama to quell insubordinate pilots in the special attack forces who planned to continue the war. Leaving nothing to chance, obedient soldiers removed the propellers from the planes before the Americans arrived.[55]

Unaware of the unstable situation in Tokyo, on August 17, MacArthur sent the Japanese a curt note telling them to stop stalling and to send a delegation to Manila immediately so that he could begin preparing for the American entry in Japan. The following day, the Japanese government replied that a delegation under Lieutenant General Kawabe Toroshiro, vice chief of the Imperial Staff, would be leaving for Manila on the nineteenth. In a separate message, the Japanese government, through Swiss intermediaries, informed the U.S. government it would be best if Japanese troops overseas be permitted to disarm themselves. They also requested that "the number of points in Japanese territory to be designated by the allies for occupation be limited to minimum number," and that "selection of the points be made in such a manner as to leave such a city as Tokyo unoccupied, and the forces to be stationed at each point be made as small as possible." The message contained a request that Japanese troops overseas be returned as quickly as possible and that they not be used as laborers by the Allies. It ended with a plea, conveyed orally to the Swiss, that the contents of this message remain confidential to avoid "catastrophic" consequences that would ensue if its contents were known to the Japanese people.

MacArthur recommended rejection of the message. He saw no need to spare the Japanese the psychological and physical burdens of defeat. Byrnes agreed. He replied that any information that the Japanese government needed to conduct the surrender arrangements would be conveyed through the Supreme Commander of the Allied Powers (SCAP). He reminded the Japanese that the Potsdam Declaration already pledged the return of Japanese troops to their homes, providing they cooperated by surrendering to the designated Allied commanders. [56]

MacArthur continued to plan for the full-scale occupation called for in the recently completed operation BLACKLIST. On August 19, while General Kawabe was in Manila, MacArthur ordered Allied commanders to refrain from accepting enemy surrenders until he conducted the main ceremony in Tokyo. The Chinese, British, and Australians protested that every day lost in asserting their control over their designated theaters would increase the potential for disorder and civil strife. No one could be certain whether the Japanese would attempt to salvage some measure of victory out of defeat by suddenly aiding the nationalist aspirations of the region's inhabitants after having postponed doing so for four years. Mountbatten was concerned that the mismatch between the vastness of the territory under his command and the paucity of the resources at his disposal would encourage insurgent nationalists to challenge the reassertion of colonial authority. Delay would only tempt them further. Of more immediate concern was the safety of the troop ships that had departed for Malaya six days earlier as part of Operation ZIPPER. To have them steam in circles or return to their ports of origin would prolong their voyages during the treacherous typhoon season. The Allies' protests were unavailing. The Combined Chiefs of Staff backed MacArthur, and the supreme commander stuck to his schedule.[57]

The Americans were slated to arrive in Japan in force on August 30. On August 27, one day ahead of an advanced party of the Eleventh Airborne Division, a plane from the carrier *Yorktown* flew through the tail end of a passing typhoon to land at Atsugi Airfield. When the paratroops arrived the next day, they were greeted by a large poster reading, "Welcome to the U.S. Army from Third Fleet." The advance party landed at the airfield on August 28 to find buffet tables and pitchers of orange juice waiting for them. The Americans feared the food might be poisoned and waited for their hosts to drink first. The mood improved only slightly after that. One American recalled that "it seemed like a party that wasn't going off very well."[58]

At dawn on August 30, the remainder of the Eleventh Airborne began arriving at Atsugi. At the same time, the Navy began landing elements of the Fourth Marines at Yokosuka Naval Base. According to one Marine officer, "Our first wave was made up entirely of officers trying to get ashore before MacArthur." MacArthur arrived at Atsugi in the afternoon. The Eleventh's military band provided the soundtrack. Standing at the top of the mobile staircase that led to the tarmac, wearing his signature shades and crush cap, corncob pipe clenched in his teeth, MacArthur paused in the doorway of the plane to survey the situation and allow photographers time to capture the moment for posterity.[59]

MacArthur proceeded to the New Grand Hotel in Yokohama, where his suite was already arranged. At daybreak on September 2, he left the hotel to conduct the surrender ceremony on board the USS *Missouri*, a 45,000-ton battleship of the *Iowa* class, that would serve as the stage for Japan's surrender. The "Mighty Mo" rested at anchor in Tokyo Bay, close to where Commodore Matthew Perry had dropped anchor ninety-two years earlier on his mission to open Japan. Although the crew of the *Missouri* had learned of their ship's role in the ceremony only days before, they had managed to scrounge enough paint to make her presentable. Commodore Perry's thirty-one-star flag was flown in from the United States in a special glass case and mounted on a bulkhead overlooking the surrender deck. Captain Stuart S. Murray, the *Missouri's* skipper, oversaw the preparations down to the last detail. His staff produced charts designating the assigned positions for Allied dignitaries and journalists and rehearsed the signing ceremony following instructions from MacArthur's staff. Worried about keeping to the strict timetable, the crew members playing Japanese Foreign Minister Shigemitsu Mamoru imitated his wooden-legged gait by shoving a mop handle down one of their trouser legs.

All seemed squared away on the morning of September 2 when, fifteen minutes before the start of the ceremony, a member of MacArthur's staff delivered the surrender documents, one in Japanese, the other in English, so that they could be placed side by side on the table provided for the occasion by British Admiral Sir Bruce Fraser. As soon as the documents were presented, it became apparent that the table was not large enough to hold them. The officers of the *Missouri* scurried about the ship searching for a substitute. In the nick of time, Murray's enterprising staff hauled a table out of the mess deck, covered it with a green tablecloth from the wardroom, and set it up on the galley deck in place of Fraser's table. "It looked very nice," recalled Murray.

The ceremony began at approximately 9:00 a.m. local time. The Japanese representatives performed their duties with stiff formality. Shigemitsu, who had lost his leg in 1932 when a Korean nationalist threw a bomb during a celebration of the emperor's birthday, struggled noticeably as he came up the gangway. At MacArthur's side were Lieutenant General Jonathan Wainwright, who had surrendered American forces in the Philippines to the Japanese after MacArthur was evacuated, and British Lieutenant General Arthur E. Percival, the defeated commander of Singapore garrison. VIPs, sailors, and cameramen crowded the decks to watch the historic proceedings. Two Russian photographers who slipped onto the surrender deck were ushered off by one of the *Missouri's* officers and several Marines. After a few minutes of silence, MacArthur stepped forward and read a brief address, ending with an eloquent plea for a world where "freedom, tolerance, and justice" would flourish.[60]

The document declared the unconditional surrender of the Imperial General Headquarters and all the armed forces under Japanese control. It further commanded all civil and military officers to obey the orders of the

Supreme Allied Commander and made the authority of the emperor and the Japanese government subject to the Supreme Commander. Each delegate was to sign both copies on the line above his country's name. The Japanese foreign minister stepped forward and then paused, uncertain of where to sign. MacArthur tersely ordered his chief of staff to point out the line awaiting Shigemitsu's signature. As he began to sit down, Shigemitsu's artificial leg struck the tie rod holding the collapsible table. Viewing the ceremony from the quarterdeck, Captain Murray heard the clatter and saw the table shudder, but, much to his relief, it remained upright. Army Chief of Staff Umezu Yoshijiro signed after Shigemitsu without taking a seat. After the Japanese signed, MacArthur signed for the Allies; Admiral Chester Nimitz for the United States; followed by military representatives of China, Britain, the Soviet Union; and the remaining allies, including France and Canada.

When the last representative finished, MacArthur offered another brief prayer for peace and pronounced the proceedings closed. At that moment the sun broke through the clouds. Just then, a flight of approximately four hundred B-29s and four hundred carrier planes passed overhead. MacArthur moved to a microphone and began a radio address to a world audience. "Today the guns are silent," began the now famous message. "A great tragedy has ended. A great victory has been won." The Allied commanders outside Japan were now free to complete the arrangements for the surrender of Japanese forces in their areas.

The surrenders conducted throughout Asia relied on displays of force and potent symbols to convey the irresistibility of Allied power and impress upon the Japanese the unconditional nature of their defeat. The Chinese ceremony took place on September 9 in the auditorium of the Whampoa Military Academy in Nanking. The Japanese were compelled to surrender to their Chinese foes in the school whose first president had been Chiang Kai-shek. On the same day, the Americans took the surrender of the Japanese authorities in Korea below the thirty-eighth parallel in the government palace in Seoul. More than twenty American officers sat behind a rectangular table with their backs to the large open windows. On the opposite side of the table the small Japanese delegation sweated under the hot lights brought in by photographers. As he signed over control of Japan's wealthiest colony, Governor General Abe Nobuyuki spit up in his handkerchief. The ceremony completed, Abe left the room and vomited outside on the marble floor.

Mountbatten finally got to conduct his own surrender ceremony at Singapore on September 12, four days after Truman received the instruments of surrender at the White House. The SEAC commander arrived at the downtown municipal building at 10:30 a.m. Stepping out of his car, Mountbatten inspected four guards of honor, one each from the Royal Navy, Air Force, Australian paratroopers, and Indian Army, while the assembled bands from the fleet played *Rule Britannia*. Major General Brian Kimmins, who Mountbatten described as the "producer" of the "marvelous show," had highlighted the international composition of the forces defeating Japan. Guards from India, Australia, the United States, and China assumed conspicuous positions inside the building. In the main chamber, long rectangular tables faced each other. Representatives of the Allies, including the Netherlands and France, sat at one table. The assembled dignitaries and spectators were instructed not to rise when the Japanese entered. Once the Japanese were seated, everyone in the room rose and stood for a minute of silence. At the end of that observance, Mountbatten entered through the double doors to take his place at a dais, later noting that he had been feeling "like some actor taking a cue at the climax of a great opera."

Speaking to the radio audience as much as to the Japanese in the room, Mountbatten made a statement in which he called attention to the one-hundred-thousand-man Allied force that had begun coming ashore on September 9. The SEAC commander explained, "The surrender today is no negotiated surrender. The Japanese are submitting to superior force now massed here." As if to underscore that point, the Chinese delegate took out a camera and began taking pictures of the Japanese at the moment of their most extreme humiliation. "Not even Hollywood," wrote Mountbatten afterward, "had they been called upon to stage such a ceremony, could have thought up the idea of the Chinese delegate taking pictures from the table."[61]

Over the next several months, local surrenders would take place across Asia and the bypassed islands of the Pacific. General Yamashita Tomoyuki had already come down from his mountain redoubt in the Philippines to surrender to the Americans at Baguio on September 3. Japanese forces in Burma surrendered the same day as Mountbatten's ceremony in Singapore. Chinese Nationalist forces did not receive the surrender of Japanese forces in north China until October 10. With the exception of Manchuria, where poor communications and Soviet aggressiveness prolonged the fighting, in defiance of the emperor's rescript, Japanese forces throughout Asia offered little resistance and surrendered unconditionally to the designated Allied commanders.

MacArthur's tenure as Supreme Commander for the Allied Powers (SCAP) began with typical flourish. As he winged his way toward Tokyo, the general casually told his staff how he planned to democratize Japan. Pacing the aisle of his plane, he explained that he would begin by destroying Japan's ability to make war. He would then enfranchise women, strengthen labor unions and agricultural organizations, destroy monopolies, establish a free press, end police repression, liberalize education, and decentralize political power.[62] The general's plans for Japan awed his admiring staff. During his soliloquy, however, MacArthur neglected to mention that the agenda he recited had been sent to him from Washington as the U.S. Initial Post-Surrender Policy. This well-known anecdote, a humorous example of the general's penchant for theatricality, reveals the sycophancy of some of his closest advisors. Even though the Initial Post-Surrender Policy was published a few weeks after this incident, Bonner Fellers and Courtney Whitney (one of MacArthur's aides) wrote years later as if the general had dreamed up the entire reform plan for Japan.

Even before he had arrived in Japan, MacArthur indicated that he expected to be the arbiter of which policies the Americans would implement during the occupation. On August 24, the War Department instructed MacArthur to order the Japanese government to tell its diplomats in neutral countries to turn over their papers and property to Allied representatives. The State Department had sent the same instructions to the Japanese, but they refused, citing the absence of any such provision in the Potsdam Declaration. MacArthur also balked at implementing the order. He noted that the Japanese would insist that the demand was beyond his authority, and he further noted that he would have no means of enforcing it, since the areas in question were outside of his command. The implication that MacArthur saw his authority so limited did not sit well with the State Department.

After some discussion in Washington, Truman approved instructions to MacArthur clarifying his authority. SCAP was informed that the authority of the Japanese government and emperor to rule were subordinate to his. "Our relations with Japan," he was told, "do not rest on a contractual basis, but on an unconditional surrender. Since your authority is Supreme, you will not entertain any question on the part of the Japanese as to its scope."

The same day, MacArthur was advised that once he had established satisfactory control in Japan, he should enforce the State Department's order. One would assume that MacArthur would have welcomed an enlargement of his powers. But the general did not take direction well, and he especially resented it when it emanated from Washington. Therefore, the War Department prefaced the message by saying the matter was not urgent. By attempting to soften the blow to MacArthur's outsized ego, the War Department gave him enough latitude to ignore the order. It was not an auspicious beginning for the relationship between Washington and Japan's new shogun.[63]

Over the next few days, MacArthur and his staff spoke and acted in ways that suggested to some observers that SCAP was taking a "kid glove" or "powder puff" approach to the occupation. In retrospect, some of these reactions seem unwarranted. MacArthur did, after all, need to establish military control over a country that contained several million military personnel. And he was not responsible for the decision to work through the emperor and the existing government, although he endorsed that policy. On the other hand, supporters of unconditional surrender remained wary that the same forces that sought to soften the surrender terms during the war were still at large. Recently picked to be undersecretary of state, Dean Acheson was especially vigilant in looking for signs of backsliding during the crucial first weeks of the occupation. Acheson's nomination hearing was scheduled for mid-September, but news of his selection led to the early exodus of Ballantine, Dooman, and Grew and their replacement with China hands unsympathetic to Japan. It remained to be seen, however, if policy created in Washington could be implemented in Tokyo.

The early indications were not promising. Speaking to the press shortly after his arrival, MacArthur predicted that Japan would become the leading trading country in Asia. On September 15, General Robert Eichelberger, commander of the Eighth Army, the main occupation force, guessed that the occupation might be "washed up in a year." Neither comment was meant to be definitive, but to America's allies, notably Great Britain, Australia, and New Zealand, the suggestion of a liberated Japan retaking its place among the leading trading nations in Asia was unwelcome news.[64] The real shock came on September 17 when MacArthur unexpectedly announced that he needed fewer men than expected to accomplish the goals of the surrender because he would be using the Japanese government to maintain social order and a functioning economy. Things were going so well in Japan, he said, that he would soon be able to reduce the occupation force by half, to two hundred thousand men. He added that a force that size could be replenished by GIs from the regular Army, and thus the occupation would not need to rely on peacetime conscription.[65]

As soon as he learned of MacArthur's surprise announcement, John McCloy alerted Dean Acheson and requested that he speak to Truman. Acheson immediately called the president. When Acheson told Truman that MacArthur said he would need fewer troops because he was relying on the Japanese government to carry out the goals of the occupation, the president interrupted to say he thought that statement was incorrect and uncalled for. Acheson explained that the War Department was already preparing a statement telling MacArthur that he and his men should refrain from further announcements and that his proposed reduction, if carried out, would disrupt their plans for the orderly replacement of troops in the Pacific. They were adding at Acheson's request that the State Department feared that MacArthur's comments would create the impression that "American power was being liquidated in the Far East and that we were relying solely on Japanese good faith." When Acheson asked Truman if the War Department's message could note that the president was concerned by MacArthur's announcement and that it did not reflect his views, Truman assented. He added that they could make that part as strong as they wanted. "This was not his policy and he intended to use as many men as were necessary to assure the complete carrying out of the surrender and the adoption of the policies which we had already outlined to General MacArthur."[66]

The desired message went out over General Marshall's signature the same day. MacArthur was informed that his statement and Eichelberger's previous comments had caused considerable consternation in the White House and State and War Departments. Marshall was particularly upset because MacArthur had yet to reply to two requests from the War Department for his estimate of troops needed in the Pacific by July 1946. MacArthur replied that he was distressed to learn of the disruption his announcement had caused. He was under tremendous pressure from the media and believed that he had the authority to speak because in a recent press conference Truman had told journalists to ask MacArthur about the expected duration of the occupation. After pinning the responsibility for the situation on the president, the general further distanced himself from the controversy by disavowing Eichelberger's comments. They were made without consulting SCAP and were "at variance with my own."[67]

MacArthur's reply was as misleading as it was disingenuous. The comment by Truman that the general had referred to in his reply to Marshall was a statement made by the president about the situation in Korea, where American occupation forces had not yet removed the Japanese colonial authorities. It was not about the size of occupation forces in Japan. MacArthur served up that feeble excuse because he could not state the real reason for his sudden prediction about force levels. The general was inspired to make his announcement after receiving warnings from Philip LaFollette, a former Wisconsin governor and onetime member of MacArthur's staff, and Robert Wood, chairman of Sears, Roebuck and a leader of the noninterventionist wing of the Republican Party. Wood and LaFollette told MacArthur that administration officials were conspiring to use MacArthur's need for a large occupation army as a justification for continuing the peacetime draft. Wood advised MacArthur that the best way to avoid being blamed for the continuation of conscription would be to make it clear that he would need fewer troops, perhaps two hundred thousand or three hundred thousand, to govern Japan. That would force the administration to find another excuse for continuing the draft and keeping men in uniform. MacArthur used the lower number and, in doing so, put additional pressure on the administration to speed the rate of demobilization.[68]

MacArthur's apology did nothing to quell the controversy caused by his announcement. The story hit the front pages of American papers the next day, September 18. In response to questions from the press, Acheson submitted a terse written statement making clear that he did not know in advance MacArthur would be making the announcement.[69] That afternoon, Truman told the press that he had not known in advance about MacArthur's statement. MacArthur initially expected he would need five hundred thousand men, said Truman, then it was four hundred thousand, and now two hundred thousand. "It helps to get as many men out of the army as possible." Truman's comments did little to clarify the situation. Some of the journalists present detected a note of sarcasm in the president's answer, but the Associated Press took it seriously and reported that the president had pulled the rug out from under the State Department.[70]

The following morning, Truman clarified his position, seeking to separate the subject of troops needed for the occupation from the politically explosive issue of demobilization. In an official statement, the president emphasized that the troops were coming home as quickly as they could be moved. If demobilization continued apace, it would be next spring before the administration would have to decide if it could fill the occupation forces with volunteers or if they would need draftees. Tucked into the statement was a subtle criticism of MacArthur: "No one now can accurately forecast what those needs are going to be."[71]

That comment may have been too subtle to satisfy Acheson. The same day, the acting secretary issued a sharp and unmistakable rebuke of MacArthur's comments. Acheson signaled the statement's importance by departing from usual practice and permitting the press to quote it directly. Acheson began by conceding that he could not speak on purely military issues, although he wondered how anyone could predict how many troops would be needed for the occupation so soon after it had begun. The important point, he said, was that American occupation policy had not changed "so far as I know— and I think I know." In a slap at MacArthur, the statement pointed out, "In carrying out that policy, the occupation forces are the instruments of that policy and not the determinants of policy." That policy, he said, was that the present economic and social system that made for a "will to war" would be eliminated and "whatever it takes to carry this out will be used to carry it out." In the follow-up, journalists double-checked with Acheson to be sure that they could quote the statement verbatim. Acheson replied that he had stated very clearly that they could quote his remarks on General MacArthur. He also said no one in Washington had been informed in advance of MacArthur's announcement and that occupation policy was made in Washington by a committee representing the State, War, and Navy Departments.[72]

Acheson's statement promptly touched off a political storm that lasted weeks. The press coverage of the story received close attention in the White House's daily news analysis, which was tracking public response to the surrender and the start of the occupation.[73] MacArthur, his aides, and supporters in the press and public were convinced, to varying degrees, that Acheson had aimed to blacken the general's reputation and that he had done so with the president's approval. In typical fashion, MacArthur had engaged in politically controversial behavior and then accused those affected by his actions of responding solely for partisan reasons.[74] The incident offered a preview of the insubordinate and self-promoting behavior that would lead to Truman's recall of MacArthur during the Korean War. It was also a dispute about the very purpose of unconditional surrender and the occupation.

It was no coincidence that Acheson, one of the administration's strongest supporters of unconditional surrender, led the administration's response to

MacArthur. It is significant that in addition to relegating MacArthur to the role of carrying out American policy as opposed to determining it, he salted the wound by revealing that SWNCC was creating that policy.[75] It is not clear whether Truman knew the contents of Acheson's statement in advance. We know that he did not disavow them, and thus we can be reasonably certain that he approved their purpose. When Truman first learned of MacArthur's announcement, his first reaction was to tell Acheson that the general was misrepresenting American policy. That is not surprising. It was Truman, after all, who had steadfastly refused to make concessions on the emperor in the final months of the war and insisted that the occupation would be conducted on the basis of Japan's unconditional surrender.

Press commentary on the MacArthur imbroglio adhered to the pattern established during the earlier debate over modification of unconditional surrender. This time, however, the rhetoric on both sides was more virulent than before, with innuendo giving way to bald accusations of disloyalty and betrayal of American principles. The left accused MacArthur and his supporters of protecting Japan's oligarchs and seeking to build the country as a bulwark to Soviet expansion. MacArthur's defenders viewed the attack of the general as the start of a new offensive by communist sympathizers. *New York Times* columnist Arthur Krock, a critic of unconditional surrender, reported that criticism of MacArthur was being advocated in the "pink publications." According to the pro-MacArthur *Chicago Tribune*, the general's critics in the administration were "sadists" promoting a policy that was counter to American "instincts and traditions." As if to clarify the *Tribune's* point, Mississippi congressman John Rankin declared that he was planning to inquire into the left-wing criticism of MacArthur's actions during upcoming hearings of the House Un-American Activities Committee. HUAC, as the committee was known, was starting a new round of hearings on communism in America.[76]

I. F. Stone, editor of the *Nation*, one of the "pink" publications, fired back at accusers with an equal amount of invective. "Soviet American relations are the fundamental factor in determining the future of Japan as in Germany," he wrote. "In Congress and the press, the old pro-Axis and anti-Soviet crowd is taking advantage of the demand for faster demobilization to plead for softer treatment of both Germany and Japan." Stone also noted that the conservative press sought to "identify advocates of a hard peace for the Axis with communism." Stone saw different links worth highlighting. The same crowd that had lulled the U.S. into complacence before Pearl Harbor was at it again. The Japanophiles Grew and Dooman were out, noted Stone, but MacArthur was "playing to the old isolationist crypto-fascist gallery."[77]

In the midst of the controversy, MacArthur's friends in Congress sought retribution against Acheson by trying, unsuccessfully, to derail his nomination as undersecretary. In the meantime, the administration published its earlier directive to MacArthur, explaining the scope of his authority in Japan. It also released SWNCC's Initial Post-Surrender Policy, outlining the extensive reform program he was expected to oversee. Publication of the directive and policy document served several purposes. It answered critics who said that MacArthur had been working in the dark without guidance from Washington and reassured allies and concerned citizens at home that the U.S. was not conducting the occupation with a gloved hand. It also created a yardstick against which MacArthur's actions could be measured.[78] The War Department gave MacArthur advanced notice that they planned to publish the Post-Surrender Policy, which was a courtesy MacArthur had not shown the department. That gave the general time to limit the damage by granting an interview with journalist Hugh Baillie that emphasized his sternness in dealing with Japan. Japan was finished as a world power, he declared. But the occupation would last years. MacArthur added that he would be there to see it through to the end. Asked if he planned to visit the United States soon, MacArthur replied, "No, I regret to say. I feel the situation here will require my personal presence for some time to come." Two days earlier he had had replied to a similar query from the Joint Chiefs by saying, "The delicate and difficult situation which prevails here, however, would make it unwise for me to leave until conditions are far more stabilized than at present."[79] If MacArthur was troubled by the obvious contradiction between his previous rosy prediction about the progress of the occupation and his sudden concern over the "delicate and difficult" situation he faced, he kept it to himself.

MacArthur's interview served its purposes. As the *Washington Post* editorialized, MacArthur was "back on the beam."[80] SCAP was now committed to imposing the terms of the Potsdam Declaration on Japan. The advocates of unconditional surrender were victorious. The debate over it, however, was far from over.

# 6

# "The A-Bomb Was Not Needed"

The Initial Post-Surrender Policy laid out a host of reforms. During the first year and a half of the occupation, what might be called its "liberal phase," General MacArthur implemented many of them. He purged business, government, and educational institutions of reactionary officials; released political prisoners, many of whom were communists; legalized unions; mandated freedom of religion; carried out an ambitious land reform program; disarmed and disbanded the military; and instituted a new constitution that transformed the emperor from ultimate authority into a symbol of the Japanese people, stripping the institution of its authority in government affairs.

In Japan, support for these measures came from the groups that comprised the country's prewar civil society—labor and farm organizations, for example—before they were suppressed by the militarists. Japan's rulers, the moderates that Herbert Hoover and Joseph Grew had supported, resisted many of these changes. Civilian politicians and business leaders did not object to the elimination of the military, but they did their best to frustrate liberal political and economic reforms. Before the Americans arrived in September, Suzuki's government had been replaced by one led by Prince Higashikuni Naruhiko, the first time a member of the royal family had held such a position. Higashikuni's government continued to honor war contracts and even opened military warehouses to systematic looting by favored businesses. The "horded goods" scandal, as this episode became known, fueled runaway inflation and added significantly to the misery of Japanese citizens.[1]

As we've seen, for the most part MacArthur fell in line with the policies drawn up in Washington. The Truman administration and the Supreme

Commander for the Allied Powers (SCAP) even reached a meeting of the minds on the handling of Hirohito. MacArthur is often portrayed as defying Washington by saving the emperor. In fact, the new regime at the State Department reluctantly concluded that it was best to keep Hirohito on the throne, so long as he facilitated the conduct of American policy. That was the arrangement Truman had in mind when he made Hirohito subordinate to MacArthur, or, as the president put it, the Americans would tell the Japanese how they could keep the emperor.[2]

MacArthur, however, was uncomfortable with this improvised arrangement and sought to make the retention of Hirohito a fait accompli. This effort began with the emperor's visit to MacArthur's residence on September 19. There is no trustworthy record of what took place at the brief meeting, but the photograph memorializing the occasion was worth a thousand words. MacArthur wore his khaki uniform unadorned by ribbons or tie and stood with his arms casually at his sides. The emperor, a full head shorter, stood stiffly in formal morning coat while he appeared uncertain what to do with his hands. No one who saw that picture could doubt who was in charge of Japan. In retrospect, however, the photograph can also be viewed as showing that MacArthur stood by the emperor.[3]

Research furnished by MacArthur's staff appeared to confirm the wisdom of that decision. Their analysis of public opinion showed that the Japanese still supported their emperor, although there is reason to suspect that the results of that research were shaped to fit SCAP's preferences. Certainly, Hirohito did everything he could to absolve himself of responsibility for the war. A stream of emissaries visited SCAP headquarters bearing assurances that the emperor had opposed the attack on Pearl Harbor and, despite being a prisoner of the militarists, had sought to end the conflict as soon as possible. As Hirohito endeavored to save himself, he also sought to preserve what he could salvage of his traditional role in the Japanese polity. On January 1, 1946, the emperor issued a rescript that halfheartedly renounced his divinity and linked his rule to the Meiji emperor and the authoritarian constitution promulgated during his reign. Couched in classical language and shrouded in ambiguity, the rescript was open to interpretation. As Herbert Bix, Hirohito's American biographer, notes, its Japanese authors clearly intended to satisfy the Americans while maintaining as much as possible of the emperor's authority. A key element of the speech was that in asserting continuity with the Meiji Constitution, he seemed to make democracy a matter of imperial will, not the will of the people.[4]

Emperor Hirohito and General MacArthur, at their first meeting, at the U.S. Embassy, Tokyo, September 27, 1945. U.S. Army Photograph, Lt. Gaetano Faillace.

This artifice was enough to satisfy MacArthur, but not everyone. As noted earlier, the Australian government had opposed any measures at the time of the surrender that would disassociate Hirohito from Japan's military debacle. The Australians continued to press for harsh treatment of Japan. In December, Canberra requested that Hirohito be added to the list of Japanese to be tried as war criminals. Secretary of State Byrnes brushed aside the request by saying that the list was being drawn up by a special agency within the occupation. Byrnes's willingness to shelter Hirohito did not mean the Americans were satisfied with the emperor's current status in Japanese society. In early January, the State Department informed MacArthur that he should either abolish the imperial institution or ensure it was reformed along "more democratic lines." MacArthur's instructions added that the ideal situation would be for the Japanese to initiate those reforms themselves.

It soon became clear, however, that that was not going to happen. The Japanese committee established to draft the constitution continued to define the imperial institution as a bastion of the status quo, a position that Hirohito endorsed. MacArthur responded by turning the job of drafting Japan's constitution over to a handful of Americans. The document was completed in a week, at which time MacArthur submitted it to the Japanese committee with the admonition that failure to accept the American draft would invite participation from the Allies, most of whom, like the Australians, would be less solicitous of the emperor's well-being.[5]

The committee relented, but Hirohito, as he had done in many instances throughout the war, played for time in the hope that the situation would improve. The emperor's family provided the final impetus for his acceptance of the new constitution. On February 27, Prince Mikasa, Hirohito's youngest brother, gave a speech in the Privy Council that indirectly urged Hirohito to abdicate. The same day, an AP correspondent noted that his interview with Prince Higashikuni, the emperor's uncle by marriage, revealed that many members of the imperial family supported Hirohito's abdication. In early March, another story linked to Hirohito's uncle indicated that there were plans to have Prince Takamatsu, Hirohito's brother, serve as regent until the emperor's son, Akihito, could assume the throne.[6] Seeing that the situation had developed not necessarily to his advantage, Hirohito finally relented and accepted the new constitution, and with it the greatly reduced role of the imperial institution in Japanese life.

The new constitution went into effect on May 3, 1947. It explicitly defined the emperor as the symbol of the state and the unity of the people and identified the people as sovereign. The constitution reduced the emperor to a figurehead performing ceremonial functions, subject to cabinet approval, and stripped the dynasty of all property and income, making it dependent on the cabinet.[7] Spared from prosecution as a war criminal—the beneficiary of selective immunity, his critics charged—Hirohito adapted to his new role in public life. With MacArthur's encouragement, Hirohito toured Tokyo's debris-strewn neighborhoods, visited department stores and factories, attended ribbon-cutting ceremonies, and threw out the first pitch at baseball games. Nevertheless, he never displayed much enthusiasm for these activities. Eventually, the Japanese referred to His Majesty as "Ah, So-san"—"Ah, So" being his usual utterance at these events. More irreverent Japanese also called him "Ten-chan," a diminutive that translates roughly as "Emp-baby."[8]

The demotion and humanization of the emperor came at a price. As historians have noted, in sparing the emperor from prosecution, the occupation also appeared to grant general immunity to the Japanese public. How could individual Japanese citizens be held responsible for the war if the emperor, in whose name they had acted, was not? In any case, the transformation of the emperor and the apparent acceptance of his new status by Japanese elites created the impression that moderate politicians and the emperor had always favored those outcomes. Critics of unconditional surrender pointed to the continuation of Hirohito on the throne and asked why, if the Truman administration was willing to preserve the imperial institution, they had not simply told the Japanese that during the war. More charitably inclined critics denounced that failure as a monstrous mistake that had cost hundreds of thousands of Americans and Japanese their lives. Others saw more sinister forces at work. For those critics, unconditional surrender was part of plot to spread communism in Asia. In the immediate postwar period, both groups sought to revise Americans' understanding of how the war had ended.

Not long after he entered Japan in the autumn of 1945, General Bonner Fellers, who had been head of MacArthur's psychological warfare program during the war, began to search for evidence showing that Hirohito and Suzuki had sought to turn the tables on the militarists and end the war. During the spring and summer of 1945, Fellers had argued, as noted, that the Japanese were ready to surrender. After he arrived in Japan, Fellers endeavored to prove that he had been right. Japanese officials were more than happy to help him make that case. Both Fellers and his supporter Herbert Hoover remained committed to their thesis that Hirohito had struggled to end the war beginning in early 1945.

During the first months of the occupation, Fellers prepared several memoranda stating that no evidence had been found to show that the emperor should be tried as a war criminal. He could say that because he did not actually look for that evidence. Instead, he accepted the word of the emperor and His Majesty's supporters that Hirohito had opposed the war and that he had not intended to have his war rescript used as Prime Minister Tojo Hideki used it.[9] Fellers displayed far more reverence for the throne than did many Japanese.[10] His support for Hirohito went beyond granting him selective immunity from prosecution. He and MacArthur also opposed having Hirohito abdicate. That made them more devout than the emperor's own kin.

Fellers told Hoover that the Soviets wanted to put Hirohito in the dock because they wanted "blood and revolution" in Japan. Hoover agreed and warned Fellers that the Soviets would be counting on help from sympathizers in the occupation government. "Among the men sent from the State Department to Japan," he wrote, "are some former Communists or fellow-travelers. One of them is named Service." That was a reference to John Stewart Service, the China specialist who had been arrested in the *Amerasia* case that summer.[11]

Over the next several months, Fellers's defense of the emperor from prosecution evolved into a larger project to inform Americans of Hirohito's heroic efforts to end the war early. The villain in this tale was Franklin Roosevelt, aka the "Sailor King," and his vindictive policy of unconditional surrender. Fellers was inspired in this effort by Hoover, with whom he met on his return to the U.S. in December, and again in May 1946 when Hoover visited Japan on a mission to assess the food situation in Asia. During his stay in Japan, Hoover had a long talk with Fellers about the need to gather historical materials on the war for safekeeping in the former president's Institution on War, Revolution, and Peace, on the campus of Stanford University.

Hoover shared with Fellers that he was certain that Suzuki's appointment in April 1945 had been the emperor's way of signaling that Japan wanted to end the war. He also told Fellers about his meeting with Truman, although he omitted mentioning that he had recommended that Japan be allowed to keep control of Korea and Taiwan. The former president maintained that Truman had agreed to have the State Department prepare a speech that would embody Hoover's recommendations on ending the war, but although Truman took notes, no speech was made. Fellers noted, "Mr. Hoover gave the clear impression that it might easily have been Soviet influence in the State Department which insisted that the war continue until the USSR entered and could have a hand in the peace and postwar settlement."[12]

Hoover also met three times with MacArthur. The two were well acquainted and had much in common, including an intense dislike of Hoover's successor as president. The general had served as Army Chief of Staff during Hoover's presidency, and the former president remained an ardent supporter of a MacArthur presidential bid. According to Hoover's summary of the meetings, the two men briefly discussed the food situation in Japan and then spent the rest of their time taking turns kicking Roosevelt's corpse. MacArthur complained that Roosevelt had favored the Navy in the Pacific and kept his forces on short rations. He told Hoover that during their conference in Hawaii in July 1944, he had demanded ten minutes alone with Roosevelt away from the prying eyes of "the Rosemans [sic] and Admiral Nimitz." Once they were alone, MacArthur supposedly told the president that if he approved the general's plans for retaking the Philippines, it would ensure Roosevelt's reelection in November. MacArthur went on to say that he told FDR that once the Japanese lost the Philippines, they would realize that they were beaten.[13]

Hoover in turn told MacArthur about his memorandum to Truman in mid-May stating that peace could be had "by which our major objectives could be accomplished." MacArthur agreed, noting, "We would have avoided all of the losses, the Atomic Bomb, and the entry of the Russians into Manchuria." All of it was so unnecessary, Hoover chimed in. "The whole Japanese war was a madman's desire to get into war," he said. The two men agreed that the occupation program pushed by the "liberals" was ruining Japan's chances of recovery, and they both worried about the spread of communism in Asia, especially with the Russians in Manchuria. Hoover urged MacArthur to run for the presidency in 1948, and when the general dismissed that idea, he suggested that MacArthur come home soon to provide moral leadership to the country. Clearly, the years had not diminished Hoover's admiration for MacArthur. And one can assume that MacArthur, basking in Hoover's admiration, reciprocated the feeling.[14]

Hoover's meetings with MacArthur and Fellers renewed old friendships, but they also established the contours of what would become the postwar conservative critique of Roosevelt and Truman's unconditional surrender policy. The story would be repeated in numerous publications and congressional hearings over the course of the next two decades. One key feature was that sometime in early 1945, Hirohito asserted himself and began to seek a way to end the war. Suzuki's appointment would become a pivotal moment in this saga. A second feature was that the only issue that prevented the emperor from agreeing to surrender was his uncertainty about the fate of the monarchy. The Truman administration refused the desired assurances on that point because communist sympathizers in the State Department sought to prolong the war until the Russians could attack Manchuria. Over the years, variations on these themes would be added. It soon became an article of faith that MacArthur had told Roosevelt before the Yalta Conference in February 1945 that the United States did not need Russian help to defeat Japan. The goals of communists and/or fellow travelers in the State Department also evolved in the retelling of this legend. In addition to seeking to prolong the war, the subversives were accused of trying to sow chaos in Japan by abolishing the monarchy and prosecuting Hirohito as a war criminal.

This version blurred important distinctions, such as the difference between peace and surrender. It ignored the evidence that Suzuki assumed office without any plan to end the war and even less desire to challenge the militarists. And it simplified a common dilemma in negotiations—how to demonstrate flexibility without appearing weak and encouraging rigidity from one's adversary. The legend of Hirohito's peace efforts also took for granted that the Japanese would have surrendered, provided the Americans permitted the emperor to retain the throne as a constitutional monarch, a term purveyors of this account seldom defined.

The first few months of the occupation showed that that was not the case. Even after Japan surrendered and the military was disbanded, the emperor and the so-called moderate political leadership clung to the role of the monarchy as established in the Meiji Constitution. Hirohito and those who derived their power through association with the throne were not willing to negotiate away Japan's unique political structure because it would destroy the foundation on which Japan's hierarchy rested. Japan's political class and Hirohito agreed to the restructuring of the monarchy only because the Americans were in control of Japan, a position they had obtained by compelling Japan's unconditional surrender.

MacArthur's assertion that he advised Roosevelt to forgo Soviet entry into the war differed from other features in the conservative critique in that it was later publicly revealed to be a bald-faced lie. Nevertheless, like the tale of MacArthur creating the occupation's liberal reform program while en route to Japan, the story of MacArthur's sage warning and Roosevelt's perfidy lived on among the general's admirers.

Fellers retired from the Army in November 1946 and took a job as director of public affairs for the Veterans of Foreign Wars (VFW), once he was assured by a friend that it was not a left wing outfit.[15] He served as the VFW's liaison to the armed forces and advisor on foreign affairs and military policy. He also remained active in the Republican Party, with most of his contacts being members of the party's prewar anti-interventionist wing. Fellers's political activities and professional responsibilities converged in early 1947 when *Harper's Magazine* published an article by Henry Stimson titled "The Decision to Use the Atomic Bomb." The article, which justified the use of the bomb, stirred Fellers to action. Stimson's reputation as a statesman and his access to classified materials endowed his essay with an authority that seemed likely to make it the standard explanation of how the war ended. Fellers viewed the article as a cynical attempt to silence growing criticism of the bomb's use by religious organizations. Truman's immediate endorsement of the article convinced Fellers that Stimson was running interference for the president. Fellers feared that if the article went unchallenged, it would smother the controversy over the war's end and remove an important obstacle to Truman's election in 1948.[16]

The former psychological warfare officer responded by pitching the idea of an article on Japan's decision to surrender to the editor of the mass-circulation *Reader's Digest*. When the editorial board expressed interest, Fellers informed Hoover that he intended to use the materials he had helped collect to reveal the inner history of Japan's surrender. The first draft, titled "Japan's Decision to Surrender," was finished in early March. Fellers sent a copy to his contact at the magazine and to Hoover. A key argument in Fellers's draft was his insistence that Suzuki's appointment in April was an indication that the peace movement was gaining strength and that, in early May, Hirohito bravely decided to seek peace using the Soviet Union as intermediary. Fellers wrote that the surest way for the Americans to aid the emperor's efforts would have been to clarify the meaning of unconditional surrender, "a most difficult and devastating phrase." The easiest way to do that would have been to tell the Japanese that the United States did not intend to abolish the monarchy or dethrone Hirohito.[17]

Hoover congratulated Fellers on the draft but advised him to sharpen his argument by "making it perfectly plain that the Japanese were prepared to negotiate all the way from February 1945," and that if the Americans had pursued those leads, there would have been no reason to use the atomic bombs. The two men met several times after that. Fellers dutifully incorporated most of Hoover's recommendations into the final draft, thereby making a flawed essay even more inaccurate. Retitled "Hirohito's Struggle to Surrender," the article informed readers that the atomic bombs did not influence Hirohito's decision to surrender or have any impact on the outcome of the war. According to Fellers, Japan surrendered because Hirohito "dared face down his own fanatic militarists," usurped their power, and compelled them by "sheer strength of will to surrender a defeated country to a superior enemy."[18]

Among the last-minute changes to the manuscript was a glowing reference to Hoover's recommendation to Truman in May 1945. Again the account omitted his proposed sacrifice of Korea and Taiwan. Fellers also revised the article to show that Hirohito had taken the initiative for ending the war in February, just as Hoover instructed, although his own sources did not support that claim. The article entirely neglected Suzuki's response to the Potsdam Declaration, even though at the time Fellers had been deeply dismayed by the prime minister's evident rejection of the ultimatum.

"Hirohito's Struggle to Surrender" was published in the *Reader's Digest* in July 1947. Fellers also arranged for publication in the Japanese edition of the magazine, a copy of which was shown to Hirohito. Communicating through one of his advisors, His Majesty expressed his sincere appreciation to Fellers for his contribution to history.[19]

Although Fellers later claimed that "Hirohito's Struggle to Surrender" generated universally favorable responses, he did not supplant Stimson's explanation for the war's end. Nor did he contribute to Republican victory in 1948. Truman became president in his own right, and Dean Acheson, one of the emperor's strongest critics, became secretary of state. The new secretary had his work cut out for him. As Acheson noted in his memoirs, when he replaced George Marshall as secretary of state, Chiang Kai-shek was about to fall from power, and when he fell, he fell on Acheson. The victory of the Chinese Communists over the Nationalists was only the most dramatic failure of American policy in the years immediately following Japan's defeat. Outside of Japan, conditions in the region had steadily deteriorated. The war with Japan had ended, but there was no peace for Asia. Korea remained divided, with a Soviet-backed communist regime in the North and an American-backed anticommunist regime in the South. Communist-led insurgencies challenged colonial rule in French Indochina, Malaya, and Indonesia. The American-sponsored government in the newly independent Philippines also faced armed opposition from communist rebels.

The dismal situation in Asia, as well as the harsh reality of Soviet domination in Eastern and Central Europe, naturally led commentators to ask how events had turned so quickly against America's interest and what, if anything, could have been done to prevent the situation now confronting American officials.[20] Hanson Baldwin, the *New York Times'* military analyst, offered one of the first examinations of the causes of America's misfortune. Baldwin charged that American strategists had focused narrowly on military policy without considering the nation's political objectives. Baldwin's trenchant critique, titled *Great Mistakes of the War*, identified unconditional surrender as the single biggest political mistake of the war.[21] Baldwin argued that it had prolonged the war with Germany and Japan by removing any incentive for those governments to seek peace. The consequences of that mistake were particularly severe in the case of Japan. By insisting on unconditional surrender and refusing to compromise on the emperor, the Roosevelt and Truman administrations failed to capitalize on Japan's willingness ·to surrender. Having rejected diplomacy, the Americans compounded that mistake by exaggerating Tokyo's capacity to continue the war. Those mistakes led them to seek Russian aid in defeating Japan when it was no longer needed. Thus, the war ended with the needless slaughter of hundreds of thousands of Japanese and Soviet domination of northeast Asia. That situation was made even more excruciating when one considered that the Truman administration ultimately compromised on the emperor.[22]

Baldwin was forceful in denouncing American strategic myopia, but he also hedged his argument in places. Unlike Fellers, he conceded that no one could know for sure if Japan would have surrendered, although he was almost certain they would.[23] At the very least, the U.S. could have bided its time to see if Japan's peace feelers produced results. Baldwin was

Hanson Baldwin. U.S. Army Pictorial Center.

especially adamant in criticizing Roosevelt's decision to seek Russia's assistance and pay for it with Chinese concessions. He did not explain how the Russians could be kept out of Manchuria, which was the crux of the problem Roosevelt and Marshall faced. As Marshall noted in his discussion with Stimson, the question was not whether the Russians would attack Japan, but whether they would attack Japanese forces when it would aid the American war effort. The Russians were coming. Was it better to effect some limits on their expansion through agreement or remain aloof and let them come in with no strings attached? One could argue that Roosevelt made the wrong choice, especially because he treated the Chinese so shabbily. But Roosevelt was playing a weak hand, and it is difficult to see how the postwar situation in northeast Asia would have been much different, whatever he chose.

There was less to Baldwin's argument than the average reader would have realized. Baldwin, like Fellers and many other critics of unconditional surrender, assumed that Japanese leaders, including Hirohito, were concerned only with preserving the monarchy as a hollowed-out symbol of the Japanese people. That was not the case, and Baldwin knew it. During the last days of the war, when the Japanese appeared to balk at Truman's demand that the emperor's authority would be subject to the Allied commander-in-chief, Baldwin wrote that "such a stipulation was absolutely essential to the purposes for which we fought, *if the Emperor were to be permitted to remain at all.*" Baldwin went on to explain how the throne was "indissolubly linked" with Japan's "reactionary and feudalistic military class" that had led the country to war.[24] Four years later, however, he ignored his own argument and asserted that a compromise on unconditional surrender would have ended the war on terms acceptable to Japan and the United States.

On several occasions in his brief treatise, Baldwin bolstered his argument by citing information collected by the United States Strategic Bombing Survey (USSBS), a government organization charged with assessing the effectiveness of strategic bombing in the war. In its summary report *Japan's Struggle to End the War*, published in 1946, the USSBS concluded that Japan would have surrendered by November 1945, even if the atomic bombs had not been used. Baldwin was one of the first of many critics to use the report to argue that the atomic bombs were not needed to defeat Japan. The report did not directly criticize the policy of unconditional surrender, but it did so by implication. Historians have since shown that the report was marred by serious errors. One of the authors' main objectives was to make the case for an independent air force. The report was written in haste, ignored contradictory evidence, and was bureaucratically self-serving.[25] Nevertheless, it appeared to give government approval to the view that Japan was close to surrendering when the bombs were used.

Admiral Leahy was another important source for Baldwin's assertion that Japan was on its last legs by early 1945 and that neither the Russians nor the atomic bombs were needed to end the war.[26] Baldwin favored Leahy's preferred strategy of blockade because the Navy's control of the sea promised to produce victory with a minimal loss of life. Baldwin did not explain, however, what Leahy meant by "victory." As has been noted, Leahy favored conceding on the emperor question even if it meant allowing Hirohito to preserve all the prerogatives of the throne. Leahy was willing to leave Japan's ruling structure intact and let the supposed moderates resume control of Japan. He also opposed an occupation of Japan, which would have made the prosecution of war criminals problematic and negated any chance of reforming Japanese society. That assertion also ignored Leahy's parochial interest in claiming that the Navy had defeated Japan, a claim that became especially important after the atomic bombs appeared to throw the viability of conventional forces in doubt.

Leahy's memoir, *I Was There*, was published in 1950. It soon became another standard source for those who believed that Japan was already defeated before the atomic bombs and Soviet entry into the war. One of the most frequently cited passages was the admiral's rueful observation that the Army did not understand that the Navy, with some help from the Air Force, had defeated Japan. Leahy's statement ignored Japan's preparations for defense of the homeland, the millions of soldiers on the Asian mainland, and the fanatical arsenal of thousands of suicide craft deployed for use against the invaders. The admiral's condescending tone and his cavalier dismissal of those circumstances led one Army historian to sarcastically declare that it was a pity that "the U.S. Navy could not surrender to the U.S. government on behalf of the Japanese army."[27]

Unconditional surrender came under attack by another admiral in the early postwar period. Ellis Zacharias, who was promoted to the rank of rear admiral upon retirement, churned out a series of articles after the war that trumpeted the potential of psychological warfare. Writing in popular magazines such as *Look* and the *Saturday Evening Post*, as well as the more specialized *United Nations World*, Zacharias went at his subject with the same freewheeling style that got him into hot water near the end of the war. In

November 1945, "Eighteen Words That Bagged Japan" told the story of how
Zacharias produced the propaganda broadcast that assured the Japanese that
surrender would entitle them to the rights guaranteed under the Atlantic
Charter. Zacharias insisted that he was authorized to make that controversial
speech by Navy secretary James Forrestal.[28] As the title implies, Zacharias
claimed that his reference to the Atlantic Charter paved the way for Japan's
willingness to surrender, although the link between his broadcast and Japan's
surrender, though asserted, was not shown. Zacharias glossed over the fact
that it took two atomic bombs and Russian entry into the war before the
Japanese offered to surrender. He also ignored completely that it was not
American policy to assure the Axis powers the protections provided by the
Atlantic Charter.

Over the next several years, Zacharias became increasingly critical of the
Navy brass and other Washington denizens who, as he saw it, had stymied
his efforts to transform war through psychological warfare. "The A-Bomb
Was Not Needed" (1949) was followed by the even more accusatory "How
We Bungled the Japanese Surrender," published in June 1950, three weeks
before the outbreak of the Korean War. Zacharias persistently claimed
that his broadcasts and other propaganda measures had prepared Japan to
surrender and that the war could have been ended sooner if his mulish
superiors and the shortsighted politicians in the administration had heeded
his advice. "We now know," he wrote, "that without those extreme measures," meaning the atomic bombs and Russian entry into the war, "Japan
would have quit by September 15." How we knew and why September 15
instead of some other day, he did not say. Nevertheless, Zacharias's salvos
clearly discomfited his former colleagues in uniform. Publication of "The
A-Bomb Was Not Needed" prompted Alfred Kohlberg, the chairman of the
pro-Chiang American China Policy Association, to ask whether Zacharias
was really a former naval officer. "I regret the admission," came the reply,
"but Zacharias' association with the Navy is bona fide."[29]

Although there were other critics of unconditional surrender and
America's use of atomic weapons writing in the immediate postwar period, Fellers, Baldwin, and Zacharias stood out for their claims of insider
knowledge. All three agreed that Japan was ripe for surrender during the
summer of 1945. And all three deplored the unnecessary loss of Japanese
lives as well as the gains made by the Soviet Union in northeast Asia.
Whereas Fellers's rebuttal to Stimson focused on decision-making in Tokyo,
Baldwin and Zacarias redirected readers' attention to Washington. Unlike

Stimson, they found much there that disturbed them. Zacharias believed that his government's bungling derived from interservice rivalry and hidebound resistance to new modes of warfare. Baldwin blamed America's "strategic astigmatism" on a lack of imagination, a sterile separation of military strategy from political objectives, and ineffective bureaucratic processes that deprived policymakers of vital information. Fellers believed that a failure to know one's enemy, racial prejudice, and a desire for vengeance blinded Americans to the opportunities for peace before August 1945. Despite his private suspicions of communist infiltration in the State Department, Fellers initially refrained from blaming subversives for Washington's inability to respond constructively to Hirohito's alleged overtures. That was about to change.

On January 21, 1950, after two years of trials, Alger Hiss, a former State Department official, was convicted of having lied under oath about his role as a Soviet agent in the 1930s. A graduate of Harvard Law School, Hiss had clerked for liberal Supreme Court justice Felix Frankfurter and served in several New Deal agencies before joining the State Department. He attended the Yalta Conference and helped organize the United Nations. Hiss's conviction provided conservative Republicans with the evidence they sought to make the connection between the New Deal, liberal internationalism, and communist subversion. On February 9, Republican Senator Joseph McCarthy announced that he had the names of fifty-seven individuals who were sympathetic to the Communist Party, and who were still making foreign policy for the United States. McCarthy declared that, like Hiss, these "bright young men who were born with silver spoons in their mouths" had betrayed their country to the Russians. According to McCarthy, those looking for an explanation for the rise of communism in Asia need look no further than these individuals. The collapse of Chiang Kai-shek, McCarthy claimed, could be traced directly to foreign service officers, the China hands, who were sympathetic to the Chinese Communists.

McCarthy's sensational allegations were immediately called into question by reporters who noted that he kept changing the number of subversives he found: initially it was 205; then 57, the number entered into the *Congressional Record*; and still later, 207. Attempting to discredit McCarthy and expose him as a fraud, the Truman administration supported hearings into his charges by a special subcommittee of the Senate Foreign Relations Committee. That effort ended in failure. Before the subcommittee could complete its work, a new crisis erupted in Asia that appeared to give credence to McCarthy's charges and intensified the hunt for subversives at home.[30]

On June 25, 1950, forces of the communist Democratic People's Republic of Korea (North Korea) attacked South Korea (the Republic of Korea) across the thirty-eighth parallel. Within days, the attack turned into a rout as American-armed South Korean troops retreated to the southern end of the peninsula. The Truman administration responded to the invasion by sending troops from Japan under MacArthur's command to the aid of South Korea. The Americans and South Koreans established a defensive perimeter around the port city of Pusan and began to build up for a counterattack. In September, MacArthur staged an amphibious landing farther up the peninsula on the western coast at the port of Inchon, near the capital of Seoul. The audacious flanking movement coincided with the breakout from Pusan and quickly routed the North Koreans. In late September the Joint Chiefs approved the advance of MacArthur's forces, designated as the United Nations Command (UNC), to cross the thirty-eighth parallel and unify Korea, providing they did not encounter Chinese or Soviet troops.

In late October MacArthur's forces clashed with elements of the Chinese People's Volunteer Force, which had entered the country to prevent the collapse of the North Korean government. The Chinese Communists launched a second, larger offensive against UNC forces in late November and eventually drove MacArthur's men back to the thirty-eighth parallel. Fighting off Chinese pursuers and bitter cold, the American Eighth Army embarked on the longest retreat in the history of the U.S. Army.

As the situation stabilized, MacArthur began calling for authority to attack air bases in China and recommended "unleashing" Chinese Nationalist forces on Taiwan against the mainland. Despite instructions to tone down his rhetoric, MacArthur persisted. In April 1951, congressman Joseph Martin read on the floor of the House of Representatives a letter from MacArthur criticizing Truman's refusal to expand the war into China. Truman had had enough and relieved MacArthur of his commands and recalled him to the United States.

MacArthur's recall infuriated the general's admirers in the United States. Republicans spoke of making the martyred hero a candidate for president. Under public pressure, the Democratic-led Senate arranged for an inquiry into MacArthur's dismissal. The hearings, held jointly by the Senate Armed Services and Foreign Affairs Committees, began on May 3 and quickly expanded into an inquest into the failure of American policy in Asia since

World War II.[31] Much of the investigation focused on America's alleged abandonment of Chiang Kai-shek, but the senators also constructed a chain of causation that began with unconditional surrender, which was linked to American unwillingness to respond to Japanese peace overtures because of a rigid refusal to compromise on the emperor, which, in turn, necessitated Soviet entry into the war to accomplish Japan's total defeat, which led, inevitably, to the downfall of the Chinese Nationalists.

There were several crucial pieces of evidence to this argument. One was the allegation, made by Iowa Republican Senator Bourke Hickenlooper, that in February 1945 Hirohito had told Soviet ambassador Malik of his desire to have Stalin act as a mediator between Japan and the United States. Hickenlooper did not cite his source for that statement, but it was most likely Fellers's article.[32] The second, introduced by California Republican William Knowland, was an article by Walter Trohan in the August 19 *Washington Times-Herald*. Trohan claimed that in January 1945, two days before Roosevelt left for Yalta, he received a Japanese peace offer "identical with the terms subsequently concluded by his successor Harry S. Truman." The offer, according to Trohan, was based of five separate overtures made to MacArthur's headquarters. MacArthur, according to the article, submitted that information to Roosevelt in a forty-page memorandum and recommended negotiations immediately. The entreaties received by MacArthur proposed "abject surrender of everything but the person of the Emperor," and included an offer that "the Emperor become a puppet in the hands of American forces."[33]

The idea that, in January 1945, the emperor authorized his representatives to tell MacArthur that he was willing to have the Americans occupy Japan, liberate Taiwan and Korea, surrender war criminals for trial, regulate Japanese industry, and abandon all prerogatives of the throne was patently ridiculous. Not surprisingly, Trohan's fantastic story received little attention when it was published amid the celebration of the war's end. Republication in the Senate hearings gave it second life. In the crisis atmosphere of the Korean War, it quickly became an article of faith among conspiratorially minded critics of Roosevelt. According to this story, by failing to act on MacArthur's recommendation and adhering stubbornly to unconditional surrender, Roosevelt had prolonged the war and opened northeast Asia to Soviet penetration. No evidence of MacArthur's supposed report was ever found. That only confirmed critics' worst fears about the lengths Roosevelt's men would go to serve the Kremlin's ends. The story survived for decades as part of the indictment against FDR.

As the MacArthur hearings were winding down, the Senate Internal Security Committee opened an investigation into Communist infiltration in the Institute of Pacific Relations (IPR), an international think tank believed to have shaped policy toward China and Japan during World War II. The hearings soon zeroed in on accusations that one of IPR's most prominent members, Owen Lattimore, had, while working for the Office of War Information and State Department, promoted policies that undermined Chiang's government and sown chaos in Japan. Also caught up in the inquiry was John Carter Vincent, a China specialist who was appointed by Acheson as head of the Office of Far Eastern Affairs after Japan surrendered. Among those offering testimony against Lattimore and Vincent was Eugene Dooman.

The thrust of Dooman's testimony centered on Lattimore's hostility toward the emperor and his recommendation, published in his *Solution in Asia*, that Hirohito be exiled to China.[34] Dooman also fingered Vincent as Lattimore's accomplice in trying to abolish the monarchy. Dooman pointed out that the Communists also wanted to depose Hirohito and destroy the monarchy. Asked why the Communists would wish to abolish the Japanese monarchy, Dooman replied that "they knew perfectly well, of course, that communism and a monarchial system were incongruous. Therefore, the first thing was to get rid of the monarchial system."[35] The Senate committee bolstered Dooman's depiction of Lattimore and Vincent as subversives by presenting as evidence articles from the Communist *Daily Worker* calling for the abolition of the monarchy and attacking Grew and Dooman.

During his testimony, Dooman also described at length the efforts that he and Joseph Grew made to modify unconditional surrender during the spring and summer of 1945. As part of that testimony, he claimed, inaccurately, that the draft statement that he and Grew wrote became the Potsdam Declaration. It will be recalled that the interservice committee that drafted the Potsdam Declaration found Dooman's document unacceptable because of its general opaqueness, especially on the fate of the emperor. It would have complicated Dooman's testimony, however, if he had had to explain why he had not been willing to include a forthright promise on the fate of the emperor in his warning to Japan. Dooman's convenient memory lapse spared him that embarrassment and kept the spotlight on Lattimore and Vincent.[36]

The Senate hearings became important foundational texts for a bevy of conspiracists seeking to find the culprits responsible for America's Far Eastern debacle. Most of those authors had been members of the anti-interventionist wing of the Republican Party before Pearl Harbor. Like Herbert Hoover, they saw a symmetry in the way the war with Japan began and ended. The prime mover in these catastrophes was Franklin Roosevelt, a man whose lust for power and socialistic tendencies provoked the attack on Pearl Harbor and prolonged the war so that Russia could exact its pound of flesh from China.[37]

John Flynn's *While You Slept: Our Tragedy in Asia and Who Made It* (1951) was an early effort to awaken Americans to the danger created by FDR's misbegotten policies. Flynn had been a columnist for the *New Republic* before World War II, and his previous books, including one on the domestic threat posed by the New Deal, had been published by major commercial houses.[38] *While You Slept* was his third book with Devin-Adair, a small firm that originally published books on ornithology and Irish poetry but shifted to listing books with a libertarian or conservative bent. In signing on with Devin-Adair, Flynn joined a small group of conservative authors determined to defend American liberty, as they understood it, from socialism and authoritarianism. Henry Regnery Publishing had a similar mission, as did the much smaller Bookmailer Press, which was started by a former CIA officer.

Together these publishing firms would keep alive the anti-interventionist conservatism of Herbert Hoover in the 1950s and 1960s. The Republican Party had been their natural home in the 1930s and 1940s, but as the GOP, led by Dwight Eisenhower, embraced the Cold War internationalism of the Truman administration, conspiracy-minded authors like Flynn drifted to the margins of American political life. Isolated from the mainstream, they formed a loosely knit community of activists. They read each other's work, publicized it, shared information and sources, and gossiped with unbridled enthusiasm.

Flynn's *While You Slept* blamed the Asian maelstrom on Roosevelt's secret urge to be "President of the World" and the Communists who "crawled out of their holes and came flooding into Washington." According to Flynn, the Communists, abetted by FDR, sold Stalin to the Americans as a trustworthy ally, filling the airwaves and printed media with tales of Russian heroism. The key moment in America's road to disaster in Asia came at the Casablanca Conference when Roosevelt announced the policy of unconditional surrender, which Flynn noted would lead to the destruction of Japanese power and secure for Stalin one of his key objectives in the war. Roosevelt, according to Flynn, made a horrible situation worse by seeking Soviet entry into the war when it was not needed. As evidence, he cited Admiral Leahy's memoir that Roosevelt, like the Army, did not seem to understand that the Navy had beaten Japan already. Nationalist China paid the price for Roosevelt's failures, but the Soviets were not finished. Flynn warned that Japan was also being readied for revolution. When Japan surrendered, Flynn explained, Reds and Pinks in the State Department, led by Dean Acheson and John Carter Vincent, openly challenged MacArthur and initiated radical reforms designed to throw the country into the waiting arms of the Communists.[39]

MacArthur was one of the few heroes of *While You Slept*. The general, according to Flynn, saved Japan from the Communist plot. By the time Flynn's book was published, MacArthur had been relieved of his commands in Asia. Most Republicans, especially anti-interventionists, believed that MacArthur was being made the scapegoat for the misdeeds of the Roosevelt and Truman administrations, most notably the decision to seek Soviet aid when Japan was already beaten. That element of the MacArthur myth became difficult to sustain with the publication in 1951 of James Forrestal's diaries and a U.S. Army publication titled *Washington Command Post*, one part of a multivolume series *The U.S. Army in World War II*. The Army's volume cited a memorandum by Brigadier General George Lincoln, the head of the Strategy and Policy Group, summarizing his meeting with MacArthur on February 25. Forrestal's diary contained the Navy secretary's summary of a meeting with MacArthur on February 28. Both sources showed that MacArthur wanted the United Sates to make sure that the Russians attacked Japanese troops in Manchuria before the Allies invaded Japan.[40]

Although both revelations received brief attention, they quietly slipped from view without much public comment. The matter was reopened in March 1955 when the State Department published its official diplomatic record of the Yalta Conference. Publication of the volume reignited the controversy over Roosevelt's handling of the Soviet Union and the question of Russian entry into the war against Japan. During one Senate session, Republican Styles Bridges attempted to refute allegations that MacArthur desired Soviet assistance against Japan by arguing that the general knew

Japan was on its last legs. Bridges offered as evidence a recent statement by MacArthur's former head of intelligence, Charles Willoughby, that two months before Yalta the general had informed his superiors that Japan was "nearing collapse," and that a month later he notified Washington that the Japanese were seeking Russian mediation to end the war.[41]

As accusations flew across the political aisle, Army historian Louis Morton asserted in *Reporter* magazine that MacArthur had told Washington that Russian aid was needed to defeat Japan. Courtney Whitney, MacArthur's former aide, promptly issued a statement denouncing Morton's claim and, for good measure, the evidence from Forrestal's diaries as well.[42] In September, the Army counterattacked by producing and releasing an internal study titled "The Entry of the Soviet Union into the War Against Japan, 1941–1945." The study, which was a compilation of documents and extracts with supporting narrative, showed that on at least three occasions in 1945, MacArthur had told the Army that a Soviet attack on Manchuria must precede the American invasion of Japan. Even more embarrassing, one of the reproduced documents showed that MacArthur expected Stalin to ask for Manchuria, Korea, and possibly part of north China, and that he, MacArthur, thought that would be acceptable, providing the Russians invaded Manchuria as soon as possible after Germany's defeat. Faced with irrefutable evidence showing that he had wanted Soviet aid against Japan, MacArthur changed the subject and said that he had never been consulted about the concessions made to Russia at Yalta. No one said he had. What had been in dispute, and was no longer, was his contention that he had not sought Soviet entry into the war in 1945.[43]

The alleged sellout at Yalta was an important issue in the Republican Party's critique of the Democrats' foreign policy. MacArthur's need to remain in good standing with the right wing of the GOP had led him to lie about his support for Russian participation in the war.[44] Although he was publicly revealed to have deceived his own supporters, that did not alter how many of MacArthur's admirers felt about the concessions made at Yalta. Elizabeth Churchill Brown, a former society columnist and wife of conservative columnist Constantine Brown, was so troubled by what she perceived as the Roosevelt administration's fawning attitude toward the Russians that she began her own inquiry into the wartime alliance. "Why did the United States have to be SO friendly?" she asked. "Why do we have to kiss them on the mouth?"[45]

In 1956, after more than two years at the task, she published her answer to those questions in *The Enemy at His Back*, an expose of the mysterious forces in American government and society that were betraying the United States on behalf of the Soviet Union. Brown was a diligent researcher, combing the *Congressional Record*, the IPR and MacArthur hearings, and numerous newspapers to develop her story. She also read the Army's "The Entry of the Soviet Union into the War Against Japan, 1941–1951" but ignored that slender volume's damning evidence against MacArthur. Instead, she took at face value the claims made in Charles Willoughby's *MacArthur, 1941–1951* that MacArthur opposed Soviet entry into the war. Brown repeated the now-familiar theme that Suzuki was appointed to arrange for Japan's surrender, and she noted the numerous Japanese peace feelers who were mysteriously ignored by Roosevelt and Truman. Japan was offering uncon ditional surrender, she said, but someone was always obstructing the chance for peace, prolonging the war, and serving Soviet interests. A completely vanquished Japan, she reminded readers, was what the Russians wanted.[16]

Elizabeth Churchill Brown. Hoover Institution Archives.

Brown was not able to interest Devin-Adair or Henry Regnery in her book, but she succeeded in getting Bookmailer to publish it. Senator William Knowland wrote the foreword, and congressman Frances E. Walter, chairman of the House Un-American Activities Committee, Albert Wedemeyer, former American commander of the China theater, and William M. McGovern, a professor at Northwestern University, were quoted on the book jacket. Brown used her own and her husband's extensive contacts to advertise the book. Syngman Rhee, wife of the president of the Republic of Korea, read the book and asked Brown to serve as a publicist for her government. Republican Senators Barry Goldwater of Arizona and William Jenner of Indiana both entered reviews of *Enemy at His Back* into the *Congressional Record*. William F. Buckley, Jr., publisher of the conservative *National Review* and already on his way to becoming one of the leading conservative intellectuals of the second half of the twentieth century, sent "Liz" a congratulatory note and arranged for a review in his journal.[47]

Buckley's magazine was more than happy to serve as a forum for authors seeking to expose the deceit they believed was at the heart of the Roosevelt and Truman administrations. In 1958, the *National Review* published "Hiroshima: Assault on a Beaten Foe," by Harry Elmer Barnes, a prolific critic of Roosevelt and a titan of what was known as historical revisionism, a mode of inquiry that challenged the establishment view of the past. A champion of many liberal causes, Barnes earned a PhD in history from Columbia University. Although he supported American entry into World War I, he subsequently became a critic of American involvement in that conflict. In the 1930s, he became an anti-interventionist. After December 1941, Barnes set out to prove that Roosevelt had provoked the Japanese and withheld from American commanders intelligence revealing Japan's plans to attack Pearl Harbor. From the 1940s until his death in 1968, Barnes self-published his books. With most publishing venues closed to him, Barnes was happy to have his work in Buckley's magazine, although he said he had nothing in common with the publisher's ideology.[48]

Barnes began his article on Hiroshima by declaring, "It has been incontrovertibly proven that Japan offered to surrender six months before the atom bombing, which Mr. Truman defends as necessary." Barnes's source for this bold claim was Walter Trohan's article of August 19, 1945. According to Barnes, an unnamed Army intelligence officer had given Trohan a copy of MacArthur's forty-page memorandum detailing the Japanese peace offers because he feared that Roosevelt would have it destroyed. The intelligence officer's one condition was that Trohan could not publish the information until after Japan surrendered. The terms allegedly authorized by the emperor satisfied virtually every American demand agreed to at the end of the war. Barnes noted that when Trohan published his scoop, it occasioned little or no comment in the press. Tellingly, neither the White House nor State Department had challenged the veracity of the story. In 1951, after he was recalled to the United States, MacArthur provided the ultimate verification of the story's accuracy. After MacArthur settled into his suite at New York's Waldorf Astoria, his neighbor, Herbert Hoover, showed the general Trohan's article. MacArthur "confirmed its accuracy in every detail and without qualification." Here was "absolutely accurate and convincing evidence" that Roosevelt knew that the Japanese were trying to surrender and were willing to do so on American terms, six months before Hiroshima. Readers wanting to know why Roosevelt would fail to act in such a situation only had to peer down at the article's next subheading for an answer: "And Stalin Profited."

Further into the article, Barnes swerved in an unexpected direction. Like Hoover and other anti-interventionists, he believed the atomic bombs were a wanton act of violence against unarmed civilians. However, he differed from the anti-interventionists in arguing that Truman had used the bombs on an already defeated Japan to intimidate the Soviet Union. In making this case, Barnes drew on articles by journalist Norman Cousins and British physicist P. M. S. Blackett. It was a complex argument. Barnes argued that Roosevelt arrogantly rejected MacArthur's entreaty to respond to the Japanese peace offers, and, because of that decision, he had to make concessions to get Russian assistance in the war. Those concessions strengthened Russia. That made Roosevelt's successor drop the atomic bombs as a form of intimidation to check Soviet aggressiveness. The sad conclusion was that hundreds of thousands of Japanese were slaughtered because of Roosevelt's foolish insistence on unconditional surrender.[49]

Barnes's article defied easy categorization. Barnes had combined elements of the right-wing critique of Roosevelt with what would come to be called New Left revisionism to excoriate Democrats for unconditional surrender and the atomic destruction of Hiroshima and Nagasaki. The unifying feature of the piece was an extraordinary hatred of Roosevelt. How else to explain his unquestioning trust in MacArthur's word after the general had been caught lying about his advice on Soviet entry into the war? Even Bonner

Fellers found Trohan's story unbelievable. In 1960, Fellers told Barnes that Trohan's story could not be true. Fellers said that he had never seen the memorandum Trohan described and that if MacArthur's staff had produced such a document, he would have known about it.[50]

By the early 1960s, conservatives continued to be the most consistent critics of unconditional surrender. They condemned the policy for prolonging the war, victimizing Japanese civilians, and benefitting the Soviet Union. There were also differences within this school of thought. East Coast internationalist Republicans like Grew, Stimson, and McCloy did not accuse proponents of unconditional surrender of following the Communist line. Eugene Dooman was an exception. He fell in with the Old Guard Republicans, the anti-interventionists, like Hoover and Fellers, who believed that unconditional surrender furthered Communist interests by exposing China to Russian intervention and destabilizing Japan. There would more right-wing critiques, but they never gained notoriety outside the right wing of the Republican Party.[51]

In 1964, Barry Goldwater thrilled conservatives by winning the Republican nomination. During the campaign, the senator tried but failed to unite the party's right wing, which included the far-right John Birch Society, with the moderate wing of the party.[52] Goldwater was trounced by the liberal Lyndon Baines Johnson. Adding insult to injury, Johnson set out to outdo his idol, and the right wing's nemesis, Franklin Roosevelt, in passing liberal legislation. On October 20, 1964, shortly before the election, Herbert Hoover died at the age of ninety.

The former president had been an extremely productive author in the last decade of his life, publishing more than seven books. It could have been eight. When he died, Hoover had all but finished what he called his magnum opus, a massive study of World War II that was eventually published in 2011 as *Freedom Betrayed*. Hoover's opus was a wide-ranging history of the coming of the war and the policies of Roosevelt and Truman. Not surprisingly, the former president was sharply critical of wartime policy toward Japan, especially unconditional surrender. Hoover's indictment of the policy reprised most of the criticisms that had been aired since 1945. The Americans failed to take advantage of the opening created by Suzuki's appointment and ignored the many peace feelers Tokyo put out. In short, American rigidity led to missed opportunities to induce Japan's early surrender and played into Russian hands by prolonging the war.[53]

In making his case, Hoover continued the pattern of most critics by treating the peace feelers as authorized by the government. In respect to the terms of surrender, he was willing to accommodate Japan far more than most Americans were. This was an honest disagreement, but Hoover was unwilling to even entertain the possibility that he might be wrong. Instead, he cited a 1960 letter from MacArthur approving Hoover's recommendation to Truman in 1945 and assuring the former president that the Japanese would have accepted it.[54] It is unclear how MacArthur could have been so certain that the Japanese would have accepted surrender under the terms recommended by Hoover. Nonetheless, it is safe to say that they would have approved of Hoover's willingness to leave them in control of Taiwan and Korea. Mercifully, there was no mention of the fabled long-lost MacArthur memorandum of January 1945.

Hoover's death and the fate of his magnum opus seemed to symbolize the passing of the conservative critique. Despite a sustained campaign over nearly twenty years to expose the tragic consequences of unconditional surrender, conservative critics had been unable to sway public opinion to accept their views. The issue was disappearing from public discourse. And then something unexpected happened. Unconditional surrender began to receive scrutiny from a new group of critics. This time, they came at their subject from the left wing of the political spectrum.

In 1965, Gar Alperovitz, a political economist and historian, published a landmark study in what would be known as New Left revisionism. Titled *Atomic Diplomacy*, Alperovitz's book amplified the argument made by Barnes and others that the atomic bombs were really used to intimidate the Soviet Union. Alperovitz outdid Barnes, however, in assigning diabolical motives to Truman. In Alperovitz's rendering, Truman knew the Japanese were trying to surrender, but he could not let them do so until he dropped the atomic bombs. Central to Alperovitz's argument was the idea that Truman sought a delayed diplomatic showdown with Stalin. Truman, according to Alperovitz, believed that use of the atomic bomb would give him diplomatic leverage to force the Russians to comply with American desires in Eastern Europe and northeast Asia. In order to implement that strategy, Truman had to ignore evidence that the Japanese were trying to surrender. Strict adherence to unconditional surrender became essential to Truman's larger strategy. Thus, even though the president had privately agreed that he would be willing to let the Japanese keep the emperor, he could not make that concession before the atomic bombs were dropped.[55]

*Atomic Diplomacy* received a level of attention that the conservative critics of unconditional surrender could only dream of. It was published by Simon and Schuster, a major commercial house, and appeared in time for the twentieth anniversary of the end of the war with Japan. It also matched the spirit of the times by questioning authority and shifting much of the blame for the Cold War on the U.S. That was a key difference between Alperovitz and the conservative critics of unconditional surrender. Alperovitz echoed the conservatives' argument that Japan was ready to surrender by early summer 1945, but he stood other elements of the conservative critique on their head. In *Atomic Diplomacy*, Truman bore responsibility for abandoning Roosevelt's policy of cooperation with Stalin. Truman, not communist sympathizers in the State Department, sought to prolong the war. Conservatives argued that a delayed surrender benefitted the Russians, but in Alperovitz's rendering, it benefitted the Americans.

It is telling that *Atomic Diplomacy* was instantly labeled revisionist, as if the conservative critics of unconditional surrender and the use of the atomic bombs had never existed.[56] Indeed, apart from Leahy and Zacharias, the conservative critics went virtually unnoticed in his study. Nevertheless, Alperovitz's thesis shared some similarities with that of the conservatives, the chief one being that Japan paid the price for American misdeeds. Alperovitz's work also followed, unknowingly, the conservatives' tendency to blur the distinction between Japan's search for peace and Truman's insistence on surrender. Like the conservatives, he underestimated Japanese determination to preserve the emperor's position, and with it their political structure, in the summer of 1945.

*Atomic Diplomacy* became a touchstone in the developing critique of America's Cold War policy. It readily fit into a growing narrative of American international aggressiveness that developed during the Vietnam War. New Left scholars, as the historians writing in this vein were called, challenged the orthodox interpretation that depicted U.S. diplomacy as a response to Soviet aggression. Subsequent historians writing about the atomic bombs and unconditional surrender modified Alperovitz's thesis. Most rejected the argument that Truman had followed a strategy of delayed showdown with Stalin. They agreed that the bombs served a political purpose in warning the Russians, but that that was a bonus; most concluded that Truman used the bombs to end the war as quickly as possible. Over the next thirty years, the critique of American policy at the end of the war shifted direction. Truman's claim that he faced a stark choice between invasion and use of the bombs was questioned, as was his assertion that the bombs saved a half million lives. Some historians argued that Soviet entry into the war, not the atomic bombs, was the decisive factor in ending the war. In this respect, they took the opposite position of the conservatives who had argued that Soviet assistance was not needed to end the war. An important part of these new debates was the argument that the United States missed a chance to end the war through diplomacy.

Those were the views that historians sought to represent in the Smithsonian Institution's 1995 exhibit commemorating the fiftieth anniversary of the end of the war. The centerpiece of the proposed exhibit was the *Enola Gay*, the B-29 that delivered the bomb that leveled Hiroshima and ushered in the nuclear age. The exhibit's organizers intended to make its exploration of the end of the war with Japan a challenging historical inquiry that inspired visitors to contemplate the complexities of the past. That objective ran headlong into the goals of the Air Force Association, a lobbying group that viewed the Smithsonian's Air and Space Museum and the *Enola Gay* as monuments to air power.[57] It is possible that no amount of negotiation could have reconciled the goals of these two groups, but the exhibit's organizers started off on the wrong foot and never recovered. In seeking to encourage visitors to see the war from the other side, the earliest drafts of the museum text presented a lopsided narrative that made the Americans look like aggressors. One of the more notorious lines in the first draft read that for Americans, this was a war of vengeance; for Japanese, "it was a war to defend their unique culture against Western imperialism."

That and other missteps outraged representatives of the Air Force Association and veterans' groups. The offended parties protested to Congress, the source of the museum's funds, and in the press, and launched a publicity campaign in defense of their position. The battle soon careened into the realm of the cultural politics of the mid-1990s. Politicians and commentators denounced the exhibit's creators as left-wing critics who perversely sought to turn America's victory in the Good War into another milestone in the cavalcade of shame they called American history. There was no chance for conciliation after that. Repeated rewrites of the exhibit text failed to satisfy the museum's opponents.[58]

One of the key elements of the exhibit deplored by critics was the early draft's suggestion that although Japanese peace feelers were tentative and confusing, "It is nonetheless possible to assert, at least in hindsight, that the United States should have paid closer attention to these signals from Japan."

"Like so many aspects of the 'decision to drop the bomb,'" it continued, "this matter will remain speculative and forever controversial." To highlight that conclusion, the exhibit devoted one of its "historical controversies" panels to the subject of unconditional surrender. The heading read "Would the war have ended sooner if the United States had guaranteed the Emperor's position?" Underneath, the text stated, "It is clear that American and Japanese leaders *might* have reached an agreement on Japanese surrender if the United States had made such an offer and the Suzuki government had been willing to communicate directly with the Truman administration."[59]

Unfortunately, that tentatively worded conjecture did not explain the differences within the Truman administration over the role of the emperor or the connections that liberals saw between unconditional surrender and the reform program they sought to implement. Absent from the exhibit's text and the ensuing debate was a discussion of the ideological roots of the debate in 1945. The text and its critics failed to explain why conservatives believed that Japan could be induced to surrender and why liberals rejected any proposals that failed to achieve Japan's unconditional surrender. Indeed, neither the exhibit's defenders nor detractors seemed aware that such an ideological division existed.

Critics lambasted the exhibit's authors as left-wing, anti-American snobs for even suggesting that there was an alternative to the bombs. Those critics seemed completely unaware that the strongest advocates of such an argument in 1945 were conservatives like Grew, Leahy, Stimson, and McCloy. They were even less aware that conservative anti-interventionists like Hoover, Bonner Fellers, and a significant number of Republican legislators favored accommodation with Japan. Conversely, the authors of the exhibit seemed unaware that liberals in 1945 viewed modification of unconditional surrender as an anti-Soviet act, the first shot in a Cold War that would rescue Japan's semi-feudal ruling class.

As the authors of the *Enola Gay* exhibit noted, the debate was likely to continue indefinitely. That prediction proved more accurate than they could have imagined. In 1995, John McManus's essay "Dropping the Bomb" revived the far-right's thesis that Japan was ready to surrender as early as January 1945 and that the atomic bombs were unnecessary. Published in the John Birch Society magazine *The New American*, McManus's essay built its case against dropping the bomb on the familiar sources employed by other far-right critics of unconditional surrender. These included Walter Trohan's article, Leahy's memoir, Barnes's essay, Brown's work, and those of other conspiracy theorists. McManus castigated historians who ignored the allegedly unimpeachable evidence that Japan was trying to surrender as early as January 1945. Roosevelt's and Truman's refusal to respond to those initiatives, he said, meant that those who died after that date were victims of "the treacherous determination to extend the conflict in order to benefit the Soviet Union and use the bomb." Nevertheless, despite its similarities with those earlier works, McManus's essay added a new wrinkle to the far right's explanation for why the bombs were used. According to McManus, the bombs were dropped to hasten the day when Americans, driven by fear of a nuclear Armageddon, would surrender their sovereignty to the United Nations. The real winners, he added, were "the conspirators who had done their very best for Josef Stalin, Mao Tse-tung, and world government."[60]

Debate and reinterpretation of unconditional surrender remained a relevant topic in the early years of the twenty-first century as the United States prepared for war against Iraq. When opponents of the war argued that the United States could not successfully occupy and democratize Iraq, members of the George W. Bush administration, including the president, pointed to the American occupation of Japan as evidence that Americans had undertaken similar tasks in the past and succeeded.[61] Iraq would not be any different. John Dower, one of America's leading historians of modern Japan, disagreed. Dower cited many reasons why Japan would not serve as a model for Iraq. The cooperation of the Japanese people, the thorough rejection of Japan's wartime leaders, and, crucially, Japan's prewar democratic movements were essential to the occupation's success. Americans could not count on those conditions in Iraq, he said. Moreover, noted Dower, the success of the occupation of Japan's liberal program owed much to its New Deal roots. Land reform, new rights for labor, revision of the civil and penal codes, reform of educational institutions, and, of course, the new constitution, were all part of a liberal agenda developed during the war. The "remarkable success" of the occupation also owed much to the "charismatic" Douglas MacArthur, in whom ultimate authority to implement the desired reforms was granted. Significantly, Dower asserted that all these changes were facilitated by Japan's "unconditional surrender," which resulted in a "nonnegotiable" grant of authority to the victors.[62] The advocates of unconditional surrender could not have said it any better.

# Conclusion
## "They Wanted to Keep the Emperor"

As we observe the seventy-fifth anniversary of the surrender of Japan, it becomes clear that the terms on which that surrender took place remain among the most central and the most contested issues—and with good reason. Unconditional surrender was destined to be controversial because it was Roosevelt's policy. It incited the same ideological divisions as his domestic policies and extended those battles to the arenas of foreign policy and military strategy. My goal in this book has been to explain the reasons for the debate over unconditional surrender, so that we can better understand the decisions that Harry Truman and his advisors made and their short- and long-term ramifications. It comes down to two main conclusions about those decisions: that they were strongly influenced by ideological considerations and that the push to modify unconditional surrender was closely tied to concern over the consequences of Soviet entry into the war. A third conclusion is that the chance for a negotiated peace in 1945 was exceedingly slim, given that before August 14, the Japanese never indicated they were willing to accept a dramatic change in their political structure that would reduce the emperor to a symbol without authority or power.

FDR had established the policy of unconditional surrender in 1943 in Casablanca, a very different time and place than the one Harry Truman found himself in after Roosevelt's death and the end of the war in Europe. Roosevelt and General Marshall had always worried that Americans' resolve would weaken after Germany was defeated. But Truman was the one who had to deal with that situation. The new president assumed office amid growing signs of war weariness at home. Greeting him as he took FDR's place in the Oval Office were an increasingly assertive Congress intent on reclaiming lost prerogatives, an anxious business community worried about the lagging pace of reconversion, and an impatient public demanding a speedier demobilization of GIs. Soviet involvement in the Pacific War and the development of atomic weapons gave Truman additional options, but not without also creating additional complications.

During this pivotal moment in the war, the new president's advisors presented him with diverse options and sought to win his support for them through persuasion and political maneuvering. Truman listened carefully and read diligently, but mostly kept his own counsel. In the end, I would argue, this was the wisest course. The president's advisors often mistook his vague acknowledgment of their recommendations as approval and seemed under the illusion that he had no views of his own. Indeed, in some personal accounts of meetings during his first three months in office, the president almost seems invisible. At best, he is presented as an onlooker buffeted by competing opinions and with no firm ideas about the long-term objectives of the war. That was not the case.

Truman had reasons to keep his own counsel. The debate over the surrender of Japan signaled the end of coalition government in the United States. It was also a reflection of the ideological struggle taking shape at home. It could not have been lost on the new president that most of those who advocated revising unconditional surrender were Republicans, who also sought to weaken or eliminate wartime regulations on the economy and roll back New Deal programs. It mattered that the supporters of unconditional surrender were mostly liberal Democrats and the opponents were not.

At the heart of the argument was how to perceive the role of Hirohito and the monarchy. "They wanted to keep the Emperor," Truman wrote during the final days of the war. The president was referring to the Japanese. He could easily have included most of his advisors in that statement. Truman did not have a sophisticated understanding of the emperor's role in Japanese society. Few in the United States did. Some felt the emperor had been supportive of—and indeed critical to—the militarists. Others thought he was a benign presence wielding only symbolic power. Truman agreed with the first group, and in that respect his perception of Hirohito's part in the war was more accurate than that of his conservative advisors. How he arrived at that view is open to question. Truman repeatedly deflected recommendations from his advisors to promise the Japanese they could maintain the monarchy following surrender, but he was not inflexible. During the summer of 1945 he made several announcements clarifying unconditional surrender, culminating in the Potsdam Declaration. Each time, he stopped short of pledging to preserve Japan's imperial system. American public opinion, which went heavily against the emperor, was influential, but it was not the only reason Truman hedged. Intercepts revealed a Japanese government determined to avoid unconditional surrender through an all-out defense of the homeland. Deciphered diplomatic messages showed that Hirohito desired peace, but not if it meant surrender.

Would Japan have surrendered before the atomic bombs and Soviet entry into the war had Truman promised to preserve the monarchy? Speculation typically dwells on interpreting political conditions in Japan in the spring and summer of 1945. The dynamics of power in Tokyo were important, but focusing on the Japanese government's response puts the cart before the horse. The place to start is to ask what, precisely, would the Americans be offering Japan? Regarding the emperor, no one offered Truman a hard answer. Joseph Grew, Eugene Dooman, Herbert Hoover, and Henry Stimson were all over the map on the subject. Grew described the imperial institution as politically neutral, but privately he thought that Hirohito should abdicate. Dooman was adamant that the emperor should remain on the throne, but his draft statement on the subject was so convoluted that it read like a threat rather than an inducement. His contributions to the interdepartmental committee that drafted the Potsdam Declaration were no better. The uniformed officers on the committee regarded him as a hindrance and were happier when he was absent.

The proponents of modification frequently spoke of leaving Japan with a constitutional monarchy—and even used that phrase in the draft of the Potsdam Declaration—but they did not say what they meant by that. Did they have in mind something like the British monarchy? If so, the Japanese would have rejected that as an unacceptable assault on the *kokutai*. Stimson, Grew, Leahy, and Hoover all believed that elimination of the militarists would turn Hirohito into a figurehead. They told Truman that once the militarists were removed, the "moderates" would return Japan to the path of peaceful progress they had followed before the 1930s. Leahy, Stimson, and Hoover were so confident of that outcome that they doubted the Americans should bother to occupy Japan. Hoover even recommended that Japan keep control of Korea and Taiwan.

Yet, as Truman came to understand, the emperor of Japan was not a figurehead akin to the British monarch. It took the occupation and an American-drafted constitution to make him one. After the war, critics of unconditional surrender pointed to the continuation of Hirohito on the throne as proof that Japan would have surrendered before August had the Americans made a concession about the emperor. But the status of the emperor under the occupation was very different from what it had been before August 14. There is no evidence that the Japanese would have agreed to subordinate the emperor and the entire government to the Supreme Commander of the Allied Powers before the atomic bombs and Soviet entry into the war. Indeed, the deliberations of the Japanese Supreme Council show that in addition to maintaining the emperor's status, they would not make peace unless they could disarm themselves and try their own war criminals, all without the interference of an Allied occupation.

In a system as closed as Japan's, divining Japanese intentions about surrender was mainly guesswork and supposition. The only way that the Americans could ascertain what the Japanese were seeking was through MAGIC, Tokyo's propaganda broadcasts, and the preparations being made for the defense of Kyushu. What they learned was that the Japanese did not want to negotiate directly with the Americans but rather with the Soviets and that they sought peace as an alternative to surrender. Even then, the Japanese failed to define their minimum terms, a point that the frustrated Ambassador Sato made more than once.

In refusing to make concessions about the emperor's role after the war, Truman refused to abandon the original purpose of unconditional surrender—the elimination of the ideologies that enabled the conquest and subjugation of other peoples. Once the occupation began, Truman held to that position, even at the risk of his popularity. He made his views abundantly clear in September when MacArthur surprised the administration by announcing that he would need fewer troops than expected for the occupation. Despite mounting public demand to bring the boys home, Truman insisted that he would use as many men as were necessary "to assure the complete carrying out of the surrender and the adoption of the policies which we had already outlined to General MacArthur."[1]

Japan's surrender had global repercussions. At war's end, the Americans had unconditional control of Japan, but they could not extend that dominance to the Asian mainland. American power peaked with the occupation of Korea and the dispatch of Marines to China. These interventions, however, could not turn back the revolutionary tide sweeping across Asia. By 1947, as the confrontation with the Soviet Union intensified and China sank into civil war, observers understandably sought explanations for what seemed like a stunningly swift reversal of America's fortunes. It is not surprising that many commentators and politicians blamed Roosevelt and Truman for the supposed failures of American policy. Nor is it surprising that these critics fixed upon unconditional surrender as one of the main reasons for the catastrophe unfolding in Asia. It was not merely a blunder, they argued; it was part of a deliberate conspiracy to foment revolution in Asia and advance the interests of the Soviet Union. To make their case, they had to show that the war could have ended before the Russians entered and that Truman and his advisors had deliberately ignored Japan's overtures to further their plan for revolution in Asia. They went about their task with gusto.

In writing their alternative history of the war's end, these earlier revisionists relied on what would later come to be known as "alternative facts." Grew, Hoover, Bonner Fellers, and Douglas MacArthur suffered convenient memory lapses, falsified the record, and, in MacArthur's case, flat-out lied. Along the way, they impugned the motives of their opponents, trashed the careers of proponents of unconditional surrender, and provided ammunition for conspiracy theorists for decades to come.

History does repeat itself, the novelist George Eliot reminds us, but not without a slight change of costume, an observation that has been borne out by the afterlife of the unconditional surrender debate. By the mid-1960s, the dangers of nuclear holocaust and the grim realities of the Vietnam War created an atmosphere conducive to a critical inquiry into the sources of America's military involvement in Asia. In this new political environment, the critique of unconditional surrender became the province of the progressive Left. In these new interpretations, a variety of explanations were offered for Truman's failure to negotiate. Their common theme was that his adherence to unconditional surrender thwarted the chances for achieving peace before the atomic bombs were used. With little sense of irony, conservatives blasted those interpretations when they appeared in the Smithsonian Museum's text for the *Enola Gay* exhibit. In the ensuing public brawl over the exhibit, neither side seemed aware that unconditional surrender had always provoked such heated ideological responses. The contemporary circumstances had changed, the teams had switched sides, but the arguments remained the same.

The further we get from the pivotal summer of 1945, the easier it has been to divorce the debate over unconditional surrender from the ideological and partisan interests that fueled it. Take, for example, the documentary history produced by Oliver Stone. Released in 2012 with an accompanying text under the title *Untold History of the United States*, Stone and his co-author began with American policy before the outbreak of World War II and devoted the third of their twelve chapters to the decision to use the atomic bomb. Much of the chapter is a sustained indictment of Truman's failure to end the war by modifying unconditional surrender. Entered as witnesses against the president are none other than Hoover and MacArthur. MacArthur, we are told, "always maintained that the war would have ended sooner if the United States had modified its surrender terms." The authors add that when Hoover told MacArthur that he had proposed just such a solution to Truman in May 1945, the general promptly agreed that the Japanese would have jumped at the offer.[2] No attempt is made to explore MacArthur's motives for that conclusion or explain the context in which it was made. Despite his numerous prevarications, hyper-partisanship, and profound hatred of Roosevelt and Truman, MacArthur remains a reliable source for some. The general, it seems, will not just fade away.

Invoking the opinions of the two Roosevelt haters contributes little to our understanding of Japan's willingness to surrender before August 1945. It does, however, return us to the point that unconditional surrender was destined to be controversial because it was Roosevelt's policy. But unconditional surrender has remained controversial because the policy is inseparable from the atomic bombs and Soviet entry into the war. The way the war ended cast a long shadow over the postwar world. Surely, the argument goes, a compromise was possible that would have been acceptable to an already defeated Japan and a victorious America. That the war's outcome was never in doubt only adds to the poignancy of this conjecture. That argument ignores the point that such a compromise would have required major concessions to the Japanese and a sacrifice of the war's objectives.

This does not mean that no one should question the wisdom of seeking Japan's unconditional surrender. The bombing of Hiroshima and Nagasaki demands that it remain open. But we also need to understand that unconditional surrender was not an end in itself. It was the first step in a process that transformed Japan from a military dictatorship into a more democratic and peaceful nation. This transformation was possible only because Truman rejected the recommendations of his conservative advisors to preserve the monarchy, limit the occupation, and leave Japan in control of portions of its empire. In short, the changes happened because of Truman's resolve that Japan's surrender be nothing less than unconditional.

# Notes

## INTRODUCTION

1. Joint Press Conference with Prime Minister Churchill at Casablanca, January 24, 1943, Online by Gerhard Peters and John T. Woolley, *The American Presidency Project*, https://www.presidency.ucsb.edu/node/210111; Paul M. Sparrow, *The Casablanca Conference—Unconditional Surrender*, Franklin D. Roosevelt Library and Museum, https://fdr.blogs.archives.gov/2017/01/10/the-casablanca-conference-unconditional-surrender/; "Leaders Go by Air: Aim at 'Unconditional Surrender' by Axis," *New York Times*, January 27, 1943, 1.


## CHAPTER 1

1. Yahara refers to the landing site as Kadena Beach, but American sources call them the Hagashi beaches. Colonel Hiromichi Yahara, *The Battle for Okinawa: A Japanese Officer's Eyewitness Account of the Last Great Campaign of World War II* (New York: John Wiley and Sons, 1995), xi–xiv; Roy E. Appleman, *Okinawa. The Last Battle of WW II* (Washington, DC: Center for Military History, 1948), 68–74

2. George Feifer, *Tennozan: The Battle of Okinawa and the Atomic Bomb* (New York: Ticknor & Fields, 1992), 8–19; Craig L. Symonds, *World War II at Sea: A Global History* (New York: Oxford University Press, 2018), 167–69, 626–27.

3. This summary of Koiso's fall and the appointment of Suzuki is taken from Robert J. C. Butow, *Japan's Decision to Surrender* (Stanford, CA: Stanford University Press, 1954), 58–72; Richard Frank, *Downfall: The End of the Imperial Japanese Empire* (New York: Penguin Books, 1999), 90–99; Herbert P. Bix, *Hirohito and the Making of Modern Japan* (New York: HarperCollins, 2000), 492–93.

4. Headquarters, USAFFE and Eighth U.S. Army (Rear), "Homeland Operations Record," Japanese Monograph, No. 17, 74–75.

5. Alonzo L. Hamby, *Man of the People: A Life of Harry S. Truman* (New York: Oxford University Press, 1995), 289–90.

6. Harry S. Truman, Address Before a Joint Session of the Congress, April 16, 1945, Online by Gerhard Peters and John T. Woolley, The American Presidency Project, https://www.presidency.ucsb.edu/node/230621.

7. Franklin D. Roosevelt, Joint Press Conference with Prime Minister Churchill at Casablanca, January 24, 1943, Online by Gerhard Peters and John T. Woolley, *The American Presidency Project*, https://www.presidency.ucsb.edu/node/210111.

8. Raymond G. O'Connor, *Diplomacy for Victory: FDR and Unconditional Surrender* (New York: W.W. Norton, 1971); Robert Dallek, *Franklin D. Roosevelt and American Foreign Policy, 1932–1945* (New York: Oxford University Press, 1979), 373–76; Robert James Maddox, *Weapons for Victory: The Hiroshima Decision Fifty Years Later* (Columbia: University of Missouri Press, 1995), 6–19.

9. Joint Chiefs of Staff Minutes of a Meeting at the White House, January 7, 1943, U.S. Department of State, *Foreign Relations of the United States: The Conferences at Washington, 1941–1942, and Casablanca, 1943* (1941–1943) (Washington, DC: Government Printing Office, 1943), 506. Accessed through http://digicoll.library.wisc.edu/cgi-bin/FRUS/FRUS-idx?type=browse&scope=FRUS. FRUS1. Hereafter cited as *FRUS*, volume title.

10. Dallek, *Franklin D. Roosevelt*, 364.

11. Charles Brower, *Defeating Japan: The Joint Chiefs of Staff and Strategy in the Pacific War, 1943–1945* (New York: Palgrave Macmillan, 2012), 10–11.

12. Franklin D. Roosevelt, Joint Press Conference with Prime Minister Churchill at Casablanca, January 24, 1943, Online by Gerhard Peters and John T. Woolley, *The American Presidency Project*, https://www.presidency.ucsb.edu/node/210111.

13. "Grant's Drive to Victory Recalled. Unconditional Surrender Decision in 1943 Compared to Campaign of 1864," *Pittsburgh Post-Gazette*, January 27, 1943, 2; Robert G. Nixon, "Smashing New Blows Expected Shortly in All Theaters of War," *Washington Post*, January 27, 1943, 1.

14. Walter Lippmann, "Casablanca," *Pittsburgh Post-Gazette*, January 29, 1943, 10.

15. Franklin D. Roosevelt, Joint Communique with Churchill and Chiang Kai-shek on the Cairo Conference, December 1, 1943, Online by Gerhard Peters and John T. Woolley, *The American Presidency Project*, https://www.presidency.ucsb.edu/node/209712.

16. Brian Loring Villa, "The U.S. Army, Unconditional Surrender, and the Potsdam Proclamation," *Journal of American History* 63, no. 1 (June 1976), 78; Robert P. Newman, *Truman and the Hiroshima Cult* (East Lansing: Michigan State University Press, 1995), 65–66.

17. Franklin D. Roosevelt, Address to Congress on the Yalta Conference, Online by Gerhard Peters and John T. Woolley, *The American Presidency Project*, https://www.presidency.ucsb.edu/node/210050.

18. Waldo Heinrichs and Marc Gallicchio, *Implacable Foes: War in the Pacific, 1944–1945* (New York: Oxford University Press, 2017), 415–24.

19. Heinrichs and Gallicchio, *Implacable Foes*, 496.

20. Michael D. Pearlman, *Warmaking and American Democracy: The Struggle over Military Strategy, 1700 to the Present* (Lawrence: University Press of Kansas, 1999), 275.

21. Heinrichs and Gallicchio, *Implacable Foes*, 424–27, 440–42, 483–95.

22. Earlier, Senator Harry Truman had privately complained to a friend that General Brehon Somervell, the Army's head of the Services of Supply, would create a fascist government if he could manage it. Hamby, *Man of the People*, 273. Drury quoted in Heinrichs and Gallicchio, *Implacable Foes*, 437–38.

23. Mark Stoler, "World War II in U.S. History and Memory," *Diplomatic History* 25, no. 3 (Summer), 383–92.

24. On Roosevelt's policies, see John Lewis Gaddis, *The Origins of the Cold War* (New York: Columbia University Press, 1972), 6–8, 86, 133–34, 197; Thomas G. Paterson, *On Every Front* (New York: W.W. Norton, 1979), 36–39; Dallek, *Roosevelt*, 507–21; John Lewis Gaddis, *Russia, the Soviet Union and the United States: An Interpretive History*, 2nd ed. (New York: McGraw Hill, 1990), 164–67; George C. Herring, *From Colony to Superpower: U.S. Foreign Relations Since 1776* (New York: Oxford University Press, 2011), 584–85.

25. Roosevelt quoted in Robert James Maddox, *Weapons for Victory: The Hiroshima Decision Fifty Years Later* (Columbia: University of Missouri Press, 1995), 17.

26. Forrestal wrote that Leahy supported Stimson but Stimson said only General Marshall sided with him. See Memorandum of Conversation by Charles E. Bohlen, April 23, 1945, *FRUS, 1945, Europe*, 5: 252–55; Entry for April 23, 1945, in Walter Millis, ed., *Forrestal Diaries* (New York: Viking Press, 1951), 48–51; Entry for April 23, 1945, Diary of Henry Lewis Stimson, Stimson Papers, Yale University Library, New Haven, Connecticut (microfilm). (Hereafter cited as Stimson Diaries.)

27. Truman quoted in Hamby, *Man of the People*, 320.

28. Entry for May 25, 1945, Diary of Eben Ayers, Eben Ayers Papers, Harry S. Truman Library, Independence, Missouri. Hereafter cited as Truman Library

29. Admiral Charles Cooke to Admiral King, April 4, 1945, Charles M. Cooke Papers, Hoover Institution on War, Revolution and Peace, Stanford, California.

30. Entry for May 1, 1945, State-War-Navy, in Millis, *Forrestal Diaries* (New York: Viking Press, 1951), 52.

31. Entry for May 11, 1945, Russo-Japanese War, in Millis, *Forrestal Diaries*, 55–56.

32. Waldo H. Heinrichs, Jr., *American Ambassador: Joseph C. Grew and the Development of the United States Diplomatic Tradition* (New York: Oxford University Press, 1986, reprint), especially 255–350; Heinrichs, *Threshold of War: Franklin D. Roosevelt and American Entry into World War II* (New York: Oxford University Press, 1988) 180–214.

33. Memorandum for the Acting Secretary of War, May 21, 1945, ABC 336 Russia (August 22, 1943), Section 3, Record Group 165, Records of the War Department General and Special Staffs Military Records, National Archives,

College Park, Maryland. Hereafter cited as file number and RG 165. Marc S. Gallicchio, *The Cold War Begins in Asia: American East Asian Policy and the Fall of the Japanese Empire* (New York: Columbia University Press, 1988), 10–11.

34. Memorandum of Conversation by the Acting Secretary of State, May 28, 1945, *FRUS, 1945*, 6: 545–47.

35. On Grew's "pendulum" theory of Japanese history, see Nakamura Masanori, *The Japanese Monarchy: Joseph Grew and the 'Symbol Emperor System,' 1931–1991* (Armonk, NY: M. E. Sharpe, 1992), 41–43.

36. John W.. Dower, *Embracing Defeat: Japan in the Wake of World War II* (New York: W. W. Norton, 1999), 346, 358; Tsuyoshi Hasegawa, *Racing the Enemy: Stalin, Truman, and the Surrender of Japan* (Cambridge, MA: Harvard University Press, 2005), 3–4; W. G. Beasley, *The Modern History of Japan*, 2nd ed. (New York: Praeger, 1973), 130–33; Ian Buruma, *Inventing Japan, 1853–1964* (New York: Modern Library, 2004), 35–40, 51–57.

37. Roger Butow observed, "Devotion to Kokutai is synonymous with devotion to the imperial family. The term embraces a galaxy of meanings, both real and implied." Robert J. C. Butow, *Japan's Decision to Surrender* (Stanford, CA: Stanford University Press, 1954), 16, n24; Dower, *Embracing Defeat*, 157; Hasegawa, *Racing the Enemy*, 3–4; John Hunter Boyle, *Modern Japan: The American Nexus* (Fort Worth, TX: Harcourt Brace Jovanovich College, 1993), 162, 173.

38. Memorandum of Conversation by the Acting Secretary of State, May 28, 1945, *FRUS, 1945*, 6: 545–46.

39. Memorandum for Chief, Strategy and Policy Group, Collapse of the Japanese Government on or about V-E Day, February 11, 1945, ABC 384.1 Japan (August 22, 1944), RG 165.

40. Joint Intelligence Staff, Unconditional Surrender of Japan, April 10, 1945, CCS 387 Japan (April 6, 1945), RG 218, Records of the United States Joint Chiefs of Staff, Military Records, National Archives, College Park, Maryland. Hereafter cited as file number and RG 218.

41. Quoted in Maddox, *Weapons for Victory*, 11–12.

42. Dale Hellegers notes that American efforts to understand Japanese motives were marred by a reliance on stereotypes. That holds true in this case. Surely the Japanese, many of whom had served abroad, knew what the Americans meant by unconditional surrender. Dale M. Hellegers, *We, the Japanese People: World War II and the Origins of the Japanese Constitution*, vol. 1, *Washington* (Stanford, CA: Stanford University Press, 2001), 10.

43. Immediate Demand for the Unconditional Surrender of Japan, Report of the Joint Staff Planners with the Joint Intelligence Committee with appendices, [ca. May 15, 1945], ABC 387 Japan (February 15, 1945), Section 1-B, RG 165.

44. Memorandum for the Deputy Chief of Staff, Exploitation of the Collapse of Germany by a Demand for the Surrender of Germany, May 7, 1945, OPD

387.4 TS, Item # 2933, Reel 119, George Catlett Marshall Library, Lynchburg, Virginia.

45. Harry S. Truman, Statement by the President Calling for Unconditional Surrender of Japan, May 8, 1945, Online by Gerhard Peters and John T. Woolley, *The American Presidency Project*, https://www.presidency.ucsb.edu/node/233823.

46. Butow, *Japan's Decision to Surrender*, 81–85.

47. Butow, *Japan's Decision to Surrender*, 90–92.

48. John J. McCloy to Chief of Staff (Marshall), May 20, 1945, ABC 387 Japan (February 15, 1945), Section 1-B, RG 165.

49. Entries for May 15 and 16, 1945, with memorandum "The Campaign Against Japan, Stimson Diaries; Leon V. Sigal, *Fighting to a Finish: The Politics of War Termination in the United States and Japan, 1945* (Ithaca, NY: Cornell University Press, 1988), 110–11.

50. The president was already somewhat aware that the U.S. was developing an explosive of enormous power through his role as head of the Senate committee overseeing military spending. Memorandum Discussed with the President, April 25, 1945, in William Burr, ed., *The Atomic Bomb and the End of World War II. A Collection of Primary Sources National Security Archive Electronic Briefing Book No. 162*; online at http://nsarchive.gwu.edu/NSAEBB/NSAEBB162/. (Hereafter cited as Burr, *Atomic Bomb and the End of World War II.*) Hamby, *Man of the People*, 324.

51. Memorandum for the Secretary of War from General L. R. Groves, "Atomic Fission Bombs," April 23, 1945, in Burr, *Atomic Bomb and the End of World War II.*

52. On Stimson's career, see Godfrey Hodgson, *The Colonel: The Life and Wars of Henry Stimson, 1867–1950* (New York: Alfred A. Knopf, 1990), and David F. Schmitz, *Henry L. Stimson: The First Wise Man* (Wilmington, DE: Scholarly Resources, 2001).

53. "Okinawa Struggle in Bloody Deadlock," *Washington Post*, May 19, 1945, 1.

54. Memorandum of Conversation by the Acting Secretary, May 29, 1945, *FRUS*, 1945, 6: 548; Entry for May 29, 1945, Stimson Diaries; Entry for May 29, 1945, in Millis, *Forrestal Diaries*, 66; Hellegers, *We, the Japanese People*, 94.

55. David McLellan and David Acheson, *Among Friends: Personal Letters of Dean Acheson* (New York: Dodd, Mead, 1980), 55; Weil, *A Pretty Good Club: The Founding Fathers of the U.S. Foreign Service* (New York: W.W. Norton, 1978), 213; Mayo, "Wartime Planning for Occupied Japan. The Role of the Experts," in Robert Wolfe, ed., *Americans as Proconsuls: U.S. Military Government in Germany and Japan, 1944–1952* (Carbondale: Southern Illinois University Press, 1984), 42–44.

56. Scott Donaldson, *Archibald MacLeish: An American Life* (Boston: Houghton Mifflin, 1992), 379.

57. 100th and 1001st meetings of the Secretary's Staff Committee, May 28, May 29, 1945, Minutes of the Secretary's Staff Committee, Record Group 59, General Records of the Department of State, National Archives, College Park, Maryland. Hereafter cited as file name and RG 59.

58. Lattimore quoted Sun Fo when he recommended puncturing the myth of the emperor's divinity. Owen Lattimore, *Solution in Asia* (Boston: Little Brown, 1945), 44–45, 189.

59. Harry S. Truman, Special Message to the Congress on Winning the War with Japan, June 1, 1945, Online by Gerhard Peters and John T. Woolley, *The American Presidency Project*, https://www.presidency.ucsb.edu/node/232206.

60. For the Navy's and Army's strategic views, see Charles Brower, *Defeating Japan*, 103, 132–35.

61. "22 Jap Planes Destroyed, 23 Damaged in 2 Blows," *Washington Post*, June 5, 1945, 1; "Yanks Stir Hornets' Nest over Kyushu: American Planes Outmaneuvered," *Washington Post*, June 4, 1945; Frank, *Downfall*, 79; Symonds, *World War II at Sea*, 632.

## CHAPTER 2

1. Yahara, *Battle for Okinawa*, 125–27; Appleman, *Okinawa*, 427–34; Major Charles S. Nichols, Jr., and Henry I. Shaw, Jr., *Okinawa: Victory in the Pacific* (Washington, DC: U.S. Government Printing Office, 1955), 217–27.

2. Edward J. Drea, *In the Service of the Emperor: Essays on the Imperial Japanese Army* (Lincoln: University of Nebraska Press, 1998), 152–53.

3. Hattori Takushiro, *The Complete History of the Greater East Asia War* (Tokyo: Headquarters United States Army Far Eastern Forces, 1953–1954), 289.

4. Butow, *Japan's Decision to Surrender*, 95–101.

5. Butow, *Japan's Decision to Surrender*, 101–2.

6. Butow, *Japan's Decision to Surrender*, 12–13, 112–16; Frank, *Downfall*, 96–98; Bix, *Hirohito*, 493–94; Tsuyoshi Hasegawa, *Racing the Enemy: Stalin, Truman, and the Surrender of Japan* (Cambridge, MA: Harvard University Press, 2005), 99–102.

7. Kido coaxed Suzuki into agreement with his proposal by telling him that the emperor had approved. Hasegawa, *Racing the Enemy*, 102.

8. Butow, *Japan's Decision to Surrender*, 118–21; Bix, *Hirohito*, 494.

9. Truman told his staff that he had written Hoover on the spur of the moment. Entry for May 24, 1945, Diary of Eben Ayers, Eben Ayers Papers, The Harry S. Truman Library and Museum, Independence, Missouri. (Hereafter cited as HST.) Years later he told an interviewer that he had called Hoover when the former president was in Washington. Robert Ferrell recounts that story but also indicates his doubts about its veracity. Robert H. Ferrell, *Harry S. Truman: A Life* (Columbia: University of Missouri Press, 1994), 194–95, 421n32. For Hoover's desire for a meeting and the preliminary arrangements,

see Gary Dean Best, *Herbert Hoover: The Post Presidential Years, 1933–1964* (Stanford, CA: Hoover Institution Press, 1983), 266–70.

10. Joan Hoff Wilson, "Herbert Hoover's Plan for Ending the Second World War," *The International History Review* 1, no. 1 (January 1979), 84–102.

11. "Moderate" was the term used to describe such advocates of cooperation with the West as Baron Shidehara Kijūrō, Suzuki Kantarō, and Admiral Nomura Kichisaburō. For the most part, they supported a parliamentary system presided over by a small elite. Their views on economics and popular sovereignty were what we would normally describe as conservative. They appeared moderate when compared with the militarists, however.

12. Hoover called Roosevelt a madman during a conversation with General Douglas MacArthur in May 1946. Haruo Iguchi, "The First Revisionists: Bonner Fellers, Herbert Hoover, and Japan's Decision to Surrender," in Gallicchio, ed., *The Unpredictability of the Past: Memories of the Asia-Pacific War in U.S.-East Asian Relations* (Durham, NC: Duke University Press, 2007), 65.

13. Critics of unconditional surrender often described the doctrine's supporters as seeking vengeance or as animated by "blind prejudice." See Joseph Grew to the Secretary of State, January 3, 194[5], U.S. Department of State, *Foreign Relations of the United States, 1945* (Washington, DC: Government Printing Office, 1969), 6: 515–16.

14. Hoff Wilson, "Hoover's Plan."

15. Robert Ferrell, ed., *Off the Record: The Private Papers of Harry S. Truman* (New York: Penguin Books, 1980), 40.

16. Best, *Herbert Hoover*, 270.

17. Entry for May 31, 1945, Eben Ayers Diary, Papers of Eben Ayers, HST.

18. Iguchi, "The First Revisionists," 66.

19. William R. Castle to Herbert Hoover, June 2, 1945, Herbert Hoover papers, Post-Presidential Individual Files, Herbert Hoover Presidential Library, West Branch, Iowa. (Hereafter cited as HHL.)

20. Castle to Hoover, quoted in Alfred Castle, *Diplomatic Realism: William R. Castle, Jr. and American Foreign Policy 1919–1953* (Honolulu: Samuel N. and Mary Castle Foundation, 1998), 139.

21. O'Laughlin to Hoover, May 12, 1945. O'Laughlin Correspondence, HHL.

22. "Truman Found Widely Popular After First Month in Office: GOP Voters Look for Him, Democrats Look to His Carrying Out FDR Aims," May 10, 1945; "Truman Wins Plaudits of Big Majority of Both Democrats and Republicans in Poll," June 30, 1945; in Records of the Institute of Public Opinion, 1945–1951, Box 1, HST.

23. A statistical analysis of Truman's Senate voting record describes him as a "moderate liberal" who defended New Deal programs during the war years. Gary M. Fink and James W. Hilty, "Prologue: The Senate Voting Record of Harry S. Truman," *Journal of Interdisciplinary History* 4, no. 2 (Autumn 1973), 207–35.

Robert J. Donovan, *Conflict and Crisis: The Presidency of Harry S Truman, 1945–1948* (New York: W.W. Norton, 1977), 26.

24. Hamby, *Man of the People*, 273.

25. *Fortune* quoted in David Kennedy, *Freedom from Fear: The American People in Depression and War, 1929–1945* (New York: Oxford University Press, 1999), 782. MacLeish quoted in Allan Winkler, *Home Front U.S.A.: America During World War II* (Arlington Heights, IL: Harlan Davidson, 1986), 85.

26. John Morton Blum, *V Was for Victory: Politics and American Culture During World War II* (New York: Harcourt Brace Jovanovich, 1976), 122.

27. Blum, *V Was for Victory*, 123.

28. Kennedy, *Freedom From Fear*, 622–23; Robert Griffith, "Forging America's Postwar Order: Domestic Politics and Political Economy in the Age of Truman," in Michael J. Lacey, ed., *The Truman Presidency* (New York: Cambridge University Press, 1989), 63.

29. Ibid.

30. "22 Groups Support Extension of OPA," *New York Times*, May 28, 1945, 21; Meg Jacobs, "'How About Some Meat?': The Office of Price Administration, Consumption Politics, and State Building from the Bottom Up, 1941–1946," *Journal of American History* 84, no. 3 (December 1997), 910–41.

31. Truman might have preferred to have shown the memorandum to James F. Byrnes, a former Senate colleague, and already a close advisor, but Byrnes was home in South Carolina during this period. Byrnes was the previous director of OWMR and the secretary of state in waiting. David Robertson, *Sly and Able: A Political Biography of James F. Byrnes* (New York: W. W. Norton, 1994), 400–403.

32. Entry for 17 June 1945, in Ferrell, *Off the Record*, 46; Donovan, *Conflict and Crisis*, 27–28.

33. Fred M. Vinson to Truman, 7 June 1945, enclosing [Herbert Hoover] "Memorandum on Ending the Japanese War," Truman to Cordell Hull, 9 June 1945; Truman to Edward Stettinius, Secretary of State; Truman to Henry Stimson; in State Department, WWII, White House Confidential File, Box 43, HST. As historian D. M. Giangreco has argued, Truman's handling of the Hoover memo, which contained dire casualty projections of 500,000–1,000,000 lives lost shows that the president did not conjure those numbers out of thin air when, after the war, he sought to justify his use of the atomic bombs. D. M. Giangreco, "'A Score of Bloody Okinawas and Iwo Jimas': President Truman and Casualty Estimates for the Invasion of Japan,'" *Pacific Historical Review* 72, no. 1 (February 2003), 93–132.

34. General Handy to Stimson, Memorandum, June 4, 1945, copy in Item 2840, microfilm reel 117, General Staff Papers, George C. Marshall Papers, George C. Marshall Research Library, Lexington, Virginia. (Hereafter cited as MRL.)

35. Marshall to Stimson, June 15, 1945, transmitting "Memorandum of Comments on "Ending the Japanese War," June 14, 1945, facsimile in Burr, *Atomic Bomb*

*and the End of the War II*, http://nsarchive.gwu.edu/NSAEBB/NSAEBB162/18.pdf.

36. Ibid. Stimson drew a vertical line in the margin and penciled a question mark next to the comments about Europe. He drew another vertical line alongside the comments about Suzuki and the liberals and wrote "no" with a "#" above it in the margin.

37. Frank, *Downfall*, 133, and endnote on 390–91.

38. Dooman was the primary author of the report on the Hoover memorandum and the draft statement that Grew handed Truman. Memorandum of Conversation, June 15, 1945, 740.00119 PW/6/- 1545, Department of State Decimal File, Record Group 59, General Records of the Department of State, National Archive, College Park, Maryland; Hellegers, *We, the Japanese People*, 97–98.

39. Joseph Grew to President Truman, June 13, 1945, State Department, WWII–1945, White House Confidential File, Box 43, HST.

40. Draft Statement submitted with Joseph Grew to President Truman, June 13, 1945, State Department, WWII, White House Confidential File, Box 43, HST.

41. American observers in China reported that the Chinese government expected the Japanese to depose Hirohito. Chinese press commentary also called for the overthrow of the monarchy. Hellegers, *We, the Japanese People*, 319n264, 319n265.

42. Grew to Rosenman, with attachment, June 16, 1945, folder: State Department, World War II-1945, White House Confidential File, HST.

43. Stettinius's message was in response to the staff work the Joint Chiefs were doing on the timing of a warning. Dale Hellegers notes that in evaluating the Hoover memorandum, Dooman had not questioned the former president's suggestion that the U.S. issue a warning without consulting the Russians or the British. Stettinius to Grew, June 15, 1945, State Department, World War II-1945, White House Confidential File, HST; Hellegers, *We, the Japanese People*, 319n261; Herbert Feis, *Japan Subdued: The Atomic Bomb and the End of the Pacific War* (Princeton, NJ: Princeton University Press, 1961), 20–21.

44. Memorandum by the Acting Secretary of State (Grew), June 18, 1945, *FRUS: The Conference of Berlin (the Potsdam Conference), 1945*, 1: 177–78 (hereafter cited as *FRUS: Conference of Berlin)*; Memorandum of Joseph Grew, June 18, 1945, 740.00119 PW/7-945, RG 59, General Records of the Department of State, NARA.

45. Truman later said he deferred discussion because he wanted to consult with the Allies. Herbert Feis suggests that Truman may have worried that issuing a warning before it could be followed by a military blow might involve the U.S. in protracted negotiations with Japan. He also notes Truman's concern over the public's reaction to a softening of unconditional surrender. Hull to Truman, June 12, 1945, folder: State Department, World War II-1945, White House Confidential File, HST; Feis, *Japan Subdued*, 21–22.

46. All quotes from the meeting are in Minutes of Meeting held at the White House, June 18, 1945, *FRUS: Conference of Berlin* 1: 903–10, http://digicoll. library.wisc.edu/cgi-bin/FRUS/FRUS-idx?type=turn&entity=FRUS.FRU S1945Berlinv01.p1044&id=FRUS.FRUS1945Berlinv01&isize=M&q1. A facsimile of the minutes from the Joint Chiefs' files can be found in Burr, *Atomic Bomb and the End of World War II.*

47. Minutes of the Meeting Held at the White House, June 18, 1945, ibid. According to McCloy's recollections, as the meeting was ending Truman asked for his opinion saying, "no one gets out of here without committing himself." McCloy recommended that the United States tell the Japanese that they could keep the emperor provided they surrendered immediately. "I think we ought to have our heads examined," he recalled saying, "if we don't let them keep the emperor." He added that the U.S. should link that offer to a warning that it would soon have the atomic bomb, which it would use against Japan. There is, however, reason to doubt McCloy's melodramatic account. The minutes show that McCloy had not been silent during the meeting; he had already expressed his views when he supported Stimson's views on seeking a diplomatic alternative to an invasion. McCloy quoted in Marc S. Gallicchio, *The Cold War Begins in Asia: American East Asian Policy and the Fall of the Japanese Empire* (New York: Columbia University Press, 1988), 14.

48. Ibid.

49. Entry for March 8, 1947, in Millis., *Forrestal Diaries*, 70–71.

50. Entry for March 8, 1947, in Millis, *Forrestal Diaries*, 70–71.

51. Forrestal's diary contains evidence that casts McCloy's story into doubt. Forrestal noted parenthetically in his diary entry, "Neither Stimson nor I were at this meeting." It is not clear from Forrestal's diary if McCloy told him that or if Forrestal inferred it, but either way, that statement is false. Unfortunately, it is easier to disprove Forrestal's parenthetical statement than it is to explain why he entered it into his official diary. If the notation was Forrestal's observation and not something McCloy told him, then it would mean that he did not realize that McCloy was talking about the June 18 meeting or that he had completely forgotten about what happened there. Neither possibility seems plausible. The meeting at the White House was of monumental importance.

Another possibility is that he and Stimson had left the room when McCloy spoke to Truman. But if they had, it is still likely that Forrestal would have remembered the meeting from McCloy's description. Nevertheless, Forrestal wrote that he and Stimson were not at the meeting, not that they had left the room. Still another possibility is that Forrestal made the parenthetical comment about his absence because he was unable to recall McCloy's version of events and assumed that he had not attended the meeting McCloy was describing. On the other hand, perhaps McCloy told Forrestal that he and Stimson were not present. If McCloy did so, it raises even more serious questions about the accuracy of his story. Either he deliberately misled Forrestal about who was present so Forrestal couldn't contradict his version of events or McCloy's recollection was so seriously flawed as to throw the whole story into doubt. The latter seems most likely. After all, why would McCloy go to great lengths to tell Forrestal about a meeting that Forrestal attended unless he, McCloy, was so seriously confused about the sequence of events that he did not recall that Forrestal was present?

52. McCloy interview with Marc Gallicchio, August 2, 1984, quoted in Gallicchio, *The Cold War Begins in Asia*, 14.

53. McCloy's larger point in telling his story was that civilian voices needed to be included in military decisions. John J. McCloy, *The Challenge to American Foreign Policy* (Cambridge, MA: Harvard University Press, 1953), 42. The prominent journalist James Reston reported McCloy's version of events in James Reston, Jr., *Deadline: A Memoir* (New York: Random House, 1991), Appendix, "McCloy and the Bomb," 495. Other works that cite McCloy's version include Gallicchio, *The Cold War Begins in Asia*, 14; Len Giovannitti and Fred Freed, *The Decision to Drop the Bomb* (New York: Coward McCann, 1965), 135–36; Hellegers, *We, the Japanese People*, 110; Hasegawa, *Racing the Enemy*, 105; and Kai Bird, *The Chairman: John J. McCloy and the Making of the American Establishment* (New York: Simon and Schuster, 1992), 246. The following authors noted inconsistencies and doubted the accuracy of McCloy's recollections: Frank, *Downfall*, 143, Sigal, *Fighting to a Finish*, 122n69; Sean L. Malloy, *Atomic Tragedy: Henry L. Stimson and the Decision to Use the Bomb Against Japan* (Ithaca, NY: Cornell University Press, 2008), 213n8; Waldo Heinrichs and Marc Gallicchio, *Implacable Foes: War in the Pacific, 1944–1945* (New York: Oxford University Press, 2017), 642n38.

54. According to the notes Gates took for Forrestal, Grew said that he thought that the president did not agree that a warning should be issued. Stimson disagreed. He said that "he felt" that the president did not want to issue such a warning "at this moment." Minutes of the Committee of Three, June 19, 1945, Committee of Three Minutes and Related Papers, War Department, General Administration, Papers of John J. McCloy, Amherst College Library, Amherst, Massachusetts; Entry for June 19, 1945, Stimson Diary; Entry for June 19, 1945, in Millis, *Forrestal Diaries*, 69–70.

55. Minutes of the Committee of Three, June 26, 1945, Committee of Three Minutes and Related Papers, War Department, McCloy Papers; Entry for June 26–30, 1945, Stimson Diaries.

56. Ballantine to Grew, June 27, 1945, with "Draft of Proposed Statement," 740.00119-PW/6- 2745, A/MES Top Secret File, RG 59; Colonel Charles Bonesteel to General Lincoln, Immediate Demand for Japanese Surrender, June 27, 1945, Lincoln to General Hull, June 28, 1945, both in ABC 387 Japan (February 15, 1945), Section 1-B, RG 165.

57. Lincoln to Hull, June 29, 1945, Demand for Japanese Surrender, ABC 387 Japan (February 15, 1945), Section 1-B, RG 165.

58. Entry for June 26–30, Stimson Diaries; Entry for June 30, 1945, McCloy Diaries.

59. McCloy to Stimson, June 29, 1945, ABC 387 Japan (February 15, 1945), Section 1-B, RG 165.

60. Timing of Proposed Demand for Japanese Surrender, June 29, 1945, ABC 387 Japan (February 15, 1945), Section 1-B, RG 165.

61. Stimson to Truman, July 2, 1945, with "Proposed Program for Japan," July 2, 1945, and "Proclamation by the Heads of State U.S.–U.K.–[U.S.S.R.]–China," July 1, 1945, ABC 387 Japan (February 15, 1945), Section1-B, RG 165.

62. "Proposed Program for Japan," July 2, 1945, ABC 387 Japan (February 15, 1945), Section 1-B, RG 165.

63. All quotes and information about the meeting are in Entry for July 2, 1945, Stimson Diaries.

64. Maddox, *Weapons for Victory*, 74–75.

65. Rosenman to Truman, with enclosures, June 14, 1955, Alphabetical File, Rosenman, Box 11, Post-Presidential Correspondence, HST.

66. Treasury Secretary Henry Morgenthau thought Truman might select Byrnes because he had been to Yalta. Entry for June 1, 1945, Presidential Diaries, Morgenthau Papers, Franklin D. Roosevelt Library, Hyde Park, New York. Harry S. Truman, *Memoirs of Harry S. Truman: Year of Decisions* (New York: Doubleday, 1955), Robert L. Messer, *The End of an Alliance: James F. Byrnes, Roosevelt, Truman, and the Origins of the Cold War* (Chapel Hill: University of North Carolina Press, 1982), 40–42; Hamby, *Man of the People*, 307.

67. MacLeish to Byrnes, July 6, 1945, *FRUS: Conference of Berlin*, 1: 903–10, 895–97.

68. Millis, *Forrestal Diaries*, 78.

69. Minutes of the Secretary's Staff Committee, July 7, 1945, *FRUS: Conference of Berlin*, 1: 900–901.

70. Memorandum by the Legal Advisor, *FRUS: Conference of Berlin*, 1: 902.

71. Truman's last conversation with Grew on the subject ended with the president declining to issue the warning that Grew showed him and asking the acting secretary to put the item on the agenda of the Big Three meeting. Grew may have inferred that if the item was to be part of the agenda, the president would need to have at least a draft of a warning in hand. But Grew did not take it that way. When Grew met with his opposite numbers on the Committee of Three the next day, June 19, the committee made no attempt to draft a warning. McCloy's minutes show only that the members agreed it would be wise to issue a warning. Stimson's diary confirms that. The notes taken by Artemus Gates are more revealing. According to Gates, "Mr. Grew was of the impression that the President had indicated he was not in accord with this point of view. Mr. Stimson said that was not his understanding but rather he felt that the President did not want to proceed with such a plan at this moment." No one, including McCloy, claimed that they had been charged

by the president to prepare a proclamation. When Gates's notes were published in Forrestal's diary, Grew objected. He referred again to Truman's comment that his thoughts were running along the same lines as Grew's and said that their only disagreement was over timing. But even when making this defense in his memoir, Grew refrained from stating that he received instructions from Truman to prepare a warning. In addition to the previously cited minutes taken by McCloy and Stimson's diary, see Gates's notes for June 19, in Millis, *Forrestal Diaries*, 69–70; and Joseph C. Grew, *Turbulent Era: A Diplomatic Record of Forty Years, 1904–1945* (Boston: Houghton Mifflin, 1952), 2: 1424.

72. Eric Rauchway, *Winter War: Hoover, Roosevelt, and the First Clash Over the New Deal* (New York: Basic Books, 2018), 156–58; Robert P. Newman, *Truman and the Hiroshima Cult* (East Lansing: Michigan State University Press, 1995), 64.

73. On Davis, see JCS and Heads of Civilian War Agencies, June 26, 1945, Joint Chiefs of Staff Papers, CCS 334 (February 2, 1945), RG 218, Records of the Combined Chiefs of Staff, Modern Military Branch, National Archives, College Park, Maryland. See also Villa, "The U.S. Army, Unconditional Surrender, and the Potsdam Proclamation," 71–72; Newman, *Truman and the Hiroshima Cult*, 64; Robert L. Beisner, *Dean Acheson: A Life in the Cold War* (New York: Oxford University Press, 2006), 19, 23–24; Marc Gallicchio, "Truman, Unconditional Surrender, and a New Deal for Japan," in James I. Matray, ed., *Northeast Asia and the Legacy of Harry S. Truman: Japan, China, and the Two Koreas* (Kirksville, MO: Truman State University Press, 2012), 15–45.

## CHAPTER 3

1. Log of the President's Trip to the Conference, *FRUS: Conference of Berlin*, 2: 4–28.

2. Entries for July 14 and 21, 1945, Folder July 1–August 26, 1945, Diary of Harold Ickes, Harold Ickes Papers, Library of Congress.

3. Quotation is in Entry for June 25, 1944, Diary of William D. Leahy (microfilm), William D. Leahy Papers, Library of Congress, Washington, DC. For biographical information, see Henry H. Adams, *Witness to Power: The Life of Fleet Admiral William D. Leahy* (Annapolis, MD: Naval Institute Press, 1985).

4. Adams, *Witness to Power*, 282–83.

5. "Unconditional Surrender of Japan . . . ," June 29, 1945; *FRUS: Conference of Berlin*, 1: 884.

6. Military Government and Attitude Toward the Emperor, with Appendix, July 3, 1945, *FRUS: Conference of Berlin*, 1: 885–87.

7. "Proclamation by the Heads of State, U.S.–U.K.–[U.S.S.R.]–China," *FRUS: Conference of Berlin*, 1: 893–94.

8. The anonymous authority, like Grew, described Japanese militarism as a "cancer" that must be cut out. "Emperor Valuable to U.S.: Japan Might Give Up, but Must Keep Face," June 7, 1945, International News Service.

9. Arthur Krock, "Our Policy Toward the Emperor of Japan," *New York Times*, July 5, 1945, 12.

10. Gallup, *Public Opinion, 1935–1971*, Survey 348, 511–12.

11. Heinrichs and Gallicchio, *Implacable Foes*, 417–22, 444–47.

12. "The God Emperor," *Time*, May 21, 1945, 33–36; Hal Brands, "Rhetoric, Public Opinion, and Policy in the American Debate over the Japanese Emperor During World War II," *Rhetoric & Public Affairs* 8, no. 3 (Fall 2005), 431–32.

13. Robert Edwin Herzstein, *Henry R. Luce, Time, and the American Crusade in Asia* (New York: Cambridge University Press, 2005), 48–50.

14. A *New York Times* article ridiculed rumors spread by Washington insiders that Japan would surrender soon. The paper warned there was still a hard fight ahead and that compromise would be dangerous. "The Japanese Answer," *New York Times*, May 10, 1945, 22; Barnet Nover, "Which Way Japan?," *Washington Post*, May 12, 1945, 4; Drew Pearson, "Washington Merry-Go-Round," May 14, 1945, 12; "Is Japan Trying to Surrender?," *Christian Century* 62 (May 23, 1945), 619; "It Is Time to Announce Surrender Terms," *Christian Century* 62 (May 23, 1945), 619. ; *Kiplinger Washington Letter*, June 2, 1945 and June 16, 1945; Brands, "American Debate over the Japanese Emperor," 439–40.

15. Hadley Cantril, ed., *Public Opinion, 1935–1946* (Princeton, NJ: Princeton University Press, 1951), Poll # 88, June 27, 1945, 1185.

16. Fortune poll cited in Ball, "Strategic Limitations of a Warring Democracy: American War Weariness and the Decision to Invade Japan, 1944–1945," Friends of the West Point Library Occasional Papers, No. 7, March 1995, West Point, NY, 3; Cantril, *Public Opinion*, Poll # 87, June 27, 1945, 1185.

17. "The American Soldier in World War II: Reactions to the Enemy and Further Duty," Directed by Dr. Samuel A. Stouffer for the Research Branch, Information and Education Division, War Department, June 1945. In a related question, the same soldiers were asked how they felt about their service in the war; 1,317 said they had done their part and should be discharged.

18. Ibid.

19. Excerpts from these letters are contained in Unconditional Surrender File, Letters referred to Department of State, June 14–August 2, 1945, General File, HST. See also John Chappell, *Before the Bomb: How American Approached the End of the Pacific War* (Lexington: University Press of Kentucky, 1996), 116–31.

20. "Testimony Before the House War Department Subcommittee," May 25, 1945, Larry I. Bland, ed., *George C. Marshall Papers*, 5, 200–204. (Hereafter cited as GCM.) Marshall's impromptu remarks are contained in 204n1.

21. "House Group Told of Blows at Japan," *New York Times*, May 27, 1945, 4.

22. Quotations in Michael S. Sweeney, *Secrets of Victory: The Office of Censorship and the Press and Radio in World War II* (Chapel Hill: University of North Carolina Press, 2001), 207–9; "Way of the Censor," *Washington Post*, May 29, 1945, 6; Drew Pearson, "Washington Merry-Go-Round," *Washington Post*, June 7, 1945, 5.

23. Robert Edwin Herzstein, *Henry R. Luce, Time, and the American Crusade in Asia* (New York: Cambridge University Press, 2005), 48–50.

24. "Colonel O'Laughlin, Publisher, Dies," *New York Times*, March 15, 1949, 1; Peter Mauch, *Sailor Diplomat: Nomura Kichisaburo and the Japanese-American War* (Cambridge, MA: Harvard University Press, 2011), 52.

25. He also mistakenly interpreted Truman's omission of any mention of the emperor in his war messages as evidence that the president was telling the Japanese they could keep the monarchy. He compounded that error by asserting that officials around Hirohito understood that was Truman's intention. O'Laughlin to Herbert Hoover, May 12, 19, 1945, Papers of John Callan O'Laughlin, Library of Congress. (Copies of O'Laughlin's newsletter can also be found in the John Callan O'Laughlin Papers in the Herbert Hoover Presidential Library and Museum, Long Branch, Iowa. (Hereafter cited as HHL.)

26. O'Laughlin to Hoover, June 2, 1945, O'Laughlin Papers.

27. Hanson Baldwin, "Russia and the Pacific: Her Intervention Is a Question Mark," *New York Times*, May 11, 1945, 10.

28. Stone offered as evidence the government's response to a December 1944 *Harper's* article by Ernest K. Lindley and Edward Weintal in which the authors used confidential government sources to defend the State Department's policy toward Spain's reactionary dictator Francisco Franco. When queried by reporters about the declassification process, Grew replied that certain officials could declassify materials whenever they thought it appropriate. Stone observed that if "top secret," materials could be declassified so arbitrarily, they could not have been very sensitive to begin with. I. F. Stone, "Arrest of 'the Six,'" *The Nation*, June 16, 1945, 666–67.

29. Truman's response to the story is in Frank McNaughton to Jack Beal, July 7, 1945, McNaughton Papers, HST. McNaughton was a correspondent for *Time*. "Grew Flatly Denies Japan Seeks Peace," *New York Times*, June 30, 1945, 3.

30. "White Urges Truman to Give Terms to Tokyo," *New York Times*, July 3, 1945, 3.

31. "Big Three Asked to Tell Foe Price of Peace," *New York Times*, July 13, 1945, 3.

32. "Power v. Statesmanship," *Time*, July 16, 1945, 15.

33. The editorial gained wider circulation when it was reported in "Japan Warned to Give Up Soon," *New York Times*, July 22, 1945, 1.

34. Marlene Mayo has noted that for some, "There was almost no worse epithet than New Deal." Marlene J. Mayo, "American Wartime Planning for Occupied Japan: The Role of Experts," in Robert Wolfe, ed. *Americans as Proconsuls: United States Military Government in Germany and Japan, 1944–1952* (Carbondale: Southern Illinois University Press, 1984), 50.

35. "Japanese Expect Concessions," *New York Times*, July 22, 1945, 4.

36. JCS and Heads of Civilian War Agencies, June 26, 1945, CCS 334 (February 2, 1945), Joint Chiefs of Staff Papers, RG 218, Combined Chiefs of Staff, NARA.

37. Quoted in John Chapell, *Before the Bomb: How America Approached the End of the Pacific War* (Lexington: University Press of Kentucky, 1996), 124.

38. Frank McNaughton to Jack Beal, July 7, 1945, McNaughton Papers, HST.

39. Reports of talks held on July 10, 13, and 16 are in "Japanese Peace Feelers in Bern," in MAGIC Diplomatic Summaries, July 23, 24, 1945; microfilm reel 14, Intercepted Japanese Messages (Operation MAGIC) RG 457, Modern Military Records, National Archives; Ronald Lewin, *The American MAGIC: Codes, Ciphers, and the Defeat of Japan* (New York: Farrar Straus & Giroux, 1982), 282.

40. William Donovan to the White House, July 18, 1945, OSS Reports to the White House, William Donovan Papers, U.S. Army Heritage and Education Center, Carlisle Barracks, Carlisle, Pennsylvania.

41. Summary of message, June 5, 1945, Proposed Peace Discussions in Bern, microfilm reel 14, Intercepted Japanese Messages (Operation MAGIC) RG 457.

42. "Magic"—Diplomatic Summary, War Department, Office of Assistant Chief of Staff, G-2, No. 1214—July 22, 1945, Top Secret Ultra, Record Group 457, facsimile in Burr, Atomic Bomb and the End of World War II, National Security Archive Electronic Briefing Book No. 525, https://nsarchive2.gwu.edu/nukevault/ebb525-The-Atomic-Bomb-and-the-End-of-World-War-II/.

43. Summary of message, July 22, 1945, in Japanese Navy Orders Bern Official to Withdraw from Peace Negotiations, MAGIC Diplomatic Summaries, July 28, 1945, microfilm reel 14, Intercepted Japanese Messages (Operation MAGIC) RG 457.

44. Donovan to the Secretary of State, July 16, 1945, *FRUS, 1945, British Commonwealth, Far East,* 6: 489–91

45. Rudolf V. A. Janssens, *"What Future for Japan?": U.S. Wartime Planning for the Postwar Era, 1942–1945* (Amsterdam: Rodopi, 1995), 368–69, 369n98.

46. Butow, *Japan's Decision to Surrender,* 103–11; Sigal, *Fighting to a Finish,* 60.

47. Bonner F. Fellers, "The Psychology of the Japanese Soldier," Fort Leavenworth, Kansas: The Command and General Staff School, 1935, Ike Skelton Combined Arms Research Library Digital Library, see 5–7.

48. Joseph W. Bendersky, *The Jewish Threat: Anti-Semitic Politics of the U.S. Army* (New York: Basic Books, 2001), 2632–63.

49. D. Clayton James, *The Years of MacArthur. Volume 2, 1941–1945* (Boston: Houghton Mifflin Company, 1975), 668–69.

50. Fellers to Hoover, June 20, 1939, Papers of Bonner Fellers, Hoover Institution on War, Revolution and Peace, Stanford, California. (Hereafter cited as Hoover Institution.)

51. Fellers to Hoover, with attached report, June 20, 1940, Fellers Papers, Hoover Institution.

52. John W. Dower, *Embracing Defeat: Japan in the Wake of World War II* (New York: W.W. Norton Co., 1999), 281–84.

53. Relations Between USSR and Japan, U.S. Army Psychological Warfare Board, March 28, 1945, Box 3, Papers of Bonner F. Fellers, Hoover Institution.

54. Fellers to Hunt, May 20, 1945, Fellers Papers, Hoover Institution.

55. Fellers to Hunt, July 21, 1945, Fellers Papers, Hoover Institution.

56. Draft of Seven Point Plan, ca. July 1945, Fellers Papers, Hoover Institution.

57. Fellers to Hunt, July 21, 1945, Fellers Papers, Hoover Institution. (Copies of the Fellers papers are also in the MacArthur Archive in Norfolk, Virginia.)

58. Much of what Fellers wrote, however, made his claim to expertise suspect. Fellers told his fellow intelligence officers, "The people of Japan who believe themselves to be gods, are unaware of and absolutely cannot understand either America or Democracy" as they were represented in the Declaration of Independence, Constitution, and such principles as racial and religious toleration, opposition to slavery, and dignity of the individual. Sounding not unlike Lothrop Stoddard, Fellers asserted that the Japanese were distinctive because of their "intense emotionality," "regimented thought," "brutality," and "attachment to home and family." Dower, *Embracing Defeat*, 284–85.

59. Dower, *Embracing Defeat*, 282; Haruo Iguchi, "Bonner Fellers and U.S. Japan Relations, June 1945–June 1946," *Journal of American and Canadian Studies* 20 (2002), 87.

60. Marc Gallicchio, "Zacharias, Ellis Mark (01 January 1890–28 June 1961)," American National Biography Online, https://doi-org.czp1.villanova.edu/ 10.1093/anb/9780198606697.article.0700340.

61. Zacharias's recommendation, that the ideal speaker should be someone familiar with Japan and some of its leaders, made it clear that he was writing his own job description.

62. Zacharias was friends with Herbert Elliston, editorial page editor of the *Washington Post*. Elliston also favored clarification of unconditional surrender. Hellegers, *We, the Japanese People*, 310n157; A Constant Reader, "Surrender Debate. A Communication," *Washington Post*, July 21, 1945, 4; David A. Pfeiffer, "Loose Cannon or Sage Prophet: Skilled Intelligence Officer in World War II Foresaw Japan's Plans But Annoyed Navy Brass," *Prologue* 40, no. 2 (Summer 2008), https://www.archives.gov/publications/prologue/2008/summer/ zacharias.html.

63. "Capt. Zacharias' Broadcast: Suzuki's View Stressed Warning to Tokyo Chiefs," *New York Times*, July 22, 1945, 4.

64. Arthur Krock, "In the Nation: Objects of Our Propaganda to Japan a Double Target on High Authority," *New York Times*, July 24, 1945, 22; Captain Ellis M. Zacharias, *Secret Missions: The Story of an Intelligence Officer* (New York: Putnam, 1946), 382.

65. David A. Pfeiffer, "Loose Cannon or Sage Prophet: Skilled Intelligence Officer in World War II Foresaw Japan's Plans But Annoyed Navy Brass," *Prologue* 40, no. 2 (Summer 2008), https://www.archives.gov/publications/prologue/ 2008/summer/zacharias.html

66. E. S. Duffield to Edward Barrett, July 24, 1945; T. L. Barnard to Duffield, July 26, 1945, both in 56–11–35, Box 98, RG 80, General Correspondence of the Secretary of the Navy (Forrestal), and James K. Vardaman, Jr., to Assistant

Secretary of the Navy, July 28, 1945, Box 139, RG 80, Operational Archives, Naval Historical Center, Washington Navy Yard, Washington, DC; Hellegers, *We, the Japanese People*, 78.

67. Krock, "In the Nation," 22.

68. "The U.S. at War," *Time*, July 13, 1945. See also Walter Lippmann, "Today and Tomorrow: Terms for Japan," *Washington Post*, July 12, 1945, 7; Constantine Brown, "These Changing Times," *Evening Star*, July 4, 1945, A-4.

69. *Kiplinger Washington Letter*, July 14 and July 21, 1945.

70. *Kiplinger Washington Letter*, July 21, 1945.

71. Like *Time*, the *Washington Letter* was designed to be accessible to busy readers. Kiplinger pioneered a clipped, staccato syntax with key points underscored for easy scanning. In the 1930s, Kiplinger benefitted from contacts in FDR's inner circle, the Brains Trust, and by the 1940s, the *Washington Letter* was on the verge of reaching two hundred thousand subscribers. "W. M. Kiplinger Is Dead at 76," *New York Times*, August 6, 1967, 29.

72. *Kiplinger Washington Letter*, July 21, 1945.

73. Grew to Byrnes, July 13, 1945, *FRUS: Conference of Berlin*, 1: 902–3.

74. I am grateful to Richard Frank for sharing with me this insight on the connection between American confidence and growing carelessness with information. Frank to Gallicchio, July 16, 2019.

75. Editor's note. *FRUS: Conference of Berlin*, 2: 245.

76. Entry for July 16, 1945, Stimson Diaries.

77. Truman-Stalin Meeting, July 17, 1945, and Bohlen Post-Conference Memorandum, March 1960, *FRUS: Conference of Berlin*, 2: 43–46, 1582–87; Robert H. Ferrell, ed., *Dear Bess: The Letters from Harry to Bess Truman, 1910–1959* (New York: Norton, 1983), 519.

78. Michael Nieberg, *Potsdam: The End of World War II and the Remaking of Europe* (New York: Basic Books, 2015), 107, 147.

79. Minutes of Meeting of the JCS, July 17, 1945, *FRUS: Conference of Berlin*, 2: 39–40.

80. Matthias Correa to James Forrestal, July 4, 1945; and Admiral King to JCS, July 6, 1945, both in file 331–21, Box 65, Forrestal-Secretary of the Navy, RG80 (General Correspondence of the Secretary of the Navy), Old Army and Navy Branch, NARA.

81. Military Aspects of Unconditional Surrender Formula, JCS 1275/6, July 19, 1945, w/enclosure, ABC 387 Japan (February 15, 1945), Section 1-B, RG 165, MMRB, NA.

82. Memorandum for General Handy from General Craig, July 14, 1945, ibid.

83. Minutes of Meeting of the JCS, July 17, 1945, *FRUS: Conference of Berlin*, 2: 39–40.

84. Memorandum for the President, July 18, 1945, *FRUS: Conference of Berlin*, 2: 1268–69.

85. Grew to Byrnes, transmitting Cordell Hull to James Byrnes, July 16, 1945; Memorandum of Conversation, Grew and Hull, July 17, 1945, *FRUS: Conference of Berlin*, 2: 1268–69.

86. Grew proposed a lengthy "elucidation" in response to a query from the Associated Press International News Agency. Grew to Byrnes, July 19, 1945, and Byrnes to Grew, July 21, 1945, *FRUS: Conference of Berlin*, 2: 1270–71, 1272; Janssens, "*What Future for Japan?*," 303–6.

87. Richard Frank explains how the process of informing Truman might have worked. Frank, *Downfall*, 241. See also Barton J. Bernstein, "The Alarming Japanese Buildup on Southern Kyushu, Growing U.S. Fears, and Counterfactual Analysis: Would the Planned November 1945 Invasion of Southern Kyushu Have Occurred?," *Pacific Historical Review* 68, no. 4 (November 1999), 576n24.

88. Continued Japanese Interest in Peace, July 26, 1945; Japanese in Switzerland Argue for Peace, July 27, 1945, Box 18, RG 457, Records of the National Security Agency/Central Security Service, National Archives, College Park, Maryland

89. Butow, *Japan's Decision to Surrender*, 123–25.

90. Japanese Peace Move, July 12, 1945; Follow-Up Message on Japanese Peace Move, July 13, 1945; both in MAGIC Diplomatic Summary, in Burr, *The Atomic Bomb and the End of World War II*, http://nsarchive.gwu.edu/NSAEBB/NSAEBB162/29.pdf.

91. Frank, *Downfall*, 225–27; Ronald Lewin, *The American MAGIC: Codes Cyphers, and the Defeat of Japan* (New York: Farrar, Straus and Giroux, 1982), 280–82.

92. The memorandum contains a message intended for Marshall. Memorandum for the Deputy Chief of Staff, Japanese Peace Offer, July 13, 1945, in Burr, *Atomic Bomb and the End of World War II*, http://nsarchive.gwu.edu/NSAEBB/NSAEBB162/30.pdf.

93. At first, the Japanese feared a direct assault on Honshu because they overestimated the speed with which the U.S. would be able to redeploy divisions from Europe. Once they recognized their error, Japanese planners predicted that the first assault would come against Kyushu. John Ray Skates, *The Invasion of Japan: The Alternative to the Bomb* (Columbia: University of South Carolina Press, 1994), 103; Edward J. Drea, *MacArthur's ULTRA: Codebreaking and the War Against Japan, 1942–1945* (Lawrence: University Press of Kansas, 1992), 203; Hattori Takushiro, *The Complete History of the Greater East Asia War* (Tokyo: Headquarters 500th Military Intelligence Service Group, 1954), 176.

94. Minutes of the Meeting Held at the White House on June 18, 1945, *FRUS: Conference of Berlin*, 1: 907.

95. Owing to the time differences, Marshall probably received the message on July 23. General H. A. Craig to Marshall, July 22, 1945, Item 2190, Reel 117, GCM; Maddox, *Weapons for Victory*, 118.

96. Tripartite Military Meeting, July 24, 1945, *FRUS: Conference at Berlin*, 2: 346.

97. For the buildup. see Drea, *MacArthur's ULTRA*, 206–21. See also Frank, *Downfall*, 198–211, especially for discrepancies in MacArthur's and the Navy's analyses and estimates.

98. Drea, *MacArthur's ULTRA*, 213.

99. Report of Imperial Headquarters Army Department, [July 1, 1945], in *Defense of the Homeland and End of the War*, volume 12 in Donald Detwiler and Charles Burdick, eds., *War in Asia and the Pacific: A Fifteen Volume Collection* (New York: Garland, 1980). This is the Japanese official history written under the supervision of the American Military Intelligence Section following the end of the war.

100. Anne O'Hare McCormick, "Abroad: Echoes of Conversations at Potsdam the Key Question Timing Significant," *New York Times*, July 25, 1945, 22.

101. "Terms for Japan," *New York Times*, July 23, 1945, 18.

102. "Japanese in Europe See U.S. Softening," July 20, 1945, Intercepted Japanese Messages (Operation MAGIC) RG 457.

103. "Radio to Japs Fails to Ease Peace Terms," *Washington Post*, July 23, 1945, 3.

104. Grew cited reports in the Associated Press, *Washington Post, Washington Evening Star, Baltimore Sun, New York Herald Tribune,* and *New York Times*. Grew to Byrnes, July 22, 1945, *FRUS: Conference of Berlin*, 2: 1273–74.

105. "Tokyo Radio Appeals to U.S. For a More Lenient Peace," *New York Times*, July 26, 1945, 1.

106. "Americans' Drive Is to Save Prestige, Tokyo Radio Says," *Washington Post*, July 25, 1945, 2.

107. "Tokyo Radio Appeals to U.S. for a More Lenient Peace," *New York Times*, July 26, 1945, 1.

108. William White, "OPA, Tariff Fights Loom in Congress," *New York Times*, June 18, 1945, 21; "Extending Price Control," *New York Times*, June 18, 1945, 18; "Terms to End War Urged on Truman," *New York Times*, July 24, 1945, 5. Wherry quoted in Eric F. Goldman, *Rendezvous with Destiny: A History of Modern American Reform* (New York: Vintage, 1977), 300.

109. "Terms to End War Urged on Truman," *New York Times*, July 24, 1945, 5.

110. "Magnuson in Senate Urges Stern Terms," *New York Times*, July 25, 1945, 3; "Washington Surprised," *New York Times*, July 27, 1945, 4. Press coverage is discussed in Uday Mohan and Sanho Tree, "Hiroshima, the American Media, and the Construction of Conventional Wisdom, *Journal of American East Asian Relations* 4, no. 2 (Summer 1995), 141–60, especially 152–56.

111. "Blow on Blow: At Japan's Homeland Threefold Attack Halsey's Strikes," *New York Times*, July 22, 1945, 59.

112. Major George Fielding Elliot, "Unknown Factors," *Evening Star*, July 23, 1945, A-8.

113. Elliot's column was carried in thirty-five newspapers and reached an estimated five million readers. Major George Fielding Elliot, "Unknown Factors,"

*Evening Star*, July 23, 1945, A-8; "George Fielding Eliot, 76, Dies; Military Writer of World War II," *New York Times*, April 22, 1971.

CHAPTER 4

1. Entry for July 25, 1945, in Ferrell, *Off the Record*, 55–56.
2. Groves's report is reproduced in Martin J. Sherwin, *A World Destroyed: The Atomic Bomb and the Grand Alliance* (New York: Vintage Books, 1977), appendix P, 308–14.
3. Gallicchio, *Cold War Begins in Asia*, 43; Maddox, *Weapons for Victory*, 102.
4. Notes of the meeting were written in an informal abbreviated form by Russian specialist and interpreter Charles Bohlen. Truman-Stalin Meeting, July 17, 1945, *FRUS: Conference of Berlin*, 2: 43–46.
5. Entry for July 17, 1945, William D. Leahy Diaries, Leahy Papers, Library of Congress (microfilm). (Hereafter cited as Leahy Diaries.)
6. Entry for July 17, 1945, Ferrell, *Off the Record*, 53.
7. Entry for July 18, 1945, Stimson Diaries.
8. Ferrell, *Dear Bess*, 519.
9. Entry for July 18, 1945, Ferrell, *Off the Record*, 53–54.
10. Eighth Plenary Meeting, July 24, 1945, *FRUS: Conference of Berlin*, 2: 362.
11. I am closely following the interpretation of the Stalin-Soong talks in Maddox, *Weapons for Victory*, 101–3.
12. Michael Neiberg, *Potsdam: The End of World War II and the Remaking of Europe* (New York: Basic Books, 2015), 234.
13. Truman to Ambassador Hurley (for Chiang Kai-shek), July 23, 1945, *FRUS, 1945. Far East, China*, 7: 950.
14. Entry for July 24, 1945, Stimson Diaries.
15. All quotes in this section from Vinson to Truman, July 19, 1945, Naval Aide to President, 1945–1953, Berlin Conference, Communications from the Map Room, July 15–25, Box 6, HST Papers, HST.
16. Vinson to Truman, July 20, 1945, Naval Aide to President, 1945–1953, Berlin Conference, Communications from the Map Room, July 15–25, Box 6, HST Papers, HST.
17. Memorandum for the President, [July 21, 1945], Correspondence with the President, 1945, Political File, 1945–1946, Box 139, Vinson Papers, HST.
18. Truman's reply is quoted in a cross reference file that recorded action on presidential correspondence. VINSON, Hon. Fred M., Official File 122 (1945), HST.
19. Entry for July 21, 1945, Stimson Diaries; Sherwin, *A World Destroyed*, 223–24.
20. Truman to Ambassador Hurley, for Chiang Kai-shek, July 24, *FRUS: Conference of Berlin*, 2: 1278.
21. Entry for July 24, 1945, Stimson Diaries.
22. Entry for July 24, 1945, Stimson Diaries.

23. Reports from witnesses vary as to what specifically Truman said to Stalin. Hasegawa, *Racing the Enemy*, 154; Maddox, *Weapons for Victory*, 99; Donovan, *Conflict and Crisis*, 93.

24. Philip Ziegler, ed., *Personal Diary of Admiral the Lord Louis Mountbatten: Supreme Allied Commander, South-East Asia, 1943–1946* (London: Collins, 1988), 230.

25. Ziegler, *Mountbatten Diary*, 231.

26. Ziegler, *Mountbatten Diary*, 232.

27. Frank, *Downfall*, 243; Maddox, *Weapons for Victory*, 118.

28. Memorandum for the Secretary of War, "Status of Demobilization Plans to Meet an Early Defeat of Japan," August 1, 1945, Item 2338, Reel 79, MRL.

29. All quotations in this section are from Memorandum for the President, [July 25, 1945], Item 2595, Reel 109, MRL.

30. Entry for July 25, 1945, Ferrell, *Off the Record*, 55–56.

31. Byrnes-Molotov Meeting, July 27, 1945, *FRUS: Conference of Berlin*, 2: 449–50; Gallicchio, *Cold War Begins*, 45; Donovan, *Conflict and Crisis*, 95.

32. Proclamation Defining Terms for Japanese, *Department of State Bulletin*, July 29, 1945, 13: 137–38; also in Proclamation by the Heads of Governments, the United States, China, and Great Britain, July 26, 1945, *FRUS: Conference of Berlin*, 2: 1474–76.

33. Proclamation by the Heads of Governments, the United States, China, and Great Britain, July 26, 1945, *FRUS: Conference of Berlin*, 2: 1474–76.

34. Entry for July 26, 1945, Leahy Diaries.

35. Gallicchio, *Cold War Begins in Asia*, 46.

36. Entry for July 28, 1945, in Millis, *Forrestal Diaries*, 78.

37. Maddox, *Weapons for Victory*, 121, 127; Charles E. Bohlen, *Witness to History, 1929–1969* (New York: W. W. Norton and Company, 1973), 236–37.

38. Some historians have suggested that in electing to release the declaration over the airwaves as a radio broadcast rather than through diplomatic channels, the Americans showed that they regarded the warning merely as propaganda. There is merit in that view. The declaration was aimed at the American home front as well as Japan. Moreover, by the time it was issued, the Japanese had given Truman and his advisors ample reason to think that any statement would be rejected. It should be noted, however, that in issuing the warning as a broadcast, the Allies followed the recommendation of the McCloy committee. The staff officers who drafted the declaration thought it would be most effective if it were treated like the Cairo Declaration and other major Allied pronouncements. In the final analysis, the medium chosen to communicate with Tokyo was not an impediment to Japan's accepting it or seeking clarification.

39. Hasegawa, *Racing the Enemy*, 162, 165–66.

40. Butow, *Japan's Decision to Surrender*, 143–45; Hasegawa, *Racing the Enemy*, 165–66, Bix, *Hirohito*, 500–501.

41. Butow, *Japan's Decision to Surrender*, 146–49; Hasegawa, *Racing the Enemy*, 167–68, Bix, *Hirohito*, 500–501.

42. The AP and *New York Times* quoted Suzuki as saying the declaration was "merely an expansion" of the Cairo Declaration. "Japan Officially Spurns Ultimatum," *Pittsburgh Post-Gazette* (United Press), July 30, 1945, 2; "Premier Plans to Fight On," *Philadelphia Inquirer* (Associated Press), July 30, 1; "Japan Officially Turns Down Allied Surrender Ultimatum," *New York Times*, July 30, 1945, 1; "Jap Premier Scorns Allied Peace Demand: Suzuki Asserts Nip Plane Production Above Anticipation," *Washington Post* (UP), July 30, 1945, 1.

43. Butow, *Japan's Decision to Surrender*, 149–50; Frank, *Downfall*, 235–38; Hasegawa, *Racing the Enemy*, 169–72.

44. Frank, *Downfall*, 234–39.

45. The mirror is kept in several wooden boxes within boxes at the Ise shrine, the sword is stored in a wooden box inside a stone container at the Atsuta shrine. Some historians refer to the sacred jewel, but Shillony refers to jewels. Replicas of the relics are stored in the palace in Tokyo, but they are hidden from view also. Ben-Ami Shillony, *Enigma of the Emperors: Sacred Subservience in Japanese History* (Kent, UK: Global Oriental, 2005), 29–31; Bix, *Hirohito*, 502–3.

46. "Jap's Potsdam Ultimatum Seen by Senators as Apt to Shorten War," *Pittsburgh Post-Gazette*, July 27, 1945, 1.

47. Constantine Brown, "This Changing World," *Evening Star*, July 30, 1945, A-6.

48. Ernest K. Lindley, "People Laud Ultimatum For Japan," *Washington Post*, July 29, 1945, B5.

49. The offenders were Grew, Nelson Rockefeller, Assistant Secretary of State James C. Dunn, and Assistant Secretary of State Julius Holmes. Thomas Casey to the President of the United States, July 21, 1945, with resolutions; William D. Hassett to Thomas Casey, July 28, 1945, Box 801, Official File 190, Potsdam Conference, HST.

50. Wallace was the herald of the "Century of the Common Man," which was the title of his most famous wartime address. He viewed the State Department as anti-Soviet and ultra-conservative. By late 1944, he harbored a fear that an American Fascism, led by business interests, was on the rise. J. Samuel Walker, *Henry A. Wallace and American Foreign Policy* (Westport, CT: Greenwood Press, 1976), 83–99; Entry for July 24, 1945, John Morton Blum, ed., *The Price of Vision: The Diary of Henry A. Wallace, 1942–1946* (Boston: Houghton Mifflin Company, 1973), 479.

51. "Birds of a Feather," *Washington Post*, July 29, 1945, 5B.

52. Suspicion about the anti-Soviet motives of those seeking to modify unconditional surrender was not limited to metropolitan liberals. See "Shall We Let Japan Off Easy?," *Roanoke Rapids Herald*, July 19, 1945, 6; "Shape of Things," *Nation*, July 28, 1945, 69.

53. "Terms for Japan," *New Republic*, July 30, 1945, 119–20.

54. "Japan's Choice," *Nation*, August 4, 1945, 103.

55. Hanson Baldwin, "Terms for Japanese," *New York Times*, July 27, 1945, 4.

56. The dates for the Gallup Polls are July 27–August 1. The Foreign Affairs Surveys are listed as August, but the questions indicate both were conducted before August 14 and most likely the first week of August. Polls obtained online through Roper Center for Public Opinion Research, *Roper Express*, I Roper Center.

57. "Army to Hit Japan with 8000 Planes," *Washington Post*, July 30, 1945, 1.

58. "Tokyo Area, Inland Sea Again Given Pounding," *Washington Post*, July 30, 1945, 1.

59. "Allied Warships Roving Off Japan Unchallenged," *Washington Post*, August 1, 1945, 1.

60. John Terraine, *The Life and Times of Lord Mountbatten* (London, 1968), 124.

61. Lt. Colonel David M. Glantz, *August Storm: The Soviet 1945 Strategic Offensive in Manchuria* (Ft. Leavenworth, KS: Combat Studies Institute, 1983); Louis Allen, *The End of the War in Asia* (London: Hart-Davis, MacGibbon, 1976), 193–96.

62. Heinrichs and Gallicchio, *Implacable Foes*, 483–503, 535–40.

63. Saburo Hayashi in collaboration with Alvin D. Coox, *Kōgun: The Japanese Army in the Pacific* (Quantico, VA: Marine Corps Association, 1959), 178–80.

64. Allen, *End of the War in Asia*, 74–75.

65. Frank, *Downfall*, 280.

66. Hasegawa, *Racing the Enemy*, 163.

67. Estimates of the attacking force vary slightly. Edward Drea places the number at about 650,000. Richard Frank cites in formation in a Sixth Army Field Order of July 28, 1945, to reach a total of 693,295. Drea, MacArthur's *ULTRA*, 217.

68. Ibid., 125; Ziegler, *Mountbatten Diary*, 231–32.

69. Samuel Eliot Morison, *The U.S. Naval Operations in World War II*, vol. 14, *Victory in the Pacific, 1945* (Boston: Little, Brown and Company, 1960), 354; D. Clayton James, *The Years of MacArthur* (Boston: Houghton Mifflin Company, 1975), 2: 771. MacArthur's several communications on the subject are summarized in Memorandum for the Chief of Staff, August 1, 1945, OPD 014.1 TS, cases 50/2, RG 165.

70. Gallicchio, *Cold War Begins in Asia*, 63.

## CHAPTER 5

1. Log of the President's Trip, *FRUS: Conference of Berlin*, 2: 3–28

2. Four days earlier, Willoughby had filed an amended intelligence assessment warning that the increase in defenders on Kyushu "if not checked, may grow to a point where we attack on a ratio of one (1) to one (1) which is not a recipe for victory." General Headquarters, U.S. Armed Forces Pacific, Military Intelligence Summary, General Staff, "Amendment No. 1 to G-2 Estimate of the Enemy Situation with Respect to Kyushu (dated April 25, 1945)," July 29, 1945, Stephen Chamberlain Papers, U.S. Army Heritage and Education

Center, Carlisle Barracks, Carlisle, Pennsylvania. A copy of the April 25 G-2 estimate is also in this file. Frank, *Downfall*, 202–4.

3. Frank, *Downfall*, 272–73.

4. Sato's message was dated July 30. MAGIC Diplomatic Summary, August 1, 1945, MAGIC Diplomatic Summaries, 1942–1945, Box 18, RG 457, Records of the National Security Agency/Central Security Agency, National Archives, College Park, Maryland.

5. MAGIC-Diplomatic Summary, August 2, 1945, MAGIC Diplomatic Summaries, 1942–1945, Box 18, RG 457.

6. MAGIC-Diplomatic Summary, August 5, 1945, MAGIC Diplomatic Summaries, 1942–1945, Box 18, RG 457.

7. This summary of conditions in Japan is based on Thomas Heavens, *Valley of Darkness: The Japanese People and World War II* (New York: W. W. Norton, 1978); Frank Gibney, ed., *Sensō. The Japanese Remember the Pacific War: Letters to the Editor of Asahi Shimbun* (Armonk, NY: M. E. Sharpe, 1995); Tessa Morris-Suzuki, *Showa: An Inside History of Hirohito's Japan* (New York: Shocken Books, 1985); John W. Dower, *Embracing Defeat: Japan in the Wake of World War II* (New York: W. W. Norton, 1999); Yukiko Koshiro, *Imperial Eclipse: Japan's Strategic Thinking About Continental Asia Before August 1945* (Ithaca, NY: Cornell University Press, 2013), 235.

8. Boyle, *Modern Japan*, 288; David Rees, *The Defeat of Japan* (Westport, CT: Praeger, 1997), 154–56; Frank, *Downfall*, 264–67.

9. "Blast Power of New Weapon Most Terrific in War Annals," *Washington Post*, August 7, 1945, 1.

10. Cabinet Meeting and Togo's Meeting with the Emperor, August 7–8, 1945. Source: Gaimusho (Ministry of Foreign Affairs), ed., *Shūsen Shiroku* (The Historical Records of the End of the War), annotated by Jun Eto, 4: 57–60 [Excerpts] [Translation by Toshihiro Higuchi]; and Diary Entry for Wednesday, August 8, 1945, Source: Takashi Itoh, ed., *Sokichi Takagi: Nikki to Joho* [Sokichi Takagi: Diary and Documents] (Tokyo, Japan: Misuzu-Shobo, 2000), 923–24 [Translation by Hikaru Tajima], in Document 55a and 55b; all in Burr, ed., *The Atomic Bomb and the End of World War II*, Archive, http://nsarchive.gwu.edu/NSAEBB/NSAEBB162/63.pdf; Morris-Suzuki, *Showa*, 139–82; Boyle, *Modern Japan*, 290.

11. Bonesteel also said that the Army had polled GIs on their opinions about the emperor. In another instance, however, he said the Army had gleaned soldiers' attitudes by reading their mail. Memorandum for General Lincoln, August 7, 1945, ABC 387 Japan (February 15, 1945) Section 1-B, NA; Bonesteel Oral History, Senior Officers' Debriefing Program, 1971, U.S. Army Heritage and Education Foundation, Carlisle Barracks, Pennsylvania; Brian Loring Villa, "The U.S. Army, Unconditional Surrender, and the Potsdam Proclamation," *Journal of American History* (June 1976), 66–92.

12. The day before, MacLeish had asked the Japan expert Joseph Ballantine for the State Department's answers to several probing questions regarding the Potsdam Declaration. The tone of that message made it clear that MacLeish was guarding against any softening of unconditional surrender. Ballantine to MacLeish, August 8, 1945, *FRUS, 1945, The British Commonwealth, the Far East*, 6: 591–92; MacLeish to Grew, August 9, 1945, Correspondence, Grew, Papers of Archibald MacLeish, Library of Congress.

13. It is not clear if MacLeish's objections would have been enough to kill the broadcast. Zacharias may not have been aware of MacLeish's outraged comments. He does not mention the broadcast in his memoir, Captain Ellis M. Zacharias, *Secret Missions: The Story of an Intelligence Officer* (New York: G. P. Putnam's Sons, 1946), 384–89.

14. Glantz, *August Storm*, 79–94; Allen, *The End of the War in Asia*, 195–96; Frank, *Downfall*, 277–83.

15. Allen, *The End of the War in Asia*, 196.

16. Cabinet Meeting and Togo's Meeting with the Emperor, August 7–8, 1945, Source: *Gaimusho* (Ministry of Foreign Affairs), ed., *Shusen Shiroku* (The Historical Records of the End of the War), annotated by Jun Eto, 4: 57–60 [Excerpts] [Translation by Toshihiro Higuchi], all in Document 55a, Burr, ed., *The Atomic Bomb and the End of World War II*, Archive, http://nsarchive. gwu.edu/NSAEBB/NSAEBB162/63.pdf; Butow, *Japan's Decision to Surrender*, 160–64; John Hunter Boyle, *Modern Japan: The American Nexus* (Fort Worth, TX: Harcourt Brace Jovanovich, 1993), 290–92; Tsuyoshi Hasegawa, *Racing the Enemy: Stalin, Truman, and the Surrender of Japan* (Cambridge, MA: Harvard University Press, 2005), 185, 203–5.

17. For reasons known only to himself, Hiranuma continued to speak. In doing so, he appeared to reverse himself and support the military's position. Anami, for one, was confused as to where Hiranuma stood. Ultimately, Hiranuma's meanderings did not matter. The emperor had already decided to accept the declaration with only one condition. "Hoshina Memorandum" on the Emperor's "Sacred Decision [*go-seidan*]," August 9–10, 1945, Source: Zenshiro Hoshina, *Daitoa Senso Hishi: Hoshina Zenshiro Kaiso-roku* [Secret History of the Greater East Asia War: Memoir of Zenshiro Hoshina] (Tokyo, Japan: Hara-Shobo, 1975), excerpts from Section 5, "The Emperor made go-seidan [= the sacred decision]—the decision to terminate the war," 139–49 [translation by Hikaru Tajima], Document 62, in Burr, ed., *The Atomic Bomb and the End of World War II*, Archive, http://nsarchive.gwu.edu/NSAEBB/NSAEBB162/ 63.pdf; Butow, *Japan's Decision to Surrender*, 164–74; Hasegawa, *Racing the Enemy*, 203–12; Frank, *Downfall*, 290–94.

18. Byrnes's memoir also inaccurately omits crucial details about how the final response to Japan was written. See John K. Emerson, *The Japanese Thread: A Life in the U.S. Foreign Service* (New York: Holt Reinhart, and Winston, 1978), 237–38.

19. Also present was John Snyder, a banker and friend of Truman's whom the president had called to Washington shortly after taking office. Byrnes's account is in Entry for August 10, 1945, folder 102, Conferences 2–1, Potsdam, Walter Brown's Book, Special Collections, Robert Muldrow Cooper Library, Clemson University, Clemson, South Carolina. Entry for August 10, 1945, Ayers Diary, Ayers Papers, HST.

20. This error may have gone unnoticed by historians because the editorial note that precedes Truman's entry states that the president arrived at the White House on August 9. Truman's ship docked at Hampton Roads at 5:25 p.m. on August 7. Editorial note and entry for August 10, 1945, in Ferrell, *Off the Record*, 59–62; "Truman Back from Europe, Holds Cabinet Conference," *New York Times*, August 8, 1945, 1; "The President's Homecoming," *New York Times*, August 8, 1945, 22. The 9:00 a.m. meeting on August 10 is also reported in "Japan Offers to Surrender: U.S. May Let Emperor Remain," *New York Times*, August 11, 1945, 1.

21. Entries for Thursday, August 9, 1945, and Friday, August 10, 1945, Appointments, Box 20, Rose Conway Files, HST. See also the entry for August 10, 1945, in Millis, *Forrestal Diaries*, 82–84.

22. Entry for August 10, 1945, Stimson Diary.

23. Entry for August 10, 1945, in James Forrestal's diary, in Millis, *Forrestal Diaries*, 82–84.

24. There are several differing accounts of this episode. According to Joseph Ballantine, Truman, Byrnes, and the other cabinet members were going to accept the Japanese offer at face value. That would have been a disaster because, as Ballantine noted, the emperor's powers were all-embracing. According to Ballantine, the Allies were saved from making this disastrous mistake by Grew, who at the urging of Dooman and Ballantine went to see Byrnes in his office. Grew was rebuffed, but Dooman and Ballantine beseeched Grew to try again. This time Ballantine and Dooman were invited in the secretary's office, and the two men quickly persuaded Ben Cohen that the Americans could not accept the Japanese reply without revision. There is no other corroboration of Ballantine's dramatic account. Neither Dooman nor Grew mention it. And there is no evidence to indicate that Byrnes was willing to accept the Japanese condition at face value. Hugh Borton, a State Department advisor and Japan scholar, noted that Ballantine was alarmed by the June opinion poll showing that Americans were adamantly opposed to keeping the emperor. After the war, Ballantine was intent on showing that he was not soft on the emperor. That concern may have affected his recollection of events as presented in his memoirs. Borton, however, adds to the confusion by saying, "Our immediate task therefore was to prepare a reply that did not restrict the Allied commander's authority but gave the Japanese assurances that the emperor's prerogatives would not be compromised." The Americans wanted to guarantee the Allied commander's supreme authority, but they were not trying to assure the Japanese that the emperor's prerogatives

would be preserved. Ballantine's memoir also includes a significant error in his description of Byrnes's reply. Ballantine omits the words "and the Japanese Government" from the phrase "the authority of the Emperor and the Japanese Government to rule the state." Tsuyoshi Hasegawa also notes the absence of any accounts supporting Ballantine's. Joseph Ballantine, Memoirs, 1888–1970, unpublished, 264–65, Joseph Ballantine Papers, Hoover Institution; Hugh Borton, *Spanning Japan's Modern Century: The Memoirs of Hugh Borton* (Lanham, MD: Lexington Books, 2002), 141–43; Hasegawa, *Racing the Enemy*, 347–48n9, Byrnes to Winant, August 10, 1945, *FRUS*, 1945, The British Commonwealth, the Far East, 6: 626.

25. Entry for August 10, 1945, Stimson Diary.
26. Blum, *The Price of Vision*, 473–75; Entry for August 10, 1945, Stimson Diary.
27. "Japan's Surrender Maneuvers," SRH-090, Record Group 457 (Special Research Histories), Modern Military Records Branch, National Archives; Bix, *Hirohito*, 517.
28. Entry for July 25, 1945, Stimson Diary.
29. Entry for August 10, 1945, in Ferrell, *Off the Record*, 61.
30. "Surrender," Frank McNaughton to Eleanor Welch, August 10, 1945, Box 9, McNaughton Papers, HST. For Mansfield's version of the meeting, see Don Oberdorfer, *Senator Mansfield: The Extraordinary Life of a Great American Statesmen and Diplomat* (Washington, DC: Smithsonian Books, 2003), 84–86.
31. "Surrender," Frank McNaughton to Eleanor Welch, August 10, 1945, Box 9, McNaughton Papers, HST. Barton Bernstein cites McNaughton's reports as evidence of Truman's "quest for American-defined justice, and appropriate punishment, not revenge, with a desire to root out Japanese totalitarianism, which Truman linked to Hirohito and the emperor system." Commentary by Barton J. Bernstein, Stanford University, on Tsuyoshi Hasegawa, in Hasegawa, *Racing the Enemy*; H-Diplo Roundtable, *Racing the Enemy Roundtable*, http://networks.h-net.org/system/files/contributed-files/bernstein-hasegawaroundtable.pdf.
32. Entry for August 10, 1945, in Ferrell, *Off the Record*, 61.
33. Commonwealth to Addison, August 12, 1945, W. J. Hudson and Wendy Way, eds., *Documents on Australian Foreign Policy, 1937–1949*, vol. 3, *1945* (Canberra: Australian Publishing Service, 1989), 336–37.
34. Maddox, *Weapons for Victory*, 140.
35. Gallicchio, *Cold War Begins in Asia*, 75–76.
36. Hasegawa, *Racing the Enemy*, 229–31; Hayashi, *Kōgun*, 181.
37. Quoted in Hasegawa, *Racing the Enemy*, 233.
38. Shillony, *Enigma of the Emperors*, 198; Toshikazu Kase, *Journey to the Missouri* (Hamden, CT: Archon Books, 1969), 250.
39. Bix, *Hirohito*, 526; Hasegawa, *Racing the Enemy*, 239–40; Kase, *Journey to the Missouri*, 252.
40. The text can be found in the Pacific Research Society, *Japan's Longest Day* (Tokyo: Kodansha, 1968), 209–11.

41. Bix, *Hirohito*, 526–27; Dower, *Embracing Defeat*, 34–39.

42. The events of August 14 are recounted in Pacific Research Society, *Japan's Longest Day*. For briefer accounts, see Hasegawa, *Racing the Enemy*, 238–46; Kase, *Journey to the Missouri*, 252–54.

43. Memorandum from Major General Clayton Bissell, Assistant Chief of Staff, G-2, for the Chief of Staff, "Estimate of Japanese Situation for Next 30 Days," August 12, 1945, Top Secret, Document 70, in Burr, ed., *The Atomic Bomb and the End of World War II*, http://nsarchive.gwu.edu/NSAEBB/NSAEBB162/70.pdf.

44. Marc Gallicchio, "After Nagasaki: General Marshall's Plan for Tactical Nuclear Weapons in Japan," *Prologue* 23 (Winter 1991), 396–404.

45. "Third Fleet Fliers Smash Suicide Blow, 138 Planes," *Washington Post*, August 14, 1945, 1.

46. Hanson Baldwin, "War Pressure Unrelaxed," *New York Times*, August 14, 1945, 2.

47. Grässli (Swiss Chargé) to James Byrnes, August 14, 1945, *FRUS*, 1945, 6: 662–63; Harry S. Truman: "The President's News Conference," August 14, 1945, Online by Gerhard Peters and John T. Woolley, The American Presidency Project, http://www.presidency.ucsb.edu/ws/?pid=12383.

48. Pacific Research Society, *Japan's Longest Day*, 215–328; Boyle, *Modern Japan*, 295–96; Hasegawa, *Racing the Enemy*, 225–28; Frank, *Downfall*, 316–21.

49. Boyle, *Modern Japan*, 295–96.

50. Gibney, *Sensō*, 215; Morris-Suzuki, *Showa*, 184–89; Samuel Hideeo Yamashita, *Daily Life in Wartime Japan* (Lawrence: University Press of Kansas, 2015), 175–79; Boyle, *Modern Japan*, 296; Dower, *Embracing Defeat*, 34–39.

51. Entry for August 14, 1945, Leahy Diaries; "1 Dead, Over 100 Injured In Victory Celebrations," *Philadelphia Inquirer*, August 15, 1945, 4; "Celebration Nationwide," *Washington Post*, August 15, 1945, 4; "New York Goes Wild 3rd Time," *New York Times*, August 15, 1945, 4; William Craig, *The Fall of Japan* (New York: Dial Press, 1967), 204–5; H. G. Nicholas, ed., *Washington Dispatches 1941–1945: Weekly Political Reports from the British Embassy* (Chicago: University of Chicago Press, 1981), 602.

52. Gallicchio, *Cold War Begins in Asia*, 80–85.

53. Gallicchio, *Cold War Begins in Asia*, 85–88; Marc Gallicchio, "The Kuriles Controversy: U.S. Diplomacy in the Soviet-Japan Border Dispute 1941–1956," *Pacific Historical Review* (February 1991), 69–101.

54. Emperor Hirohito's Surrender Rescript to Japanese Troops, August 17, 1945, Taiwan Documents Project, http://www.taiwandocuments.org/surrender07.htm.

55. The head count of Japanese forces is an approximation. Sources vary as to the numbers. Kase, *Journey to the Missouri*, 262–64; Hayashi, *Kōgun*, 182; James, *Years of MacArthur*, 3: 779–80.

56. Washington to Commander in Chief Army Forces Pacific, August 18, 1945, Blue Binders, Box 9, RG 9, MacArthur Archives, Norfolk, Virginia; War Department to MacArthur, August 17, 1945, TS, Incoming-Outgoing Messages, OPD, Box 57, RG 165, National Archives and Record Administration (NARA), College Park, Maryland;; "MacArthur's Blunt Note Gets Results," *Washington Post*, August 18, 1945, 1; James, *Years of MacArthur*, 2: 778–79.

57. Ronald H. Spector, *In the Ruins of Empire: The Japanese Surrender and the Battle for Postwar Asia* (New York: Random House, 2007), 74–75; Peter Dennis, *Troubled Days of Peace: Mountbatten and South East Asia Command, 1945–1946* (Manchester, UK: Manchester University Press, 1987), 13–15.

58. Michael Schaller, *Douglas MacArthur: The Far Eastern General* (New York: Oxford University Press, 1989), 118–19.

59. James, *Years of MacArthur*, 2: 784–85.

60. This description of the surrender proceedings is taken from Morison, *Victory in the Pacific*, 360–70; James, *Years of MacArthur*, 2: 784–92; Denis A. Clift, "Be Sure Everything Clicks and Clicks on Time," *United States Naval Institute Proceedings* 141, no. 8 (August 2015), 70–73, and the *New York Times'* coverage of the ceremony.

61. The description of the Singapore ceremony and the related quotations are in Ziegler, *Mountbatten Diary*, 245–50. See also "Surrender Signed in Singapore," *Times* (London), September 13, 1945, 4.

62. Michael Schaller, *The American Occupation of Japan: The Origins of the Cold War in Asia* (New York: Oxford University Press, 1985), 24; Fellers wrote that MacArthur outlined his reform plan on his porch while making a layover on Okinawa, Entry for August 29, 1945, Official Diary, Military Secretary, Fellers Papers. He recounted the story five years later for a radio broadcast. Japan Friend or Enemy, notes for Broadcast WGPA, Bethlehem, Pennsylvania, February 22, 1950, Writings of Bonner Fellers, Fellers Papers, MacArthur Memorial Archives. (Hereafter cited as MMA.)

63. Acheson to Truman, September 5, 1945, transmitting SWNCC 181/2, *FRUS*, 1945, 6: 712–14; JCS to MacArthur (JCS 5), September 7, 1945, and JCS to MacArthur, (JCS 6), September 7, 1945, Blue Binders, Box 160, RG 9, MMA.

64. Edwin James, "Too Early to Assess Japanese Occupation," *New York Times*, September 16, 1945, E3; "Put Japs in Their Place and Keep Them There," *Philadelphia Inquirer*, September 6, 1945, 6B; The President's News Conference, September 12, 1945, Harry S. Truman Library and Museum, https://www. trumanlibrary.gov/library/public-papers/132/presidents-news-conference; Nicholas, Washington Dispatches, 615.

65. Text of Statement issued by SCAP (MacArthur), September 17, 1945, *FRUS*, 1945, 6: 715–16.

66. Memorandum of Telephone Conversation, September 17, 1945, *FRUS*, 1945, 6: 716–17.

67. Chief of Staff (Marshall) to MacArthur, September 17, 1945, and MacArthur to Marshall, September 18, 1945, *FRUS*, 1945, 6: 717–18, 718–19.

68. MacArthur's statement ignored information he received from Marshall explaining the outlines of a policy regarding the Allied control machinery for the Japanese empire. The policy would require SCAP to consult with the occupying powers before announcing adjustments in the occupation force. The JCS probably also assumed that MacArthur would discuss those adjustments with Washington before announcing them. Marshall to MacArthur, August 22, 1945, Blue Binders, Box 160, RG 9, MacArthur Memorial Archives; The President's News Conference, September 12, 1945, Harry S. Truman Library and Museum, https://www.trumanlibrary.gov/library/public-papers/132/presidents-news-conference; Schaller, Far Eastern General, 135–36; James, Years of MacArthur, 3: 17–25.

69. "MacArthur Sees Cut of Force to 200,000 Within Six Months," New York Times, September 18, 1945, 1; "MacArthur's Plan for Small Occupation Force Stirs Storm," Pittsburgh-Post Gazette, September 18, 1945, 1; "General M'Arthur to Need Only 200,000 Men, Philadelphia Inquirer Public Ledger," September 18, 1945, 1; "Acheson Voices Concern over Unheralded Declaration," and "MacArthur Says 200,000 Regulars May Take over Job in 6 Months," both in Washington Post, September 18, 1945, 1.

70. For an analysis of press reaction to Truman's comments, see Time correspondent Frank McNaughton to Art Monroe, September 21, 1945, McNaughton Reports File, 1941–1949, Box 9, Frank McNaughton Papers, HST. The President's News Conference, September 18, 1945, https://www.trumanlibrary.gov/library/public-papers/137/presidents-news-conference; "Occupation Plan Upheld by Truman," Pittsburgh Post-Gazette, September 19, 1945, 1.

71. Statement by the President Concerning Demobilization of the Armed Forces September 19, 1945, https://www.trumanlibrary.gov/library/public-papers/138/statement-president-concerning-demobilization-armed-forces.

72. "Acheson Sets Path," New York Times, September 20, 1945, 1.

73. Stories from several papers were sent to Acheson by the White House under the heading "Acheson Policy favored in U.S. MacArthur a Republican Flop," Pacific Policy, Box 59, Papers of Dean Acheson, HST. Summaries of Radio Comment and Newspaper Editorials, December 1945, Rose Conway Files, Box 12, HST.

74. Russell Buhite has shown that MacArthur often exhibited behavior consistent with the clinical diagnosis of narcissistic personality disorder. Russell D. Buhite, Douglas MacArthur: Statecraft and Stagecraft in America's East Asian Policy (Lanham, MD: Rowman and Littlefield, 2008).

75. On September 18, members of his staff showed Truman a cartoon that depicted MacArthur as responsible for everything being done in Japan. Truman later commented that he was "going to do something about that fellow" who was balling things up. Entry for September 18, 1945, Ayers Diary, HST.

76. "Krock, Acheson-MacArthur Tilt Raises Disunity Issue," *New York Times,* September 23, 1945, 71; "Our Army in Germany," *Chicago Tribune,* September 24, 1945, 12; "House Hearing on Communism Opens Today," *Washington Post,* September 26, 1945, 3. Edwin James also thought criticism of MacArthur was coming mostly from "red and pink sources." "James, Too Early to Assess Japanese Occupation," *New York Times,* September 16, 1945, E3.

77. "Stone, Behind the MacArthur Row," *Nation,* September 29, 1945, 77–79.

78. "Text of Statement on Control of Japs," *Washington Post,* September 23, 1945, M4; "MacArthur's Powers Defined by Truman," *New York Times,* September 25, 1945, 3.

79. MacArthur supported publication of the Initial Post-Surrender Policy, MacArthur to Marshall, September 20, 1945, MacArthur to JCS, September 19, 1945, both in Blue Binders, Box 160, RG 9, MacArthur Archives; Hugh Baillie, "MacArthur Declares Japan Finished as a Great Power," *New York Times,* September 22, 1945, 1.

80. "Back On The Beam," *Washington Post,* September 23, 1945, B4.

## CHAPTER 6

1. Bix, *Hirohito,* 540–41; Schaller, *American Occupation of Japan,* 30–50; Dower, *Embracing Defeat,* 112–20; Boyle, *Modern Japan,* 324–41; Howard Schonberger, *Aftermath of War: Americans and the Remaking of Japan* (Kent, OH: Kent State University Press, 1989), 55–67.

2. Remarkably, Joseph Grew, now in retirement, told his former secretary, Robert Fearey, that he thought Hirohito should be tried as a war criminal for issuing the rescript that started the war. Fearey to George Atcheson, October 13, 1945, Box 1, Robert Fearey Papers, Hoover Institute. Hal Brands, "Who Saved Hirohito? The MacArthur Myth and U.S. Policy Toward Hirohito and the Japanese Imperial Institution, 1942–1946," *Pacific Historical Review* (May 2006), 271–305.

3. Dower, *Embracing Defeat,* 293–98; Bix, *Hirohito,* 543–48.

4. Bix, *Hirohito,* 560–64; Dower, *Embracing Defeat,* 313–14.

5. Brands, "Who Saved Hirohito?," 288–90, 295–97; Bix, *Hirohito,* 565–76; Dower, *Embracing Defeat,* 374–78.

6. "Prince Suggested that Hirohito Quit," *New York Times,* March 4, 1946, 6.

7. Shillony, *Enigma of the Emperors,* 224.

8. Boyle, *Modern Japan,* 322–24.

9. Bix, *Hirohito,* 567; Dower, *Embracing Defeat,* 322–24.

10. Memo to Commander-in-Chief, October 2, 1945, Hoover File, Fellers Papers, MMA.

11. Fellers to Hoover, October 3, 1945; Hoover to Fellers, October 15, 1945; Fellers to Hoover, November 15, 1945, all in Hoover File, Fellers Papers, MMA.

12. [Notes Hoover-Fellers conversation], May 7, 1946, Hoover File, Fellers Papers, MMA.

13. Japan, May 4, 5, 6, 1946, MacArthur File, Post Presidential Papers, HHL.

14. Japan, May 4, 5, 6, 1946, MacArthur File, Post Presidential Papers, HHL.

15. Frazer Hunt Fellers, April 25, 1946, Veterans of Foreign Wars file, Fellers Papers, MMA.

16. For a discussion of Stimson's motives, production, and reception of Stimson's article, see Barton J. Bernstein, "Seizing the Contested Terrain of Early Nuclear History: Stimson, Conant, and Their Allies Explain the Decision to Use the Atomic Bomb," *Diplomatic History* (Winter 1993), 35–72. For the article, see Henry Lewis Stimson, "The Decision to Use the Atomic Bomb," *Harper's Magazine* (February 1947), reproduced in http://afe.easia.columbia.edu/ps/japan/stimson_harpers.pdf.

17. "Japan's Decision to Surrender," Writings of Bonner Fellers, Fellers Papers, MMA.

18. For Hoover's contributions to Fellers's article, see Haruo Iguchi, "The First Revisionist: Bonner Fellers, Herbert Hoover, and Japan's Decision to Surrender," in Marc Gallicchio, ed., *The Unpredictability of the Past. Memories of the Asia-Pacific War in U.S.-East Asian Relations* (Durham, NC: Duke University Press, 2017), 52–84.

19. The article appeared first in the VFW's magazine *Foreign Service* and was immediately reprinted in *Reader's Digest*.

20. For congressional reaction and sharpening of partisan division over Roosevelt's and Truman's foreign policy, see Athan G. Theoharis, *The Yalta Myths. An Issue in U.S. Politics, 1945–1955* (Columbia: University of Missouri Press, 1970), 70–86..

21. Hanson W. Baldwin, *Great Mistakes of the War* (New York: Harper & Brothers, 1949), 14.

22. Baldwin, *Great Mistakes of the War*, 77–109.

23. Baldwin, *Great Mistakes of the War*, 90.

24. Emphasis is mine. Hanson Baldwin, "War Pressure Unrelaxed," *New York Times*, August 14, 1945, 2.

25. The conclusion read that it was the survey group's opinion "that certainly prior to 31 December 1945, and in all probability prior to 1 November 1945, Japan would have surrendered even if the atomic bombs had not been dropped, even if Russia had not entered the war, and even if no invasion had been planned or contemplated." USSBS, "Japan's Struggle to End the War," https://www.ibiblio.org/hyperwar/AAF/USSBS/JapansStruggle/index.html#A5; Robert P. Newman, *Truman and the Hiroshima Cult* (East Lansing: Michigan State University Press, 1995), 33–56.

26. It appears that Baldwin interviewed Leahy. The admiral's memoir was published the year after Baldwin's book. Baldwin, *Great Mistakes*, 90–93.

27. Michael Pearlman, *Warmaking and American Democracy: The Struggle Over Military Strategy, 1700 to the Present* (Lawrence: University Press of Kansas, 1999), 265.

28. Zacharias, "Eighteen Words That Bagged Japan," *Saturday Evening Post,* November 17, 1945.

29. Zacharias, "How We Bungled the Japanese Surrender," *Look Magazine* (June 6, 1950); Rear Admiral Isaac C. Johnson (Rtd.) to Alfred Kohlberg, August 29, 1949, Zacharias File, Box 207, Alfred Kohlberg Papers, Hoover Institute.

30. Contrary to McCarthy's depiction of all foreign service officers as products of the Eastern elite, many came from middle-class backgrounds. John Carter Vincent was born in Kansas and graduated from Mercer College in Georgia. John Stewart Service was born in China and graduated from Oberlin College in Ohio. John Patton Davies was born in China, attended the University of Wisconsin for two years, spent a year at Yenching University in China, and then graduated from Columbia University. All three were dismissed from the foreign service despite being cleared of charges of disloyalty by numerous review boards, although Service was eventually reinstated. Warren I. Cohen, *American Foreign Relations in the Age of Soviet Power, 1945–1991* (New York: Cambridge University Press, 1993), 52–53; Kathryn S. Olmsted, *Real Enemies: Conspiracy Theories and American Democracy, World War I to 9/11* (New York: Oxford University Press, 2009), 96–104; Ellen Schrecker, *The Age of McCarthyism: A Brief History with Documents* (Boston: Bedford Books, 1994), 26–31, 62–65, 210–14.

31. United States Congress, Senate Armed Services Committee, and Senate Foreign Affairs Committee, *The Military Situation in the Far East* (Washington, DC: Government Printing Office, 1951). Hereafter cited as MacArthur Hearings.

32. Hickenlooper also referred to the USSBS report. MacArthur Hearings, 2196.

33. The article was also published in the *Chicago Tribune.* MacArthur Hearings, 561.

34. Institute of Pacific Relations, *Report of the Internal Security Committee* (Washington, DC: Government Printing Office, 1952), 194fn22.

35. Dooman nursed a long-standing grudge against Vincent and was prone to grossly inaccurate statements. For example, he incorrectly blamed Vincent for altering the Initial Post-Surrender Policy. Years after he retired, he was still telling friends that he was the victim of a conspiracy directed by Vincent. Institute of Pacific Relations, U.S. Congress. *Internal Security Committee. Hearings Held July 25, 1951–June 20, 1952.* Washington, DC: Government Printing Office, 1952, 705; Gary May, *China Scapegoat: The Diplomatic Ordeal of John Carter Vincent* (Prospect Heights, IL: Waveland Press, 1979), 250–53.

36. Grew also credited Dooman with authorship of the declaration in his memoir. A State Department historian verified later that Dooman's draft was not the basis of the Potsdam Declaration. E. Taylor Parks to Herbert Feis, October 6, 1959, Herbert Feis Papers, Library of Congress, Washington, DC.

Dooman's testimony is in Institute of Pacific Relations, U.S. Congress. *Internal Security Committee. Hearings Held July 25, 1951–June 20, 1952.* Washington, DC: Government Printing Office, 1952, 728–33.

37. Justus Doenecke, "Rehearsal for Cold War: United States Anti-Interventionists and the Soviet Union, 1939–1941," *International Journal of Politics, Culture, and Society* (Spring 1994), 375–92; Olmstead, *Real Enemies,* 74–81, 94–95.

38. On Flynn, see Olmstead, *Real Enemies,* 32, 47–49, 60–65, 103–107.

39. John T. Flynn, *While You Slept: Our Tragedy in Asia and Who Made It* (New York: Devin-Adair, 1951), 26–27, 41–43, 48, 169–70.

40. Millis, *Forrestal Diaries,* 31; Ray S. Cline, *Washington Command Post: The Operations Division* (Washington, DC: Government Printing Office, 1951), 308.

41. *U.S. Congressional Record,* 84th Cong., 1st session, 1955, C1, Part 3, 3374–3376; Theoharis, *Yalta Myths,* 70–86.

42. "Aide Scores Linking Yalta and MacArthur," *Washington Post,* April 6, 1955, 6; "Article Assailed by MacArthur Aide," *New York Times,* April 6, 1955, 17.

43. D. Clayton James writes in his generally sympathetic biography of this episode that one of the general's traits, as many close to him sadly learned, was "a desperate need to save face, even if it involved lying." James, *Years of MacArthur,* 2: 763–65; "MacArthur: More from the Record," *Washington Post,* October 21, 1955, 50; "M'Arthur Asserts Documents Prove His Yalta Stand," *New York Times,* October 21, 1955, 1.

44. "MacArthur and Yalta," *Commonweal,* November 4, 1955, 109; James, *Years of MacArthur,* 2: 765.

45. Elizabeth Churchill Brown, *Enemy at His Back* (New York: Bookmailer, 1956), xiv.

46. Brown was aided by Dr. Edna Fluegel, a professor of political science at Trinity College in Washington, DC. Fluegel worked as a divisional assistant in the State Department 1942–1945 with Alger Hiss and attended the founding conferences of the United Nations. She testified at the IPR hearings in 1952. Brown, *Enemy at His Back,* xxi, 9–10, 22–23, 30, 74, 87.

47. *Enemy at His Back* was reviewed in the Catholic magazine *Wanderer* by Senator Pat McCarran's sister, Sister Mary Patricia. Pat McCarran chaired the Senate Internal Security Committee. It was also reviewed in the conservative journals *American Mercury* and *National Review.* It was listed as recommended reading by the *American Legion Magazine* and *Navy League* magazine. Newsweek columnist Raymond Moley promised Brown a mention in his *Newsweek* column. Moley was a former member of FDR's Brains Trust turned conservative. Clippings and letters in Brown Papers, HHL.

48. Justus Doenecke, "Harry Elmer Barnes," *Wisconsin Magazine of History* (Summer 1973), 311–23; Warren I. Cohen, *The American Revisionists: The Lessons of Interventionism in World War I* (Chicago: University of Chicago Press, 36, 216–18; Olmstead, *Real Enemies,* 22–23, 60–63, 79.

49. Harry Elmer Barnes, "Hiroshima: Assault on a Beaten Foe," *National Review*, May 10, 1958, 441–43.

50. Fellers described the report in question as a long cablegram to Roosevelt urging that Russia not be brought into the war. Fellers also said he was told that when Hoover asked MacArthur about it, the general said the Army had taken all his papers so he could not verify the story. Bonner Fellers to Harry Elmer Barnes, March 2, 1960, Box 1, Fellers Papers, MML.

51. Anthony Kubek, *How the Far East Was Lost: American Policy and the Creation of Communist China, 1941–1949* (Chicago: Henry Regnery, 1963); Cornell Simpson, *The Death of James Forrestal* (Belmont, MA: Western Islands, 1966).

52. Donald T. Critchlow, *The Conservative Ascendancy: How the Republicans Rose to Power in Modern America*, 2nd ed. (Lawrence: University Press of Kansas, 2011), 58–76.

53. George H. Nash, ed., *Freedom Betrayed: Herbert Hoover's Secret History of the Second World War and Its Aftermath* (Stanford, CA: Hoover Institution Press, 2011), 489–93, 536–38, 560–65.

54. Nash, *Freedom Betrayed*, 537n4.

55. Gar Alperovtiz, *Atomic Diplomacy: Hiroshima and Potsdam; The Use of the Atomic Bomb and the American Confrontation with Soviet Power* (New York: Simon and Schuster, 1965), 176–87.

56. For a brief discussion, see J. Samuel Walker, *Prompt and Utter Destruction: Truman and the Use of the Atomic Bombs Against Japan* (Chapel Hill: University of North Carolina Press, 1997), 104–5.

57. Waldo Heinrichs, "The Enola Gay and Contested Public Memory," in Gallicchio, *Unpredictability of the Past*, 201–33.

58. A sample of newspaper coverage of the controversy has been collected by the Air Force Association in a bound volume titled *Enola Gay Coverage*, 1994. That and other Association materials were deposited in the Special Collections of the library at the University of Massachusetts at Amherst. For additional discussion of the controversy that is strongly supportive of the curators, see Philip Nobile, ed., *Judgment at the Smithsonian: The Bombing of Hiroshima and Nagasaki* (New York: Marlowe, 1995), xviii–xcvii.

59. Emphasis in original. "The Crossroads: The End of World War II, the Atomic Bomb, and the Origins of the Cold War," First Script for the *Enola Gay* Exhibit, January 1994, Air Force Association collection.

60. The atomic bombings of Hiroshima and Nagasaki stimulated widespread calls for world government in the immediate postwar years. There is no evidence, of course, that unconditional surrender was promoted with that end in mind. Wesley T. Wooley, *Alternatives to Anarchy: American Supranationalism Since World War II* (Bloomington: Indiana University Press, 1988), 3–82; John F. McManus, "Dropping the Bomb," *New American* (August 21, 1997), https://www.thenewamerican.com/culture/history/item/23288-dropping-the-bomb-why-did-the-u-s-unleash-its-terrible-weapon.

61. Gallicchio, "The Search for a Usable Past: The U.S. and the Lessons of the Occupation of Japan," *IJOS: International Journal of Okinawan Studies* (December 2016), 83–98.

62. Dower began by noting that the terrorist attack on 9/11 had prompted comparisons to Pearl Harbor and added that the Bush administration appeared to be taking a page from Japan's playbook by adopting a strategy of preemption. John W. Dower, "Lessons from Japan About War's Aftermath," *New York Times*, October 27, 2002, 13C.

## CONCLUSION

1. Memorandum of Telephone Conversation, September 17, 1945, *FRUS*, 1945, *The British Commonwealth, the Far East* 6: 716–17.

2. Oliver Stone and Peter Kuznick, *The Untold History of the United States* (New York: Gallery Books, 2012), 176.

# Index

*For the benefit of digital users, indexed terms that span two pages (e.g., 52–53) may, on occasion, appear on only one of those pages.*